TEN SQUADRONS
OF HURRICANES

To my fellow Hurricane admirers/enthusiasts/fanatics.

TEN SQUADRONS OF HURRICANES

ADRIAN STEWART

Pen & Sword
AVIATION

First published in Great Britain in 2016 by
PEN & SWORD MILITARY
an imprint of
Pen & Sword Books Ltd
47 Church Street
Barnsley
South Yorkshire S70 2AS

Copyright © Adrian Stewart, 2016

ISBN 978 1 47384 842 9

Typeset in Ehrhardt by Chic Graphics

Printed and bound in England
by CPI Group (UK) Ltd, Croydon, CR0 4YY

Pen & Sword Books Ltd incorporates the imprints of
Pen & Sword Archaeology, Atlas, Aviation, Battleground, Discovery,
Family History, History, Maritime, Military, Naval, Politics, Railways,
Select, Social History, Transport, True Crime, Claymore Press,
Frontline Books, Leo Cooper, Praetorian Press, Remember When,
Seaforth Publishing and Wharncliffe..

For a complete list of Pen & Sword titles please contact
PEN & SWORD BOOKS LIMITED
47 Church Street, Barnsley, South Yorkshire, S70 2AS, England
E-mail: enquiries@pen-and-sword.co.uk
Website: www.pen-and-sword.co.uk

Contents

Acknowledgements

I must, as always, express my indebtedness:

For the production of the book, to Brigadier Henry Wilson, Matt Jones and their colleagues at Pen & Sword Books Limited; Andrew Hewson and his colleagues at Johnson & Alcock Limited; and my editor Pamela Covey, whom nothing daunted.

For the manuscript, to Sylvia Menzies; for the cover, to Jon Wilkinson; for the photographs, to Christopher Shores, Philip Fisher and his staff at the Birmingham & Midland Institute & Library and the staff of the Taylor Library.

For additional information to:
Squadron Leader Bryan Colston,
Colin & Mary Cook,
F.W.T. Davis,
Christopher Shores,
John Michael Thayer,
James Thornley Marshall.

To all the above, my sincere thanks.

The front cover, designed by Jon Wilkinson, shows aircraft of 85 Squadron returning to base after combat during the Battle of Britain. It pays tribute to the Hurricane's well-deserved reputation for surviving massive damage and still bringing its pilot home safely.

Prologue

The World's Finest Flying Club

For the officers and men of the young Royal Air Force, the years from 1922 to 1933 were a golden age. By 1922, the new service had successfully resisted all attempts to destroy its independent existence. Admittedly, the pious conviction that the First World War had been 'a war to end wars' had resulted in a drastic reduction of its strength. This, though, had increased its community spirit and self-reliance by turning it into a small, select fellowship in which almost everyone knew everyone else and friends in different squadrons were kept fully informed about each other's activities. It was frequently stated that the RAF resembled a close-knit flying club; not only that but the finest one in the world.

Service morale was increased still further when RAF actions in Somaliland, Turkey and Iraq and on the North-West Frontier of India effectively prevented or quelled uprisings, raids, banditry and the threat of major hostilities with very few casualties and, as the politicians gratefully noted, at strictly limited expense. It was sustained by the interest and support shown by the general public, particularly at the Royal Air Force Display held every year at Hendon, chiefly to raise money for the RAF Benevolent Fund. Generously favoured by the weather, even in the otherwise notoriously dreadful summer of 1931, the display attracted huge crowds who delightedly watched set-piece bombing attacks on 'enemy' strongholds that invariably disintegrated in a spectacular explosion, aerial drill by squadrons of brightly-coloured fighters and individual exhibitions of aerobatics including, in 1931, a particularly highly-praised one by a certain Pilot Officer Douglas Bader.

Both the bomber and the fighter aircraft of the time were biplanes. Back in September 1912, two monoplanes had broken up in the air, as a consequence of which, in the following month, the Royal Flying Corps had banned the use of military monoplanes. The ban was lifted five months later, but the belief that monoplanes lacked sufficient structural integrity long persisted. Moreover, most aircraft manufacturers preferred to continue with the production of biplanes, to which they were accustomed and with which they were experienced. So when in February 1925 Sydney (later Sir Sydney) Camm, who that year became Chief Designer at H.G. Hawker Engineering, the privately-owned predecessor of Hawker Aircraft Limited, proposed a monoplane fighter to be armed with two Vickers machine guns and powered by a Bristol Jupiter engine, his suggestion met with no favour and never progressed beyond the drawing board.

Camm therefore continued with his biplane designs, and in July 1929 there appeared on the Hawker stand at the Olympia Aero Show a light bomber and an interceptor fighter, both of course biplanes, both with a Rolls-Royce Kestrel engine and both winning widespread admiration from all who saw them. Camm is said to have maintained that an aircraft designer must have 'a knowledge of aerodynamics, some elementary mathematics and an eye for beauty' and in both these aircraft all three requirements, but especially the last, were clear for all to see.

Camm is also reputed to have expressed a preference for designing fighters, so he must have taken great pleasure in his Hawker Hornet which, after further trials and the installation of a more powerful version of the Kestrel engine, became the Fury; this entered RAF squadron service in May 1931. Yet his Hawker Hart light bomber was only marginally less beautiful and would have a far greater influence on the future.

The Hart had first flown in June 1928 with a top speed of 184 mph, some 10 mph in excess of any existing RAF fighter. Over 1,000 Harts would be built – a huge number in peacetime – and in addition it formed the basis for a number of derivative types, collectively called Hart Variants, of which over 1,800 were produced. There was an improved bomber version called the Hind, a fighter version named the Demon, a naval reconnaissance aircraft with folding wings and floats known as the Osprey and the army co-operation Audax. The latter in turn led to the Hector, an improved version, the Hardy for use in Iraq and the Hartbees (or Hartebeeste as it was sometimes known) for use in South Africa.

In February 1930 Harts entered service with 33 Squadron and in that year's Annual Air Defence Exercises they proved quite impossible to intercept. They repeated their successes in 1931, hitting Northolt aerodrome with tennis balls marked 'bombs' before they could be engaged. Only the Harts' fighter cousins, the Demons, were capable of intercepting them and their performance was only marginally superior. Even the Fury, shortly to enter RAF service, would not solve the problem posed by the Harts, for with a top speed of 207 mph and an inadequate armament of two Vickers machine guns, it could be regarded as no more than a useful 'stop-gap'.

It was clear that the Royal Air Force desperately needed a new, improved fighter and in an attempt to obtain one, the Air Ministry issued Specification F7/30. This called for an interceptor that would be capable of operating by day or by night, attain a top speed of 250 mph, mount four Vickers machine guns and, it was suggested, be powered by the new Rolls-Royce Goshawk engine. Encouraged by the promise of large production contracts, several aircraft manufacturers attempted to meet the F7/30 requirements. Camm's candidate was the PV3, an improved version of the Fury with a Goshawk engine but the eventual worthy winner was the Gloster Gladiator. The most significant effect of the Specification, though, was to convince many people that no further development of the biplane could be expected, so future advances must be sought elsewhere. The need for these would soon become increasingly apparent.

On 30 January 1933, Adolf Hitler became Chancellor of Germany and promptly began to tear up the Versailles Treaty of 1919 that had marked the end of the First World War. Under the terms of this, Germany was forbidden to have a military air force. She was allowed to build and fly civil aircraft, however, and a number of determined officers used this as a smokescreen under which they could pave the way for their air force's revival. In 1926 a state-owned airline, Lufthansa, was created and given aircraft, extensive ground facilities and what seemed unnecessarily large numbers of air-crew. This all appeared harmless but it concealed a sinister purpose: it was intended that Lufthansa should provide the basis for a future bomber force.

To swell the ranks of trained airmen, the German government also sponsored numerous flying clubs that quickly proved more popular than their equivalents in Britain. Experienced pilots were allowed to preserve their skills by flying military aircraft in friendly foreign countries. Major Hermann Göring, for instance, spent a total of six years at various times with the Swedish Air Force. As a final touch, in December 1923, with the connivance of Soviet Russia, a secret flying school came into existence at Lipetsk, south-east of Moscow, where German officers received advanced training in military aviation.

Consequently, much preparatory work had been done well before the Nazi Party came into power and thereafter events moved with alarming rapidity. In October 1933, Germany withdrew from the Geneva Disarmament Conference and the League of Nations. It was not until March 1935 that Hitler formally proclaimed the formation of a new German military air force, the Luftwaffe, with Göring as its commander-in-chief, but the German aircraft industry, assisted by massive State loans, had for the past two years already been embarking on a huge increase in production, designed to give the Luftwaffe superiority over any possible rival.

Faced with an atmosphere of growing international tension, Britain's then National Government, on 19 July 1934, proposed that the Royal Air Force should be increased by forty-one squadrons within five years. A pact between the Labour and Liberal parties to prevent this was, mercifully, defeated on 30 July by 404 votes to 60. Nonetheless, while the RAF certainly needed to expand if it was to face the mounting threat from Germany, it was also vital that it should do so with aircraft of vastly improved quality.

Sydney Camm's reaction to the situation was simple and practical. He does not appear to have been one of those who felt that war was inevitable, nor did he entertain any particular animosity towards the Germans. However, if the Royal Air Force needed a better fighter than the Gladiator, then he would provide one. With resolution, if perhaps also with a shade of regret, Sydney Camm abandoned his beautiful biplanes and turned to the future and the monoplane, and to a tough little killer that he called the Hurricane.

Chapter 1

A New Kind of Fighter
III Squadron

One summer afternoon in 1938, an American college student and future fighter pilot named Edwards Park was enjoying a biking holiday in England when he saw his first Hawker Hurricanes. Some sixty years later, writing his *Fighters: The World's Great Aces and Their Aeroplanes*, he could still recall them vividly. 'To us Yanks,' he says, 'they were a revelation. To everyone who glanced at them that peaceful day, they were a somewhat chilling glimpse of the future.'

The Hurricanes belonged to 111 Squadron based at Northolt, the first RAF unit to receive them and hence the first to receive any modern monoplane fighters. Four of them arrived in December 1937 and the first pilot to fly one was the CO, Squadron Leader John Gillan. The first pilot to fly any Hurricane had been Hawkers' chief test pilot. His real name was Paul Ward Spencer Bulman but because he could never remember the names of other people and addressed them all as 'George' – presumably reflecting that this was the name of a large percentage of the male inhabitants of Great Britain in the interwar years, so he had a fair chance of being right – his friends retorted by adopting it for him. So universally was he known as 'George' that in some accounts of the early development of the Hurricane it is assumed, not unreasonably, that it was his proper Christian name.

'George' Bulman first took off from Brooklands aerodrome in the

Hurricane prototype, registered serial number K5083, on 6 November 1935. This, it will be noted, was over two years before the Hurricane entered RAF service and it may surprise many to learn that the main reason for this delay was the problems encountered with the early versions of the Rolls-Royce Merlin engine that had been chosen as its power-plant. Then when a suitable engine, the Merlin G or Mark II, was created by Rolls-Royce, further delay resulted from the consequent need to alter the aircraft's nose, propeller, air-intake, engine cowlings, engine mounting, glycol tank and hand-starting system.

Fortunately the problems in no way affected the confidence of both Hawkers and the Air Ministry in the Hurricane project, and their faith was sustained by the performance of the prototype. This had a speed of 318 mph at 15,500ft; it could climb to 15,000ft in 5.7 minutes and to 20,000ft in 8.4 minutes; and its service ceiling was 34,500ft and estimated absolute ceiling 35,400ft. Moreover it was rightly anticipated that lessons learned with K5083 would result in a further increased performance in the production version.

Bulman and the pilots at the Aircraft and Armament Experimental Establishment at Martlesham Heath, Suffolk to which K5083 had been sent for service evaluation all gave highly favourable reports, and as a result, in March 1936 the Air Ministry provisionally decided to place an order for 600 Hurricanes. This decision, which it is interesting to learn was strongly supported by Mr Neville Chamberlain, then Chancellor of the Exchequer, was probably no great surprise to Hawkers who were being urged by the Air Ministry to speed up Hurricane production. In a superb illustration of private enterprise, in every sense of the word, Hawkers therefore determined not to wait for the anticipated contract but to commence production drawings immediately and prepare for an output of 1,000 aeroplanes, confident that export orders would cover any excess over RAF requirements.

Future events quickly justified this action. The formal contract for 600 Hurricanes, then the largest order ever placed for a military aircraft in peacetime, was issued on 3 June 1936. Hurricanes were indeed exported to Canada, South Africa, Yugoslavia, Belgium, Turkey, Rumania, Persia and Poland, and after war had broken out, to Finland, Portugal and Eire, although in retrospect it seems extraordinary that a single one was allowed out of the country, and on 1 November 1938 the Air Ministry gave an order for another 1,000 Hurricanes.

By then, much more had happened. On 12 October 1937 the first production Hurricane Mark I, L1547, flown by Hawkers' test pilot Philip Lucas, had taken off from Brooklands aerodrome. Two months later, as previously mentioned, four Mark Is were delivered to 111 Squadron and during the early months of 1938, 111 was built up to its full establishment strength: sixteen aircraft at that date, though increased to twenty not long afterwards.

'Treble One' had previously been equipped with the Gloster Gauntlet that was in effect an earlier edition of the Gladiator: a biplane with an open cockpit, a fixed undercarriage, an armament of two machine guns and a top speed of 230 mph. The Hurricane was quite different, appearing both formidable and frightening. It was a monoplane with a top speed of 328 mph and a closed cockpit. Its undercarriage was wide and immensely strong but could be retracted. It carried eight 0.303in Browning machine guns, closely grouped in two batteries of four, one on each wing; this made the Hurricane a marvellously steady gun platform and one that could be rearmed quickly and easily. To pilots used to an open cockpit and a top wing above them, it appeared terrifyingly fast and at first many preferred to fly with the undercarriage down in order to reduce their speed to a more acceptable level.

Squadron Leader Gillan appreciated the situation and carefully prepared his pilots for their new responsibilities. He would allow nobody else to fly a Hurricane until he had acquired experience on one himself and ensured that every pilot received detailed personal instructions about the machine's capabilities before he took off. He also forbade aerobatics until his men had built up a suitable number of flying hours on the type, although not all of them obeyed this injunction. Nonetheless, the Hurricane had inevitable 'teething problems' to solve. On 1 February 1938, Flying Officer Bocquet became the first man to die in a Hurricane when he apparently lost control in a dive while making a mock attack on a ground target. Soon afterwards, Pilot Officer Roy Dutton became the first man to land a Hurricane on its belly when his undercarriage failed to function correctly; fortunately he survived and went on to become an air commodore. Later still, three more pilots were killed as the result of an undetected fault in the Hurricane's altimeter.

It may therefore have been with the intention of improving morale that, on 10 February, Gillan embarked on the flight for which he would become famous. He had been ordered to make a high-speed trial flight from Northolt to Turnhouse near Edinburgh and back. The outward half was not very pleasant, being made in heavy cloud and in the teeth of a gale of considerable velocity, but realizing that this would assist him on his return to Northolt, he ordered his aircraft refuelled immediately and shortly after 1700 hours he took off again into the gathering dusk. He touched down at Northolt with the aid of landing lights and signal flares forty-eight minutes later, having covered the 327 miles from Turnhouse at an average ground speed of 408.75 mph or almost 7 miles a minute.

It was perhaps inevitable that subsequent reports of this record-breaking achievement made little mention of the gale that had made it possible, though Gillan's men were well aware of it and gave their leader the nickname of 'Downwind' that he would carry for the rest of his life. Equally, however, the gale should not be allowed to conceal Gillan's brilliant airmanship. The flight had been made in cloud and darkness, the windscreen had iced over and only started to clear when the Hurricane began its descent, and Gillan had therefore had to rely almost entirely on his instruments. He had also wholly achieved his aim of installing confidence into his pilots. Despite the battering it had received from the elements, Hurricane L1555 – henceforth always known as 'State Express 555' – had triumphantly demonstrated its rugged reliability, particularly that of its Merlin engine which had been at full throttle throughout the flight and had never once faltered.

Almost overnight, 111 Squadron, as Francis K. Mason remarks in *The Hawker Hurricane*, became a 'corps d'élite'. It received a series of distinguished visitors, including King George VI, and was called on to give numerous demonstrations that earned high praise both from the press and the general public. Unfortunately, exaggerated accounts tended to suggest that only men of supreme skill at the peak of physical fitness and mental alertness could control the Hurricane and, as a result, young pilots learning to fly it frequently lacked confidence in their ability to master the monster. It should be emphasized that Gillan played no part in furthering this myth and in reports to the Air Ministry and to Hawkers he stated firmly that 'The Hurricane is a simple aircraft to fly.'

Gillan's thorough training and leadership by example had been acknowledged by the award of an Air Force Cross and it seemed that a glittering career lay before him. Unhappily though, he had fallen for an American actress named Clare Luce and deserted his post in order to pursue her to New York. His visit was an unmitigated disaster. It is reported that the lady hit him over the head with a bottle of champagne. It seems unlikely that this could have happened without his sustaining serious injury; however, he wined and dined the lady but did not win her. As if that was not enough, he was court-martialled for his rash action and ceased to command 111 in January 1939. He did later rise to the rank of wing commander but was killed in action, flying a Spitfire, on 29 August 1941.

Although Gillan had no further connection with the Hawker fighter after his departure from 111, he is always associated with it and it is fitting that his name should have been recorded on individual Hurricanes. During the war, many RAF aircraft were 'sponsored' by British colonies, protectorates, cities, industrial concerns, newspapers and individuals, all of which provided the money needed to build them.[1] One such subscriber was Wing Commander Gillan's mother, who presented three Hurricanes to the nation in memory of her son at a cost of about £5,000 apiece. All of them were inscribed 'Our John' under the cockpit.

Gillan's place as CO of 111, and incidentally his 'State Express 555', were taken over by an officer who, so he would later state 'happened to be passing at the time.' We may take the liberty of believing that there were better reasons for appointing the new head of the RAF's most prestigious fighter unit. Squadron Leader Harry Broadhurst already had a varied and highly successful record as an airman and as a staff officer, during the course of which he had won the Brooke-Popham Trophy, awarded for proficiency in air gunnery, three years running, and had earned an Air Force Cross. He would command 111 during the remaining months of peace and the early months of the Second World War.

As war drew inexorably closer, the RAF could find consolation in the knowledge that Hurricanes were reaching the squadrons from Hawkers' factories at Kingston, Brooklands and a new one at Langley, built in 1939 specifically for their production, and pilots were being trained to fly them. Improvements were also being made to the Hurricanes' fighting capability, if not always as rapidly as the Air Ministry desired, because there were understandable concerns about the effect these might have on the smooth running of the production lines.

Despite this, the number of improvements was impressive. Hurricanes were fitted with better radios, better exhausts, better fuel, rear-view mirrors, and enlarged rudders and new underfins that dramatically assisted their recovery from a spin. Protection for the pilots was provided by strengthened windscreens and the fitting of armour-plate at the front of and later also the rear of the cockpit. Self-sealing fuel tank covers reduced the dangers of fire. The original wings, fitted with a fabric covering that tended to 'balloon' at high speeds or if damaged, were replaced by much stronger metal wings; these also greatly increased the Hurricanes' speed in a dive and included heating units for the gun-bays that had previously been unusable above 15,000ft, even in summer.

Perhaps the greatest improvements were those to the Hurricanes' power-plant. Gillan appears to have been lucky during his record-breaking flight, for other pilots found the Merlin II engine less reliable. Worse still, it drove a fixed-pitch two-bladed wooden propeller that condemned its Hurricanes to a very long take-off run and a poor rate of climb; moreover, it was alarmingly apt to disintegrate without warning under pressure.

These defects were now put right by the arrival of a De Havilland metal three-bladed two-pitch propeller. This enabled the pilot to alter the pitch - in other words the angle – of the blades so as to use fine (low) pitch for take-off and coarse (high) pitch for greater speeds, in much the same way as gears are used in a car. As well as its other benefits, this brought about a reduction of the Hurricanes' fuel consumption. Later, Hurricanes were given a Rotol constant-speed propeller that adjusted the pitch to the engine speed automatically.

This was accompanied by the introduction of the Merlin III engine that was not only very reliable but featured a shaft capable of use with either the De Havilland or Rotol propellers. Not all Hurricanes had received all these improvements by the time war was finally declared on 3 September 1939, but most of them had been converted by early 1940 and all by the start of the Battle of Britain.

The outbreak of war found 111 Squadron still at Northolt, helping to mount guard over London. The squadron practised operating after dark and on 8 September suffered its first wartime casualty when Pilot Officer the Hon. St Clair Erskine crashed and was killed. During daylight hours the Hurricanes were principally employed in dealing with barrage balloons, a number of which broke away from their moorings in high winds, threatening to cause damage with their trailing steel cables. On 20 September Flight Lieutenant Powell fired 111's first shots in anger – 2,200 of them – to bring down a runaway balloon. Broadhurst destroyed two more on 28 and 29 September, and on 4 October 111 became 'balloon-busting' champions with a score of eleven for the day.

Enemy aircraft at this time were conspicuous by their absence, but in November 111 was ordered north to Acklington in Northumberland and on the 29th Squadron Leader Broadhurst took off to intercept enemy reconnaissance machines approaching the coast. This was a day of heavy cloud and thick fog; Broadhurst had to rely solely on his instruments and was quite prepared to be unable to land on his return to base and be compelled to bale out. Some 8 miles east of Alnwick he sighted a Heinkel He 111 that quickly dived into cloud while its gunners fired back at the Hurricane. Broadhurst, however, caught up with it and two bursts of fire sent the Heinkel plunging into the sea, trailing smoke and flames. Broadhurst then had to pull up sharply and narrowly avoided following it into the water. His ground control managed to direct him to a safe landing and he later received a Distinguished Flying Cross.

Soon after this, Broadhurst led 111 to Drem airfield just south of the Firth of Forth and early in 1940, the squadron moved on to Wick in the extreme north of Scotland. Broadhurst, though, did not accompany it, having been promoted to wing commander and subsequently being transferred to France to take charge of 60 Wing, controlling 85 and 87 (Hurricane) Squadrons, about which more will follow. He did not restrict himself to administrative duties but flew whenever possible and on 20 May he believed he had shot down a Messerschmitt Bf 110.[2]

By that date, the German blitzkrieg on France and the Low Countries that began on 10 May had overrun most of the RAF's bases, heavy losses had been suffered and the surviving pilots were in the last stages of exhaustion. On the 21st, on which day German tanks reached the English Channel at Abbeville, it was decided to evacuate 60 Wing's remaining Hurricanes. These gathered at Merville airfield where Broadhurst also took over responsibility for 61 Wing, consisting of two more battered Hurricane squadrons, 607 and 615, both of which had converted from Gladiators just in time to meet the German onslaught.

Broadhurst completed the evacuation of both wings without incident, except that, being the last to leave, he was on his own when attacked by several enemy fighters. Luckily, as the pilots and ground crews of any Hurricane squadron could testify, Camm's fighter could endure an extraordinary amount of punishment and Broadhurst's Hurricane, despite damage to an elevator, an aileron, the cockpit canopy and both wings, brought him safely across the Channel to land at Northolt. He then went on a lecture tour of fighter squadrons in which he urged, successfully, that the line of fire of the Hurricanes' guns, then directed to converge at a range of 400 yards, should instead do so at 250 yards as had already been adopted by the most experienced squadrons in France.

His lecture tour completed, Broadhurst was appointed station commander at Wittering, where he learned that the Hurricane he had flown back from France, though officially 'written off', had in fact been repaired. According to Broadhurst, as reported by Edward Bishop in *Hurricane*:

It suddenly dawned on me that I had my own Hurricane! So I collected it and had it painted black with my initials on it, and used it at night. Meanwhile Rolls-Royce, whom I knew well, offered to re-engine it with the most up to date Merlin[3] which revolutionised its performance.

In December 1940 Broadhurst was posted to Hornchurch to command a Spitfire wing, but he took his private Hurricane with him and continued to fly it at night until mid-1941 when it was reclaimed by the Air Ministry. During daylight hours he accompanied his wing on sweeps over France, gaining several further successes. In May 1942 he became a group captain but this did not prevent him from participating in the raid on Dieppe on 19 August, flying high above the beaches to watch the progress of the fighting and warn if reinforcements were required or a change of tactics was necessary. As with his missions over France, he was then flying a Spitfire but his part in the Hurricane story would resume later.

While Broadhurst was with 60 Wing in France, at Wick his former squadron, now under Squadron Leader John Thompson, together with 43 and 605 (Hurricane) Squadrons, was mounting guard over the British Home Fleet's main base at Scapa Flow in the Orkney Islands. It shot down three enemy bombers at different times before the blitzkrieg led to its recall to Northolt on 13 May 1940. Thereafter it was in almost constant action, first helping to protect the hard-pressed British Expeditionary Force (BEF), often operating temporarily from airfields in France, and later helping to cover the BEF's evacuation.

On 18 May 111 Squadron had its most active day of the war to date, clashing with German bombers escorted by Messerschmitt Bf 109s and Bf 110s. A number of enemy aircraft were destroyed but after Sergeant Craig had shot down a 110, his Hurricane was badly damaged and he was compelled to crash-land. He was unhurt and was able to rejoin his squadron in time to down another 110 on the 24th.

Craig was not the only Treble One pilot to come down in France. On the 19th the squadron made a successful attack on a force of Heinkel He 111s but was then engaged from above by the escorting 110s. This time it was Squadron Leader Thompson who crash-landed but he too was unhurt and returned to England by boat. In a week of intensive combat, 111 was believed to have destroyed sixteen enemy aircraft and had helped the RAF, as the Germans admitted, to gain temporary air supremacy over the Pas de Calais.

After a brief rest 111 was back in action, this time covering the

Dunkirk evacuation that had begun on 26 May. Göring had guaranteed that not one British soldier would escape and his men tried hard to make good his boast but without success. On the 31st most of 111's pilots were kept away from the German bombers by the escorting 109s, although Sergeant Robinson was able to attack a Junkers Ju 88; he shot this down but was wounded by return fire and crash-landed on his return to base. On 1 June the Luftwaffe attacked the rescuing vessels between the RAF fighters' patrols, sinking eleven ships including one French and three British destroyers. Next day, though, 111 was again able to engage enemy raiders and their escort. In an encounter with 109s, the Canadian Pilot Officer Wilson destroyed one but suffered many hits on his Hurricane. Nonetheless, this brought him most of the way back to England and he finally baled out just short of the coast and was rescued unhurt.

Even after the completion of the Dunkirk evacuation, the Hurricanes based in southern England continued to operate over France, escorting Allied bombers or reconnaissance machines and covering lesser evacuations at Le Havre and Le Tréport. On both 6 and 7 June Treble One had battles with 109s, its pilots believing they had destroyed a total of seven of these, and on the 11th the squadron successfully intercepted Dornier Do 17s, escorted by 109s, over Le Havre.

One of the squadron's most accomplished pilots during this period was Flying Officer Henry Michael Ferris who was awarded a DFC, having shot down six or seven enemy aircraft, all of them Messerschmitt Bf 109 or Bf 110 fighters. Unfortunately he has another more dubious claim to fame. As Christopher Shores and Clive Williams reveal in *Aces High*, their magnificent survey of the RAF's leading fighter pilots, when the crew of a 110 that Ferris had brought down on 18 May had baled out and were going to land in German-occupied territory 'he had shot them on their parachutes'.

Since Ferris openly declared this in his Combat Report, he clearly felt his action was justified. However, few RAF pilots would have shared his belief. Most of them regarded themselves as attacking enemy machines, not enemy airmen, were pleased when they saw a parachute open and refrained from firing at an aircraft that was already clearly doomed. They tended, probably deliberately, not to think of what their fire was doing to the men inside the machine they were engaging and were often horrified when they saw the ghastly consequences, consoling themselves with the thought that 'it was either him or me.' They were enraged and disgusted when, as sometimes happened, RAF pilots were killed by enemy fighters while coming down on their parachutes. They were embarrassed by the Polish pilots of 302 and 303 (Hurricane) Squadrons who, during the Battle of Britain, tried to kill Luftwaffe crews after they had baled out.

Air Chief Marshal Sir Hugh Dowding, head of Fighter Command in the Battle of Britain, thought that airmen who had baled out over enemy territory and so were likely to become prisoners of war should not be harmed but those who would be able to return to the fight were 'fair game'. This view would provide justification for Ferris and for German pilots who attacked airmen escaping by parachute over England – though not for the Poles who, in fairness, had better cause to hate their foes than either the British or the Germans – but the question remains why Ferris was prepared to take a course of action of which so few of his fellow pilots could approve.

It appears that Ferris had no personal reason for hating the Germans, so it can only be assumed that he was an exceptionally aggressive character who was desperately eager to get at his foes. On 10 July, for instance, he downed a 109 but, says the Squadron Diary, he 'was in turn attacked by three others who shot away an aileron control; he was persistently attacked for about twenty miles but managed to avoid further damage.' Determined not to be left out of the fight, he decided not to land at a forward airfield but instead made for Croydon, where 111 was then based. Here, the Squadron Diary continues, 'he picked up a fresh Hurricane and immediately set off to join his squadron.'

It was perhaps inevitable that Ferris would not long survive. On 16 August the end came when his Hurricane, thrusting ahead of the rest of the squadron, collided head-on with a Dornier Do 17. 'There was a tremendous explosion,' reported Squadron Leader Thompson, 'and very little left, except a few pieces floating down.'

By 16 August the Battle of Britain had already been in progress for over a month and John Thompson had long since proved himself a worthy successor to Gillan and Broadhurst. As well as his own experiences at Dunkirk, he had had conversations with the surviving pilots of Hurricane squadrons that had fought in the Battle of France but had now all returned to British soil. As a result, he had abandoned the inflexible 'Vee' or 'Vic' formations that involved spending more time keeping station than watching out for enemy aircraft and the recommended standard attacks that the Hurricane squadrons in France had long realized were unsuited to combat at high speeds. Instead, if possible he would lead 111's pilots in head-on charges at their enemies. This tactic resulted in the death of Ferris on 16 August; however, it repeatedly disrupted and scattered hostile formations and was made more effective by an unusual talent that Thompson was lucky enough to possess.

As is well known, Fighter Command was normally given priceless early warning by radar but the experience and efficiency of its operators varied. Some low-flying formations were not detected at all. Reports of enemy numbers were often inaccurate and their height was so notoriously underestimated that most controllers automatically added a few thousand feet to the altitude estimated and many squadron commanders added a further few thousand on their own initiative. Radar also could not tell whether the intruders were making an attack or a diversion or whether they were the main or only a preliminary striking force, or perhaps a 'free chase' as it was called, containing only 109s. Moreover, once the Germans had crossed the coast, radar did not operate and despite the gallant efforts of the Observer Corps volunteers, the defence could be confused by sharp changes of course or the splitting up of formations.

For these reasons, just as valuable as radar were 'Pip-Squeak', a device that automatically reported a British fighter's position to the ground controllers, and a very high-frequency radio that allowed pilots and controllers to keep in touch with each other. These enabled the defenders to remain flexible and carry out changes of plan. Nonetheless, RAF squadrons frequently sighted hostile formations only to find themselves badly-placed to intercept; for instance, still climbing and liable to be attacked from above. Treble

One, though, almost invariably managed to reach a position from which it could attack effectively. This was due in no small measure to Squadron Leader Thompson whose intuitive ability to determine the location and intention of enemy units is described by Basil Collier in *The Battle of Britain* as 'almost uncanny'.

Thompson's men made their first interception in the Battle of Britain on 10 July, officially reckoned to be the day on which it commenced. During July the Luftwaffe concentrated mainly on attacking British shipping, partly in order to gain air superiority over the Channel, partly in order to whittle down Fighter Command, both of which would help prepare the way for the German army to carry out a landing in Britain in about mid-September. Nor were these preliminary raids made in vain: as well as causing much harm to British coastal convoys, the German airmen had sunk four destroyers by the end of July, causing the Royal Navy to abandon Dover as a base, thus leaving the shores of Kent and Sussex wide open to the intended invasion.

To engage the raiders and protect the convoys was the task of Air Vice-Marshal Keith Park, a tall lean New Zealander who commanded No. 11 Group that in these early days before the creation of a separate 10 Group in the south-west was responsible for the defence of the whole of southern England. Park controlled Spitfires and Blenheims as well as Hurricanes but the Hawker fighters made up three-fifths of his strength: fifteen squadrons in all including, of course, 111 at Croydon.

On 10 July No. 11 Group's main task was to defend a large convoy, unromantically code-named BREAD, from attacks by Dornier Do 17s escorted by Messerschmitt Bf 109s and Bf 110s. That only one small ship was sunk owed much to 111 Squadron's terrifying head-on charge that scattered the Dorniers, prevented them from bombing accurately and resulted in one of them being shot down, as was one of the 109s. A second Dornier was lost when Flying Officer Higgs crashed into it. Some accounts suggest that Higgs baled out, only to be drowned, although the Squadron Diary states only that a rescue launch was at once sent to the scene of the collision 'but no sign was found of either Higgs or the Dornier's crew'; in any event, the young pilot lost his life, the only RAF pilot to die on this first day of the battle. The Luftwaffe lost eleven aircraft: one by means unknown, one by AA fire, two by Spitfires and seven by Hurricanes.

Not all the early days were as satisfactory. On 19 July, for instance, a swarm of Messerschmitt Bf 109s attacked nine Defiants of 141 Squadron. The Boulton Paul Defiant was a two-seater monoplane without forward guns that relied on a rear turret containing four 0.303in machine guns. During the Dunkirk evacuation, Defiants had shot down several 109s that had dived straight into the fire of their rear guns, having mistaken them for Hurricanes. In the jubilation caused by this, it was forgotten that in October 1939 Treble One had taken part in comparative trials of the Hurricane and the Defiant and had concluded that any average Hurricane pilot would be able to master a Defiant, as would any 109 pilot who met it more than once.

On 19 July, this judgement proved horribly accurate. Six Defiants were shot down and a seventh so damaged that it was 'written off' and lost its gunner who had baled out, never to be seen again. Ironically, it was 111 Squadron that saved 141 from complete destruction: its Hurricanes arrived just in time to engage the 109s, one of which was shot down by Pilot Officer Simpson, and give the surviving Defiants a chance to escape.

Thereafter 111's fortunes were somewhat mixed. On 25 July its famous head-on attack drove a formation of Junkers Ju 88s away from a convoy it was attempting to bomb and shot down one of the escorting 109s. By contrast, on 11 August 111 was for once engaged by 109s before it could gain height and lost five Hurricanes and four pilots, accounting for only one of the enemy in return. Two days later, the Luftwaffe embarked on its major offensive against Fighter Command but 'Eagle Day', as it was grandly entitled, proved a fiasco as a result of bad weather. This time, 111 was lucky enough to engage a formation of Dornier Do 17s that was not only unescorted but had already been scattered by the Hurricanes of 151 Squadron and lost one of its number. A charge by 111 completed the rout, four more Dorniers falling to its Hurricanes' guns.

Treble One's greatest air battle lay just ahead but before dealing with it, it seems convenient to examine more closely the structure of the Luftwaffe. It was divided into Luftflotten (Air Fleets), of which the two usually engaged with Fighter Command in the Battle of Britain were Luftflotte 2 under Field Marshal Albert Kesselring, stationed in north-east France and the Low Countries, and Luftflotte 3 under Field Marshal Hugo Sperrle in north-west France. Luftflotten in turn were divided into Fliegerkorps and those again into Geschwader of 90 to 120 aircraft.

These Geschwader were designated according to their functions. Those containing bombers, at this time mainly Heinkel He 111s, Dornier Do 17s and Junkers Ju 88s, were called Kampfgeschwader or KG for short. The Junkers Ju 87 dive-bombers formed Stukageschwader (StG). The single-engined Messerschmitt Bf 109s formed Jagdgeschwader (JG). The twin-engined Messerschmitt Bf 110s, of which Göring thought highly and were known as Zerstörern (Destroyers) made up Zerstörergeschwader or ZG. All Geschwader controlled three or four Gruppen, and each Gruppe three or four Staffeln of 10 to 12 machines; the equivalent of though weaker than a typical RAF Squadron. There were also independent Gruppen not attached to any Geschwader and in 1940 by far the most important of these was Erprobungsgruppe 210.

'Test Group 210', to translate its title into English, had been formed on 1 July to provide the Luftwaffe with a unit capable of making low-level attacks on precision targets such as fast convoys, aircraft factories and radar stations. It was divided into three Staffeln, two with Bf 110s and the third with Bf 109s, all of them, including the 109s, carrying bombs. The Gruppe had a brilliant, chivalrous and much-respected leader in the Swiss-born Hauptmann (Captain) Rubensdörffer and he was supported by brave, experienced and able junior officers.

Rubensdörffer's fighter-bombers carried out their most remarkable mission on 12 August. In preparation for Eagle Day, the Germans had decided to disrupt Britain's chain of radar stations and since these were small, difficult and well-defended targets, Erprobungsgruppe 210 was chosen for the task. Its crews certainly did their best. In a cleverly co-ordinated assault on the radar stations at Dover, Rye, Pevensey and Dunkirk near Faversham in north Kent, they hit every one of them and put all except Dunkirk out of action. All were 'back on air' within a few hours but in the meantime a major raid broke through to inflict serious damage on Portsmouth dockyard and knock out the radar station at Ventnor on the Isle of Wight for three days.[4]

As we saw, Eagle Day was not a happy one for the Luftwaffe but on 15 August it made its greatest effort, flying over 2,000 sorties. Naturally Erprobungsgruppe 210 was not left out and early that afternoon it made another brilliant low-level raid on the airfield at Martlesham Heath, achieving complete surprise and so damaging the base that it was not fully operational for forty-eight hours. Then just before 1900, fifteen of its Bf 110s and eight of its 109s swooped down on Croydon airfield. This, of course, was the home of 111 (Hurricane) Squadron which had so far not had a good day, having lost Pilot Officer Fisher in the morning's fighting.

Moments before Erprobungsgruppe 210's assault, Squadron Leader Thompson had taken off at the head of nine Hurricanes and these were just clear of the aerodrome when bombs crashed into it with murderous efficiency. At much the same time, the Hurricanes of 32 Squadron, based at nearby Biggin Hill, attacked Erprobungsgruppe 210 from the flank, shooting down a 110 and a 109. The 109s were in any event short of fuel and were unable to help the 110s as Treble One's avenging Hurricanes also struck these in their usual head-on charge.

Rubensdörffer's able pilots reacted quickly, forming a defensive circle while edging towards the protection of some clouds, then suddenly splitting up into small groups that raced away to the south. Yet the Hurricanes were not taken by surprise and were instantly in pursuit. Five more Messerschmitt Bf 110s were shot down and Thompson personally downed the one flown by Rubensdörffer who perished along with his gunner Feldwebel (Sergeant Major) Ehekercher. Rubensdörffer's last action was to pull his doomed machine away from a cottage on which it was falling, to crash on the far side of it.

The loss of its finest bomber pilot completed the Luftwaffe's depression on 'Black Thursday', as it called 15 August, but the spirit he had inspired in his own airmen lived on. They continued their daring and determined attacks throughout the Battle of Britain but the Hurricanes of other squadrons would, like 111, prove to be just too good for them. Their new leader, Hauptmann von Boltenstern, was killed in a fight with Hurricanes of 601 Squadron on 4 September. It was Spitfires that killed Erprobungsgruppe 210's next leader, Hauptmann Lutz, on 27 September but his successor, Oberleutnant (Lieutenant) Weimann, became another victim of Hurricanes, in this case those of 303 (Polish) Squadron on 5 October.

Erprobungsgruppe 210 made its final assault of the battle on 29 October when its Staffel of bomb-carrying Bf 109s, led by Oberleutnant Hintze, attacked North Weald airfield just as the Hurricanes of 257 Squadron were taking off. Two of these were destroyed and one pilot killed. The Hurricanes of 249 Squadron, also based at North Weald, gave chase to the raiders and Flight Lieutenant Barton shot down the 109 flown by Hintze. The latter escaped by parachute, to become a prisoner of war.

Hermann Göring, who since the start of the battle had enjoyed the newly-created rank of Reichsmarschall, with a king-sized baton to prove it, had promised his Führer that four days of maximum effort by his Luftwaffe would smash Fighter Command. Neither 13 nor 15 August had achieved this but, hoping that the defenders might at least have been exhausted, Göring tried again - and failed again - on 16 and 18 August.

It need hardly be said that 111 was in the thick of the fighting on both days. On the 16th, which happened to be his birthday, Squadron Leader Thompson made another perfect interception of a formation of Dornier Do 17s that 111 was able to scatter before the escorting Messerschmitt Bf 109s could intervene. Two Dorniers were shot down and a third destroyed by collision (this was the incident that resulted in the death of Ferris). Oberleutnant Rudolf Lamberty, who as the pilot of the leading bomber was in an unpleasantly good position to see 111's attack, was immensely impressed by the Hurricanes' performance, which he considered far superior to that of the 109s.[5]

When the 109s did belatedly engage 111, they shot down one Hurricane in flames but Sergeant Carnall escaped by parachute. Pilot Officer Walker evened the score by downing a 109. Sergeant Thomas Wallace, an aggressive South African who had recently joined 111 and was anxious to make up for lost time, pursued a group of Dorniers as far as the French coast. He then encountered six Messerschmitt Bf 109s but outmanoeuvred them and evaded all attacks until five of his foes, presumably short of fuel or ammunition or both, broke off the action. The sixth persisted but despite later statements – British as well as German – no Hurricane pilot feared a 109 in an even duel. Wallace promptly attacked head-on and shot the 109 into the sea. He then returned to base, where his Hurricane was found to be practically undamaged.

On 18 August 111 was sent to the aid of Kenley airfield, threatened by strong formations of Dornier Do 17s and Junkers Ju 88s. Thompson's men shot down at least one Dornier and one Ju 88 and damaged several others but their gunners fought back determinedly, downing two Hurricanes, although both the pilots baled out, and so damaging a third that it crash-landed on a golf course, again without injury to the pilot. Tragically, one of the squadron's finest pilots, Flight Lieutenant Connors, was also shot down and killed, not by the enemy but by 'friendly' AA fire.

Next day, 111 was transferred to Debden, changing places with another Hurricane squadron, No. 85. They also exchanged ground crews who remained at their old bases, though neither noticed any difference as the ground crews of all RAF squadrons of this date were exceptionally good. Debden, though still in No. 11 Group, was supposed to be a less perilous base than Croydon but 111 did not find it particularly restful and on 24, 26 and 31 August and 2 September its pilots intercepted enemy formations, destroying a number of Dornier Do 17s and Messerschmitt Bf 110s, although another of the squadron's best men, Sergeant Dymond, was killed on 2 September. In any case, 111 was ordered back to Croydon on 3 September and on the following day was involved in a violent battle with Bf 109s. It destroyed two of these but lost two Hurricanes, both pilots being killed, one by the enemy fighters after he had taken to his parachute.

Further clashes occurred over the next three days and by now 111's pilots were under intense strain and becoming exhausted. On 5 September, for example, Flying Officer 'Ben' Bowring led eight Hurricanes against more than 100 enemy aircraft and shot down a

109. Early next morning, he downed a Junkers Ju 88 but had his windscreen shattered by return fire. In the late afternoon he was again in action, was forced to bale out and was temporarily put off the squadron strength with a wounded arm.

It was all becoming too much to endure and on 8 September 111 was withdrawn to Drem and later to other bases in Scotland. Since it had flown south to No. 11 Group on 13 May, it had been credited with the destruction of ninety-four enemy aircraft, though this was undoubtedly an exaggeration as a result of duplicated claims for the same 'kill' made by more than one pilot and by what the RAF understandingly called the 'enthusiasm factor'. Fifteen of its pilots had died in action and it now had only seven serviceable Hurricanes left.

Treble One's glory days were over for the time being. John Thompson left in October for a staff post at No. 11 Group and in due course became an air commodore; his men settled down in the role of a 'C Class' squadron, the primary duty of which was training new pilots. On 25 October a raid by Heinkel He 111s on their base at Montrose destroyed seven Hurricanes on the ground, killed six airmen and wounded twenty-one others. The squadron gained some revenge during November by shooting down several Heinkels, two of them being disposed of by Sergeant Kucera, a Czech pilot who had come to Britain by way of the Balkans, the Middle East and France and been posted to 111 in early October.

New Year's Day 1941 was marked by 111 with the destruction of a Junkers Ju 88 over the sea, east of Aberdeen. For the first three months of the year there were similar encounters, becoming increasingly rare, until in April 1941 the first squadron to have received Hurricanes ceased to fly them and re-equipped with Spitfires.

That, though, would not be the last time that 111 Squadron flew Hawker aircraft, for in June 1955 it received Sydney Camm's most beautiful fighter: the slim, elegant Hunter with its swept-back wings, fin and tailplane that was the first RAF aircraft to exceed the speed of sound. In addition to its normal duties, 111 devoted every spare moment to practising formation aerobatics and for three years gave inspired demonstrations at various air shows, culminating at

Farnborough in 1958 when no fewer than twenty-two of its all-black Hunters, the 'Black Arrows' as they were called, performed an incredible tight roll in perfect unison.

For many who saw the Black Arrows, 111 Squadron will always be associated with the Hawker Hunter, but its place in aviation history is most firmly secured by its association with the Hawker Hurricane. Nor was that association forgotten by the men who flew the Hunters. On 8 August 1955 their brilliant leader, Squadron Leader Roger Topp, honoured it by repeating Gillan's famous flight from Turnhouse to Northolt. Gillan's 'State Express 555' had made this at an average speed of 408.75 mph. Topp's Hunter WT739 averaged 717.50 mph. Such was the advance in less than twenty years of the aircraft designed by Sydney Camm.

Notes

1. The various Indian states, for instance, donated the money for over 200 RAF fighters. The most poignant individual gifts were surely those of Lady Rachel MacRobert who lost all three of her pilot sons and who provided the country with a Stirling bomber and four Hurricanes. The 'MacRobert Hurricanes', as they were collectively called, flew with 94 Squadron, on which Flight Lieutenant Sir Roderic MacRobert had been serving when he was killed in action on 21 May 1941.
2. Both the twin-engined Messerschmitt Bf 110 and the single-engined Messerschmitt Bf 109 were made by the Bavarian Aircraft Company, or *Bayerische Flugzeugwerke* in German, hence the abbreviation 'Bf'. Allied airmen almost invariably called them the 'Me 110' and the 'Me 109' but this was not technically correct until 1944.
3. This was the Merlin XX that subsequently powered the Mark II Hurricanes.
4. Ventnor radar station, having just been restored, was again put out of action on 16 August, this time for seven days, while on the 18th that at Poling was knocked out for over a week. It is a tribute to the flexibility of Fighter Command that some of its finest achievements took place when its radar cover was least effective.
5. Lamberty had a still better reason for appreciating the Hurricanes' capabilities two days later, when those of 615 Squadron shot down his Dornier and he became a prisoner of war.

Chapter 2

Action by Day, Action by Night: 87 Squadron

Not only was Treble One the first RAF squadron to fly Hurricanes, but for some time it was the only RAF squadron to fly them. The motto of No. 3 Squadron is *Tertius primus erit* ('The third shall be first') but with regard to Hurricanes, No. 3 had to be content with being second and that only briefly. It obtained its first Hurricanes in March 1938 but its base, Kenley, was then too small for the aircraft, especially the early ones hampered by their wooden two-bladed propellers and needing a long take-off and landing run. A series of accidents culminated in the death of Pilot Officer Henry-May after which the squadron lost its Hurricanes, only getting them back in May 1939.

Next to be equipped with Hurricanes was 56 Squadron. It received them in May 1938 and became fully operational in August. Thus at the time of the Munich Crisis in late September, Fighter Command had just two Hurricane squadrons available, only one of which was experienced and neither of which could fight above 15,000ft since the heating for their gun-bays had not been installed. It had no Spitfires at all, was supported by inadequate numbers of anti-aircraft guns and had not yet completed either its chain of radar stations or the ground-control system that would prove so important later on.

Had war come at this time, therefore, there is no doubt that the Luftwaffe, already powerful and with priceless practical experience gained by its Condor Legion in the Spanish Civil War, would have been able to inflict very heavy damage on Britain, even though its bombers would have been unescorted since its fighters lacked sufficient range. Certainly Dowding was devoutly grateful that his Fighter Command was not yet to be tested and strove to make all possible use of the time gained. As mentioned earlier, in November 1938 an order for 1,000 more Hurricanes was placed and urgent attempts were made to get more Hurricane squadrons into service without delay.

One very important squadron was the fourth to fly the Hawker fighter: No. 87, commanded by Squadron Leader John Rhys-Jones. Not only had it received Hurricanes in place of Gladiators by early July 1938 – though it did not become fully operational until after Munich – but it had previously detached a flight that would form the basis of another famous Hurricane squadron, No. 85. Both 87 and its 'daughter' squadron were sent to France soon after the war that Munich had postponed began on 3 September 1939.

The BEF was promptly shipped across the Channel to support the French and the RAF prepared to support the BEF with six army co-operation squadrons of Blenheims or Lysanders and four squadrons of Hurricanes, all together called the Air Component. In October, however, 1 and 73 (Hurricane) Squadrons were transferred to help protect the Advanced Air Striking Force, a group of twelve Blenheim or Battle squadrons stationed in Lorraine behind the Maginot Line to carry out bombing or reconnaissance missions across the German frontier. This left only 87 and 85 as the fighter contingent of the Air Component. They were not reinforced until November and then only by the Gladiators of 607 and 615 Squadrons.

It had been decided to send Hurricanes to France because they had already become noted for their reliability and their wide, strong undercarriages were thought to be particularly valuable. The wisdom of this decision was quickly discovered by 87 Squadron. It was moved round a series of airfields that had only grass runways and these were at first so frequently waterlogged that the Hurricanes took off and landed amidst sheets of spray and later, with the coming of winter, were covered with snow and ice.

In these circumstances, the gallant ground crews had to toil ceaselessly to keep their aircraft serviceable. That they succeeded in doing so was a great compliment to them and also to the Hurricanes, for they were of the unanimous opinion that no other fighters would have endured such conditions. It was a pointer to the future when Hurricanes would operate in Norway and Russia and fly from rough desert strips, from clearings hacked out of the jungle and from the decks of aircraft carriers.

For the first months of the war, 87 had little chance to show its mettle and suffered its first casualty on 6 October when Sergeant Witty inexplicably crashed when landing and was killed. On 2 November, however, the squadron was at last in action against some reconnaissance Heinkel He 111s and Flight Lieutenant Robert Voase-Jeff shot down one of these, for which the French awarded him a Croix de Guerre. This was the first victory, not only for 87 but also for the Air Component as a whole.

On the same day, three of 87's Hurricanes attacked another Heinkel He 111. This put up a fine fight, damaging two of the Hurricanes and eventually returned to its base, albeit in a somewhat battered condition. The British pilots wrongly believed that it had force-landed in Belgium and its crew would therefore be interned, but in fact it would be 87 that would have problems with Belgium's neutrality. On 10 November Pilot Officer Dunn pursued a Dornier Do 17 over Belgium and damaged it so badly that it crashed later, killing all the crew. Dunn, however, being desperately short of petrol, was compelled to land in Belgium and was duly interned. Four days later he was joined by Squadron Leader Coope and Flying Officer Glyde who had similarly run out of fuel. All three were taken to a fort in Antwerp but allowed to visit the city on parole.

What happened next is vividly described by Perry Adams in *Hurricane Squadron: No. 87 Squadron at War 1939-1941*. Allied Intelligence had learned of what had happened and when the three pilots were sitting in a café, they were joined by a lady who introduced herself as a British 'agent'. A plan for their escape was quickly arranged. They began to take exercise runs around the fort every evening after dark. When a week of this activity had accustomed the guards to it, the same resourceful lady met them again and guided them over the French frontier. 'All were safely back at their airfield on 27 November,' Mr Adams reports triumphantly.

Despite the worsening weather, 87 continued to fly, although not without some unpleasant incidents. On 9 December Sergeant Frank Howell, flying a replacement Hurricane to the squadron, got lost in dreadful visibility and force-landed in Belgium. However, he did not have to receive help from the Secret Service for a friendly Belgian citizen arrived immediately and at once took him to the French frontier. On 3 January 1940 Flying Officer Joyce crashed on landing, happily without injury, but on 12 February Sergeant Thurgar also crashed while attempting an emergency landing and was killed.

The coming of spring brought better weather but also the return of German 'recce' aircraft. On 9 May Pilot Officer Dunn and Sergeant Gareth Nowell attacked a Messerschmitt Bf 110 and so damaged it that it crashed on landing and was 'written off'. Dunn then engaged a Dornier Do 17. His Hurricane was hit by return fire from the rear gunner and he force-landed, luckily with only minor injuries. He was unaware of the success of his own fire but in fact the Dornier also crash-landed and became a total loss.

This enemy activity was no doubt in preparation for what happened on 10 May: Germany's blitzkrieg in the west. 'War really starts,' wrote 87's Pilot Officer Dennis David in his logbook. It certainly did for him. It is reported that he flew six times that day and gained his first victories, so damaging a Heinkel He 111 and a Dornier Do 17 that both crash-landed and were written off. It was the start of a period of ten more days of frantic action that saw him destroy at least six more enemy aircraft and win a DFC and bar. When 87 was eventually evacuated to England and had a chance to rest, he went to bed and slept continuously for thirty-six hours.

David's experiences were typical of those of the pilots of 87 Squadron during these early days of May 1940. Now commanded by Squadron Leader John Dewar, who would soon earn a DSO and a DFC, they found themselves in constant action with enemy aircraft. On 10 May Sergeant Nowell shot down a pair of Henschel Hs 126 observation aircraft and the squadron destroyed two or three more later on in the fighting. Normally, though, 87 was battling against depressingly heavy numbers of German bombers, often strongly escorted.

On 11 May there were several clashes with Dornier Do 17s, of which 87 undoubtedly shot down three. The squadron also attacked Junkers Ju 87 Stuka dive-bombers, of which it destroyed three and damaged three others so severely that they crash-landed. On the 12th Heinkel He 111s were successfully engaged, and the 13th, an otherwise unhappy day, saw the start of the most remarkably varied career of any pilot who flew Hurricanes.

The 19-year-old Pilot Officer Roland Prosper 'Bee' Beamont[1] had not yet been able to claim a 'kill' when, on 13 May, 87 Squadron attacked a formation of Dornier Do 17s. The bombers were escorted by Messerschmitt Bf 110s that promptly counter-attacked the Hurricanes. One dived towards Beamont but he evaded this by turning tightly, resumed his own assault on the Dorniers and shot one of them down. Satisfaction turned to alarm as he came under fire from behind and then to astonishment on seeing that this came from the front gunner of another Dornier whose pilot clearly thought attack the best means of defence. Though Beamont would later acknowledge that 'the German flew his bomber with skill and tenacity', the Hurricane easily outmanoeuvred it and Beamont gained 'a perfect position' to open fire in his turn. 'Three rounds went off – then silence.' He was out of ammunition!

Already being engaged by the Dornier's gunners, Beamont broke away sharply and headed for base. His determined enemy even chased after him, getting off a few more shots before the Hurricane pulled away. Beamont reflected rather grimly that while the Dornier might claim a 'moral victory', he would make sure he soon gained some more real ones. This he did, downing a further three enemy aircraft in the course of the next four days.

These dramatic days in May saw plenty of successes for 87's pilots but also heavy losses, among them Flight Lieutenant Campbell who was shot down and killed by Messerschmitt Bf 109s on the 13th. On the 16th and 17th, however, a batch of fresh pilots joined 87, including Campbell's replacement Flight Lieutenant Ian Gleed. Though a small man, nicknamed 'Widge' – RAF slang for 'Midget' – he was extremely aggressive and immensely confident. 'Bee' Beamont says that Gleed's 'spirit was exactly what was needed' to revive 87's somewhat shaken morale.

Despite his aggressive attitude, Gleed, like Beamont before him, had not yet made a 'kill' when he took off on 18 May on his first sortie with 87 Squadron. He was flying a brand-new Hurricane that had also only arrived on the previous day and his confidence was boosted by the fact that 'already a black cat – my mascot – was painted on its side.' It appears to have brought him luck, for when 87 encountered a formation of Messerschmitt Bf 110s, he personally shot down two of these. Over the next couple of days he destroyed three more enemy aircraft and shared in the destruction of two others.

By 20 May, with its bases being overrun, it was clear that the Air Component's squadrons could do nothing more, so while 87's ground crews were carried home in transport aircraft, all serviceable Hurricanes were also flown out. There were now only seven of these left, some of which were not in a healthy state. One, indeed, was in so perilous a condition that, as Maurice Allward points out in his *Hurricane Special*, it was made the subject of an official Air Ministry Bulletin.

This particular machine belonged to Flying Officer Derek Ward, a New Zealander who had formerly flown Hurricanes with 151 Squadron and had joined 87 on 16 May, bringing a new Hurricane with him. It had subsequently seen much combat and, as the bulletin relates, was already 'severely damaged before the pilot left on his journey home.' In addition, Ward had decorated it with a 'coat of arms' that tempted fate: it consisted of a shield with its four quarters showing emblems of ill luck, namely a broken mirror, three cigarettes being lighted with one match, a man walking under a ladder and a large figure 13. The motto underneath was: 'So What the Hell'.

It was perhaps inevitable that Ward's journey home was a nightmare, culminating in his meeting six Messerschmitt Bf 109s when he was almost out of both petrol and ammunition. His luck was not all bad, however, for he did get back to Britain where, says the bulletin, 'the Hurricane was examined' and 'numerous bullet holes were found in the wings, fuselage and tail.'

During the fighting in May, 87 Squadron claimed to have

destroyed at least eighty enemy aircraft, though no doubt this figure was exaggerated. Nine of its pilots had been killed, including Flight Lieutenant Campbell as already mentioned. Flying Officer Joyce had been shot down and so badly injured that one leg had to be amputated. Sergeants Howell and Nowell had both been 'missing' for some days but had baled out and crash-landed respectively and subsequently rejoined the squadron. Pilot Officer Dunn had twice landed a badly-damaged Hurricane and finally, on 19 May, after shooting down a 109, he was himself shot down in flames but baled out, suffering burns. He returned to Britain safely but, horrible to relate, was killed soon afterwards in a flying accident.

Such statistics soon become meaningless and it would be morbid to examine all the losses but perhaps the death of Pilot Officer Christopher 'Kit' Mackworth on 14 May, the details of which are given by Perry Adams in *Hurricane Squadron*, may stand for all of them. Mackworth had been ordered to investigate enemy activity in the Brussels area and sighted seven German aircraft shooting up an advanced dressing station manned by a company from the Royal Army Medical Corps (RAMC). Although he was alone, Mackworth attacked the seven but was shot down and killed. His body was buried in a nearby cemetery and covered with flowers by local Belgian ladies. Mackworth had been married only a few months earlier and 'was wearing a silver locket round his neck.' Inside it was found a photograph of his wife and a strand of fair hair.

Nonetheless, for all its cruel losses, 87 was still a strong squadron. It was still led by the immensely competent John Dewar. It was still inspired by the indomitable spirit of 'Widge' Gleed. It still contained experienced men like Dennis David, Roland Beamont, Flight Lieutenant Robert Voase-Jeff who had gained its first victory and Derek Ward who would himself become a flight lieutenant in August. It would be strengthened by 'new boys' like young Pilot Officer Trevor Jay, a South African who would soon prove one of its most successful pilots. Moreover, a fortunate quiet period while the Germans completed their conquest of France gave it an opportunity for rest and recovery.

During this interval of calm between the Battle of France and the Battle of Britain, 87 was based first at Debden and then at Church

Fenton in Yorkshire, but on 4 July it moved to Exeter which it shared with another Hurricane squadron, No. 213. This was then in No. 11 Group but was shortly to be transferred to a new No. 10 Group led by a South African, Air Vice-Marshal Sir Christopher Quintin Brand, responsible for the protection of the south-west and the country on both sides of the Bristol Channel. This group had been hastily formed on the realization that the German occupation of north-western France would enable the Luftwaffe to turn 11 Group's flank as well as to strike at convoys in the area; 87 Squadron would soon discover that there was good reason for this apprehension.

On 11 July Squadron Leader Dewar, Flying Officer Glyde and Pilot Officer Jay were ordered off against a formation of Junkers Ju 87s, escorted by Messerschmitt Bf 110s, attacking shipping off Portland. Hurricanes from 238 and 601 Squadrons were also sent against this formation and 601, the first to arrive, shot down one dive-bomber, whereupon the others dropped their bombs at random and fled. Pilots from all three squadrons then engaged the 110s, four of which were shot down. The 87 Squadron trio believed that they had had a hand in all these victories.

Squadron Leader Dewar certainly helped to down one of the Messerschmitts. Two more then attacked him but he outmanoeuvred them and damaged one. Another Hurricane then closed in and finished it off. This was Dewar's last combat as 87 Squadron's CO, but not his last with it. Promoted to wing commander, as station commander at Exeter he could still fly with his old unit – now under a New Zealander, Squadron Leader Terence Lovell-Gregg – and did so whenever possible.

On 24 July Roland Beamont had an encounter that says a good deal about his character. He sighted a Junkers Ju 88 with a Spitfire (from 92 Squadron) pursuing it. This then pulled away, presumably out of ammunition, so Beamont took up the chase, putting one of the Ju 88's engines out of action. The rear gunner baled out and Beamont stopped firing as his quarry seemed about to attempt a crash-landing. This it duly did and then caught fire. Beamont had a 'momentary fear' that the rest of its crew might be trapped and was relieved to see them struggle clear. On returning to base he did not claim a victory, believing this should go to the Spitfire pilot as the first one to attack. However, it is pleasant to record that he was credited with a 'half-share' anyway.

Two days later, 87 Squadron embarked on a new activity: intercepting enemy raiders at night as well as by day. These were called 'cat's eye' missions, rather to the pilots' disgust, and although certainly not ideal, the Hurricane was by far the most suitable single-seat night-fighter available. John Gillan had once declared it to be 'a simple aeroplane to fly by night' and it did have the advantages of a fine forward view, steadiness as a gun platform, viceless response to its pilot's instructions and – a cynic might say best of all – a wide, strong undercarriage that could endure a very forceful landing without ill effects.

Indeed, the Hurricane could cope with night-fighting better than most of its pilots. They had to train their eyes to make use of whatever light was available.[2] They learned to wear goggles with dark lenses and keep away from any bright glares. They learned to use searchlights and AA bursts as guides to the progress of German aircraft. They learned to pick out enemy machines silhouetted against the fires their bombs had started. Yet all this knowledge came from experience and that was difficult and dangerous to acquire.

The activities of No. 87 on the night of 26/27 July 1940 provide a portrait in miniature of Hurricane night patrols. One of its flights had been sent to Hullavington near Bristol and was ordered to intercept a group of enemy bombers that had hoped to outflank the defences by flying up the Bristol Channel. The first pilot to take off was Sergeant Culverwell, but it seems that he lost his bearings for he climbed much too steeply. The Hurricane stalled, crashed and burst into flames, killing the unlucky sergeant. The Australian Pilot Officer John Cock was more fortunate. He took off safely, found one of the raiders, shot it down and completed the good work by landing safely.

Throughout the Battle of Britain 87 Squadron flew occasional night patrols, during which it damaged at least four more enemy aircraft, but these missions naturally became few and far between when the day-fighting rose in intensity. On 11 August six of 87's Hurricanes engaged a massive raid of Junkers Ju 88s and Messerschmitt Bf 109s, once more over Portland. Dennis David and

John Cock each destroyed a Ju 88 but then the 109s dived on the Hurricanes from above. Flight Lieutenant Voase-Jeff was killed, his Hurricane plunging into the sea with just a few pieces of wreckage to mark the spot. David, Pilot Officer McLure and Flight Sergeant Badger, however, all shot down 109s and although McLure's aircraft was damaged, all returned safely to base, as did Flying Officer Glyde.

Pilot Officer Cock was less successful but very lucky. Having downed his Junkers, he was attacked from behind and baled out with some difficulty. A 109 fired on him while he was descending by parachute but missed and was itself shot down by David. Cock came down in the sea but managed to get to shore after kicking off his boots and trousers for easier swimming. The Squadron Diary recorded with delight his return 'dressed in a tunic and blue underpants – a somewhat fearsome spectacle.'

Two days later came Eagle Day and more combats for 87 Squadron. It destroyed at least one bomber but Flying Officer Glyde was shot down and killed by return fire. Then two days after that came 15 August, which saw the Luftwaffe's greatest effort. Among the squadrons that met the raiders was No. 87, the pilots of which believed they had inflicted considerable damage on them. Trevor Jay, for instance, believed he had downed a pair of Junkers Ju 87s. He may well have contributed to their destruction but so confused was the fighting that it is impossible to be certain of who did what. Jay was next in action against five 109s. He damaged one but, as he nonchalantly recorded in his Combat Report: 'I then finished my ammunition and was shot down.' In fact, he force-landed and his Hurricane was later repaired.

Squadron Leader Lovell-Gregg, 87's CO, was less fortunate. His Hurricane was set on fire and he was wounded in his arms and legs. It appears that he tried to land his aircraft but crashed into a small copse and was killed. Pilot Officer Comely died also, his Hurricane going into the sea, and several other pilots owed their lives to their Hurricanes' ability to withstand combat damage. Wing Commander Dewar, for example, was flying with 87 on this occasion and brought his battered Hurricane home safely, reporting casually that it was 'not seriously hit except in the engine and wings.'

Dewar would also be found leading 87 in its next major clash with the enemy on 25 August, again over Portland. He personally shot down a Junkers Ju 88, while his pilots destroyed a second Junkers and three 109s. Sadly, though, 87 lost another pilot: Sergeant Wakeling baled out of his burning Hurricane but was killed when his parachute failed to open.

No doubt much to the relief of 87's men, by now inevitably suffering under the constant mental strain, 25 August was the squadron's last day of really intense activity. On 15 September its only contribution to Fighter Command's great victory was a single reconnaissance Heinkel shot down in the early morning by David and Jay. On 30 September, however, it did help to repel a raid on the aircraft factory at Yeovil so effectively that not a single bomb hit the target.

Sad to relate, 87 was to have two more cruel losses before the Battle of Britain officially ended on 31 October. On 2 September Wing Commander Dewar borrowed one of 87's Hurricanes for a flight to Tangmere. It appears that he encountered enemy aircraft near Southampton, was shot down and baled out but was drowned. His body was recovered later. On 24 October, on a routine patrol, Trevor Jay's machine collided with the one flown by John Cock. The latter returned to base safely despite having a good deal of its tail missing but Jay, with his propeller shattered, had no choice other than to bale out. He climbed onto his aircraft's wing, waved to other members of the squadron and jumped. Apparently he hit the tailplane of his Hurricane and was either knocked out or so injured that he was unable to open his parachute. He was just 19 years old.

Trevor Jay's death was all the more tragic because by that time 87's pilots were flying few routine patrols in daylight. They did carry out the occasional one well into 1941, mainly in the protection of convoys, and on 12 April lost Sergeant Stirling who was forced to 'ditch', was rescued by the enemy and became a prisoner of war. In October 1940, however, as the heavy daylight raids died away, a number of Hurricane squadrons, including 87, now based at Charmy Down near Bath, were detailed for use chiefly as night-fighters. The squadron met with very little success at first but, on the night of 4/5 January 1941, Flying Officer Denis 'Splinters'

Smallwood, soon to be promoted to flight lieutenant, attacked a Junkers Ju 88 that crashed at its base as a result of the damage he had inflicted. A similar fate befell a Heinkel He 111 engaged by Flight Lieutenant 'Roddy' Rayner on the night of 10/11 April and a number of other raiders suffered lesser damage during the same month.

These minor achievements did not satisfy 'Widge' Gleed, who had become CO of 87 Squadron in December 1940 and he therefore turned his attention to the possibility of going onto the offensive at night. The RAF had already introduced night-intruder missions by twin-engined fighters that prowled over German aerodromes in the hope of ambushing bombers returning after raids on Britain. Fighter Command now felt that Hurricanes would be ideal for engaging German aircraft over their own bases and also for 'shooting up' those bases with the aid of the full moon.

When tentative approaches on this subject were made to Squadron Leader Gleed, he took them up with enthusiasm. On the night of 14/15 March, Gleed and 'Roddy' Rayner struck at the airfield at Carpiquet near Caen, destroying or damaging several Dorniers and Ju 88s and causing considerable disruption and alarm. A second attack on Carpiquet was made by Derek Ward and Roland Beamont, who also strafed a locomotive at Caen Railway Station, leaving it half-hidden in smoke and steam.

From then until early August, Gleed and his more experienced pilots kept up the pressure on the enemy during the hours of darkness. On 7 May, for instance, Gleed, accompanied by Sergeant Lawrence 'Rubber' Thorogood, set off to raid Maupertus aerodrome near Cherbourg but, when halfway across the Channel, Gleed glimpsed 'a dark shape' heading towards England. He turned in pursuit of it, identified it as a Dornier Do 17 and shot it down in flames. The two Hurricanes then returned to base but Maupertus was not to escape attention, for later that night Beamont and Pilot Officer Geoffrey Roscoe raided it and, braving heavy flak, fired at gunposts, searchlights and 109s on the ground. On the return flight, Beamont sighted a fast German patrol boat and strafed this as well.

Still not content, the tireless Gleed found another sphere of action. German aircraft engaged on bombing, reconnaissance or mine-laying missions had become accustomed to sweeping well beyond the south-west of England and then approaching up the Bristol Channel. Gleed proposed to lead a detachment of Hurricanes to St Mary's in the Scilly Isles, from which these raiders could be intercepted. The one landing ground available to the Hurricanes was a small grass strip, only 450 yards long, but the Hawker machines had already shown that they could operate from fields, and trials at Charmy Down showed that it was possible for them to take off and land within this strictly limited distance.

Accordingly, on 19 May 1941, Gleed's detachment arrived at St Mary's, all landing safely. Its loyal ground crews had been shipped to the island earlier and now set about refuelling and servicing the Hurricanes, but only one was ready for action when the local Coastguard Station fired a red flare that was the agreed warning of an approaching enemy aircraft. Pilot Officer Badger – the former flight sergeant had just been commissioned – hastily took off and vanished over the cliff at the edge of the landing strip, causing a momentary fear that he was about to crash into the sea. Mercifully, he gained height in time and sighted an Arado Ar 196 floatplane, which he promptly shot down. Gleed was himself in action on 24 May, when he and Sergeant Thorogood destroyed a Dornier Do 18 flying boat.

During all its wartime experiences so far, 87 Squadron had flown Hurricanes and was very glad to have done so. Roland Beamont relates in his *Phoenix into Ashes*[3] that during the Battle of Britain, there was a suggestion that the squadron be re-equipped with Spitfires. This did not meet with approval. The pilots knew their Hurricanes and trusted them completely. They knew little of the Spitfire and from what they did know, believed it to be a less effective warplane. Certainly it was faster but it was also less manoeuvrable, a less steady gun platform, less capable of taking battle damage and less easily repaired when it had been damaged. Pilots and ground crews alike asked to retain their Hurricanes and their request was granted.

They may have had second thoughts a little later when Michael Lister Robinson, the CO of 609 Squadron and, Beamont tells us, 'an acknowledged virtuoso of the Spitfire', paid a visit in a Mark II, the very type that 87 would have received. It was 'much admired', says Beamont, and well it might have been. Air Marshal Sir Peter Wykeham, who flew both aircraft, declares in *Fighter Command* that 'The Hurricane inspired solid affection and respect; the Spitfire devotion', and of all the beautiful 'Spits', the Mark II was the most beautiful.

Fortunately for everyone's peace of mind, two of 87's Hurricanes engaged Lister Robinson in a mock dogfight; it is with a sense of inevitability that one learns they were flown by Gleed and Beamont. 'Within one and a half turns', both Hurricanes were on the Spitfire's tail and nothing Lister Robinson could do would shake them off. Finally he headed for home and at last began to escape his pursuers as the Spitfire's superior speed slowly pulled it away from them. The pilots of 87 Squadron were reassured that they had made the right decision.

In early 1941, 87 Squadron had the pleasure of obtaining better aircraft and still flying Hurricanes. Sydney Camm had always looked for ways in which he could improve the Hurricane's performance, range and hitting power. The first of these requirements was met when Rolls-Royce produced the Merlin XX engine that raised the Hurricane's speed to 342 mph and gave it a better rate of climb and a service ceiling of 36,000ft; it was also extremely reliable and easy to produce. The Hurricane's range could be increased by fitting attachments to the wings that would enable it to carry fixed or jettisonable fuel tanks and, as early as January 1940, Camm had proposed that the Hurricane's armament be increased from eight to twelve Browning machine guns.

An anticipated shortage of Brownings (that did not in fact occur) led to this last improvement being postponed. As an interim measure, in late 1940 the RAF received the Hurricane IIA with the Merlin XX and later the ability to carry the extra fuel tanks as well. Early in 1941 the twelve-gun version, the Mark IIB, followed it into squadron service. By mid-summer, most of the squadrons then equipped with Hurricanes had converted to these early Mark IIs but No. 87 would go straight from Mark Is to a later Mark II version.

As far back as 1935, Camm had considered mounting four

cannons in his Hurricane and had formally submitted a design for this version on 23 April 1936. It was rejected, perhaps because the Air Ministry wanted no delays in the production of Hurricanes.

All the same, Hawkers did not lose sight of the idea and, during the Battle of Britain, a Hurricane fitted with two 20mm Oerlikon cannons, one under each wing – originally for air-testing them – served with 151 Squadron, destroying one enemy aircraft and damaging another beyond repair. Even more significantly, a Hurricane that had suffered battle damage was converted by Hawkers to carry four 20mm cannons in the wings. This aircraft went to 46 Squadron and on 5 September its new weapons blew a Messerschmitt Bf 109 to pieces.

Both these modified machines had their speed much reduced by the weight of their weapons, but in February 1941 a Hurricane carrying four 20mm cannons and powered by the new Merlin XX engine attained a maximum speed of 336 mph. By this time the Germans had begun to provide their warplanes with more protective armour and Hawkers now received every encouragement to get Hurricanes carrying cannons, which had a greater penetrative power than the old Browning machine guns, into production as soon as possible.

By mid-summer of 1941 Hurricane Mark IICs, as the cannon-armed aircraft were called, were equipping seven squadrons including No. 87. They were used very effectively by the 87 detachments that continued to be sent at intervals to the Scilly Isles. Before winter brought these operations to an end, 87 had destroyed four more enemy aircraft, the last of them on 21 October.

Not long afterwards, 'Widge' Gleed was promoted to wing commander and left 87, to his own profound regret. He would always remember his time with 87, about which he would shortly write a book entitled *Arise to Conquer* that consists of a series of what can only be called 'action replays'. The squadron's new CO was 'Splinters' Smallwood, now a squadron leader. He would eventually become Air Chief Marshal Sir Denis Smallwood, Commander-in-Chief of Strike Command, which included all Britain's NATO Air Forces, and it is not intended in any way as a criticism of him to say that Gleed's flying skills, tactical knowledge and inspirational personality could never be fully replaced.

Smallwood's task was made no easier by the fact that Gleed was only the last of 87's most brilliant pilots to go elsewhere. Dennis David had been posted to 213 (Hurricane) Squadron back in October 1940. 'Bee' Beamont went to 79 Squadron in June 1941 and while with this was court-martialled for giving a WAAF officer a joy-ride in his Hurricane; however, he escaped with a reprimand. In December 1941 he was seconded to Hawkers, where he test-flew Hurricanes prior to their entry into squadron service, thus starting a new career that would run parallel with his existing one of fighter pilot. Finally 87 Squadron lost Flight Lieutenant Derek Ward in September 1941 when he was promoted and left for the Middle East where he would command another famous Hurricane squadron, No. 73.

Sadly also, 87, having suffered no fatal casualty since the death of Trevor Jay in October 1940, lost four pilots killed in flying accidents in the last four months of 1941. In February 1942 Geoffrey Roscoe, by then a flight lieutenant, also died. Smallwood and his men were therefore delighted when in August 1942 they were transferred to Tangmere and ordered to repaint their all-black Hurricanes in daytime camouflage in preparation for an important daylight operation.

This turned out to be Operation JUBILEE, the raid on Dieppe carried out on 19 August by mainly Canadian soldiers. These suffered very heavy casualties and gained hardly any of their objectives, although it is only right to recall that it was always intended that the troops should be ashore for only one day during which they would do as much damage as they could. The RAF's duties were to prevent the Luftwaffe from interfering and to provide close support. The former was given mainly to Spitfires, the latter to eight squadrons of Hurricanes including 87. Both tasks were fulfilled but at the high cost of over sixty Spitfires and twenty Hurricanes, almost all the Hurricanes to vicious anti-aircraft fire.

During the day 87 Squadron flew three close support missions, hitting German defensive positions, machine-gun posts and army lorries with its 20mm cannons. Several Hurricanes were hit by flak and three of them failed to return to base. Pilot Officer Baker baled out and was rescued by one of the Royal Navy vessels supporting the landings but Sergeant Gibson and a Polish pilot, Flying Officer Waltos, were killed. Soon afterwards, the squadron was given a period of rest that it was probably not sorry to take.

On 8 November 1942 a series of more successful landings, collectively called Operation TORCH, put Allied soldiers ashore in Vichy French Morocco and Algeria. These were quickly overrun but hopes of an advance eastward were dashed by the swift arrival of Axis forces in Tunisia. Then in early December the weather broke, turning Allied lines of communication into a sea of mud. A long struggle for Tunisia followed, from which the Allies only emerged triumphant in early May 1943.

As the chance of a quick victory faded, the RAF began to increase the squadrons in north-eastern Algeria. Among them was 87 which arrived on 17 December and added to its reputation as a night-fighter unit in the early hours of 22 January 1943 when Flight Lieutenant Arthur Cochrane intercepted an Italian Savoia Marchetti SM 79 that he shot into the sea. Cochrane had only joined 87 at the end of August 1942 but during the Battle of Britain had been credited with the destruction of six German aircraft while flying with 257 (Hurricane) Squadron. He had adorned his machine with six swastikas below the cockpit to celebrate these successes and he now added an ice-cream cone to represent the SM 79.

Normally, though, 87 Squadron flew convoy protection patrols in daylight that offered few opportunities for combat. On 27 March, however, a raid on a convoy by Heinkel He 111s was intercepted by Flying Officers Johnson and Thompson, each of whom downed one of the attackers. Unhappily, the squadron's pleasure was considerably reduced four days later when Flight Lieutenant Cochrane failed to return from an early-morning patrol for reasons that were never to be explained.

The squadron's Hurricanes gained their last victories in early April. On the 11th Pilot Officer Bawden shot down a reconnaissance Junkers Ju 88 and next day, another Ju 88 was destroyed by Flying Officer Gibbs. Yet it was also in April that Spitfires began to reach 87 and though some detachments retained Hurricanes for a few more months, the 'Spits' had taken over completely by September.

In that same April of 1943, 87 received bad news about one of its most famous 'old boys'. After leaving 87, Wing Commander Ian 'Widge' Gleed had led Spitfire wings on cross-Channel sweeps in 1942 and on operations supporting the British Eighth Army in North Africa in 1943. On 16 April, however, he was shot down and killed, probably by a worthy foe, Leutnant Ernst-Wilhelm Reinert, the Luftwaffe's top-scoring 'ace' of the Tunisian campaign. Despite all that he had achieved, 'Widge' was only 26 years old.

Happily, two other leading 87 pilots survived the war and for a long time after it. Dennis David served the RAF well in many different capacities, both flying and as a staff officer in Britain, the Western Desert, Ceylon and Burma, rising to the rank of group captain. After the war he remained in the RAF, holding a number of Air Ministry posts until 1956 when he was transferred as Air Attaché to Budapest where he had his most exciting experiences since flying Hurricanes.

In 1956 a spontaneous uprising in Budapest, followed by similar events throughout Hungary, demanded the withdrawal of the Russian troops that had occupied the country since the Second World War and the end of Communist rule. The 'revolt' was mercilessly crushed by the Red Army, Budapest was heavily bombed by Soviet warplanes and thousands of Hungarians sought asylum in Austria and Yugoslavia. David was instrumental in assisting more than 400 of these refugees to escape the clutches of the Soviet and Hungarian Secret Police. For this he received an honorary knighthood from the Grand Duke of Hapsburg, head of the Hungarian Royal Family in exile and the unofficial title of 'The Light Blue Pimpernel' from his RAF colleagues.

Dennis David always retained great admiration for the Hurricane, repeatedly emphasizing that in the Battle of Britain 'Hurricanes shot down more enemy aircraft than all the Spitfires, anti-aircraft and other aircraft combined.' His allegiance was also well demonstrated by his becoming President of the Hurricane Society and proudly accepting another title that the RAF had given him: Dennis 'Hurricane' David.

Still more remarkable were the careers of Roland 'Bee' Beamont. 'Careers' (plural) because, as mentioned earlier, he followed those of both fighter pilot and test pilot. We left him at the end of 1941 at

Hawkers, ensuring that Hurricanes were ready for delivery to their squadrons, and he was soon to perform a similar role with the Hawker Typhoon. This was no light task. The Typhoon was fast and powerful but it had a poor rate of climb and a poor performance generally above 20,000ft; it suffered from a great many 'teething troubles' including, in its early days, structural failure; and unlike most of Sydney Camm's creations, it was far from beautiful. It entered service in September 1941 – with 56 Squadron – but it became operational only in May 1942 and was highly unpopular with its pilots.

Beamont, though, remembered the night-time sorties against targets on the ground that he had flown with 87 Squadron and was convinced that the Typhoon would be ideal in this role. He was not displeased to join 56 and later the second Typhoon squadron, No. 609, as a flight lieutenant, took part in the Dieppe operation and, in October 1942, became 609's CO. In November he brought 609 to Manston in Kent and led it on night-intruder missions, specializing in 'train-busting'. By May 1943, when Beamont was appointed wing commander and left 609, it had blown up at least 100 locomotives, of which he had personally accounted for about thirty, and had given a demonstration of the Typhoon's value as a ground-attack aircraft that would lead to spectacular results prior to and during the campaigns in North-West Europe in 1944.

Beamont was now 'rested', which in his case meant returning to Hawkers to test-fly more Typhoons and also examples of Sydney Camm's third great wartime 'storm', the Hawker Tempest. This was in essence a much-improved Typhoon, more slender, more streamlined and with slim elliptical wings. With a speed of about 430 mph and four 20mm cannons, it was a magnificent interceptor fighter as well as a ground-attacker and it is easy to imagine Beamont's pleasure when, in April 1944, he was chosen to lead 150 Wing, the first to be formed with three Tempest squadrons.

Beamont's wing was quickly in action against enemy aircraft – he personally made the first Tempest 'kill', a Messerschmitt Bf 109 over Normandy on 8 June – and later against the V-1 flying bombs. Once again Beamont showed the way by shooting down the wing's first V-1 on 16 June. When the flying bombs' threat had died away in

September as their launch sites were overrun by the Allied armies, 150 Wing had destroyed about 600 of them. Beamont's own score, including 'shared' successes, was about thirty. He then led his men first to Brussels, then to Volkel in Holland, where they changed their designation to 122 Wing of the Second Tactical Air Force.

On 2 October 1944 Beamont gained his final victory, downing a Focke-Wulf Fw 190, and soon afterwards Hawkers asked him to become its Chief Test Pilot. Beamont was willing to accept but had now flown ninety-four sorties over enemy or enemy-occupied territory and wished to bring up his century before taking up his new post. This proved not to be a good decision. On his next sortie on 12 October he was hit by AA fire while attacking an enemy aerodrome, crash-landed and spent the rest of the European conflict as a prisoner of war.

At the close of hostilities, the liberated Beamont decided to leave the Royal Air Force and concentrate on his career as a test pilot, believing that in peacetime this would prove more interesting and exciting, if probably more dangerous. An appointment at Gloster Aircraft Company was not a happy one and it is perhaps not unfair to suggest that, having been in command for so long, Beamont was not well-suited to a subordinate position. In 1947, therefore, he left to join the newly-formed English Electric Company.

This time the decision was an excellent one. Not only was Beamont made Chief Test Pilot, but in May 1948 he was able to pay a visit to the United States where he was allowed to fly the second prototype of the North American Sabre. In this he became the first British pilot and only the fourth pilot of any nation to exceed the speed of sound. It was an extraordinary achievement, yet one that, strangely enough, was almost completely ignored in Britain at the time and has remained largely ignored ever since.

This is not to say that Beamont did not become honoured in his own country. In December 1949 at the Farnborough Air Show, he introduced the Canberra jet bomber to the general public in a display that staggered the most hardened onlookers, throwing it about the sky in manoeuvres he had once executed in his Hurricane. After that, one achievement followed another: his record flights in the Canberra, such as the first double crossing of the Atlantic – to

Newfoundland and back – in a single day in August 1952; his being the first to fly the English Electric Lightning fighter, the first British aircraft to go through the sound barrier in level flight and to attain twice the speed of sound; his being the first to fly the brilliant but ill-fated TSR2 supersonic bomber in September 1964; and finally, from 1970 to 1979, his supervision of the international Panavia Tornado.

Yet for all his achievements, the most remarkable of Hurricane pilots never forgot his first love. Like Dennis David, he constantly emphasized that the Hurricane bore the brunt of the fighting in the Battle of Britain and 'was exceptionally well fitted to do so'. Finally, on 6 November 1985, he attended the Hurricane Jubilee Symposium, held by the Royal Aeronautical Society at Brooklands to commemorate the 50th anniversary of the Hurricane's first flight, and declared that in 1940 the Hurricane was 'the finest fighter of the day' and thanked Hawkers for 'enabling me to fly such a wonderful aeroplane.'

Notes
1. 'Beamont', not 'Beaumont', as that officer always insisted on pointing out, hence his nickname.
2. Contrary to general belief, it is physiologically impossible for men (or even cats!) to see in complete and utter darkness, but in practice there is always a small amount of light even on the blackest of nights.
3. Beamont chose this rather odd title because the book is mainly concerned with the decline of the British aircraft industry after the war.

Chapter 3

The Hardest Days
85 Squadron

As well as its own services to the Allied cause, 87 Squadron could claim indirect credit for those of another very notable Hurricane unit. On 1 June 1938, a group of its pilots and ground crews, led by Flight Lieutenant Donald Turner, revived No. 85 Squadron that had been disbanded in July 1919. They brought with them the Gladiators that were about to be replaced by Hurricanes at 87 but it was always intended that 85 should also be a Hurricane squadron. The Hawker fighters started to arrive in September and by November 85 had reached its full establishment strength, was completely re-equipped and was commanded by Squadron Leader David Atcherley who would eventually become an air vice-marshal.

The early career of 85 Squadron, perhaps appropriately, was very similar to that of 87. On the outbreak of the Second World War, both went to France where both were units of the Air Component of the BEF. Here 85, like 87, coped with the difficulties of the French grass airfields and later the rigours of a savage winter, in its case having even fewer encounters with enemy aircraft to break the boredom.

Indeed, it was not until 21 November 1939 that 85 gained its first success when Flight Lieutenant 'Dickie' Lee intercepted a reconnaissance Heinkel He 111 over the sea near Boulogne. This he promptly shot down in flames, later being awarded a Distinguished

Flying Cross for his achievement. It was one of only two occasions on which 85 saw action in the first eight months of the war, and on the other one on 23 November the enemy 'recce' machine escaped from a pair of 85's Hurricanes with some damage and one crewman wounded. Consequently much attention was concentrated on Lee who had in fact been destined for a career in the Royal Air Force – which he had joined in 1935 at the age of 18 – almost from birth. He was the son of Lieutenant Colonel Charles Lee, once the adjutant of General Lord Trenchard, the commander of the Royal Flying Corps in France and later Chief of the Air Staff of the newly-formed Royal Air Force, and the great man was young Lee's godfather.

It may be that Trenchard was not entirely pleased by Lee's desire to be a fighter pilot, for the 'Father of the Royal Air Force' directed most of his energy towards building up a strategic bomber force and showed little interest in the fighter defence of Britain. Probably he excused Lee's choice as youthful high spirits. In any case, he was immensely proud of 'that great boy' as he called his godson and he would soon to have every reason to be.

On 10 May 1940, 85 Squadron's quiet existence ended with shocking suddenness as the German blitzkrieg smashed into France and the Low Countries. Early that morning, its Hurricanes took off to engage a force of Heinkel He 111s, of which they destroyed four. They then returned to refuel and rearm, only to have to take off again as another wave of bombers approached. Throughout the day, 85 mounted sortie after sortie to oppose an almost continuous series of raids, as it would do on most of the days following. When night brought a welcome relief, it believed it had destroyed seventeen enemy aircraft, though no doubt this was an exaggeration, and it had lost three Hurricanes, the pilots of which all mercifully survived.

Flight Lieutenant Lee was in the thick of the fighting. He helped to shoot down one Heinkel He 111 and injure another but his Hurricane was severely damaged by return fire and he was slightly wounded. Nonetheless, he was able to get back safely and next day was again in action. That afternoon, 85 was operating over German-occupied territory when Lee was hit by AA fire and crash-landed in a field. Oddly but incredibly luckily, he had chosen to wear an overcoat above his uniform and the German soldiers he encountered thought he was a refugee. He was able to get away and return to his squadron where, undaunted by his experiences, he continued to inflict losses on the enemy: though records are scanty, it is believed that he gained a total of eight victories while serving with 85 during this period and he was shortly to be awarded a DSO.

Lee was not the only 85 pilot to take a heavy toll on the Luftwaffe. On the same 11 May when he was so nearly taken prisoner, it is believed that the squadron destroyed or damaged eight German aircraft. The next day, it is estimated to have destroyed or damaged seven more. On the 13th Squadron Leader John Oliver, who had become 85's CO in January and had gained at least four victories in the previous three days, destroyed a pair of Heinkel He 111s but was then forced to bale out. He was somewhat prematurely reported 'missing' but happily returned to his squadron later that same day.

Yet the squadron's most successful pilot during this period was Sergeant Geoffrey Allard: a tall, slim Yorkshireman with ginger hair, whom E.C.R. Baker in *The Fighter Aces of the RAF* calls 'The Pride of 85'. He had served with the squadron from the start, being one of those transferred from 87 to re-found it. Unlike some young pilots, he was not in the least scared by the Hurricane's exaggerated reputation and before the war he was noted as an aerobatics expert. On 10 May he shot down a Heinkel He 111 and by the end of the 16th, he had certainly destroyed six more Heinkels; probably nine more.

By the 16th, though, the physical and mental strain of four or five sorties and at least three combats a day had had an inevitable and startling effect. Late that evening, Allard landed his Hurricane perfectly after yet another mission but failed to get out of his cockpit. He had collapsed from exhaustion and was in a deep sleep that amounted almost to a coma. It was decided to let him rest in his cockpit overnight but next morning he was still unconscious. He was lifted out of his Hurricane and put to bed. In all he slept for thirty hours and sensibly it was decided he should be sent back to England for a short stay in hospital.

By this time the Allied situation was starting to disintegrate, losses of men and machines were mounting and on 18 May 85 was cruelly deprived of the services of Flight Lieutenant Boothby, who also returned to England to recover from injuries, in his case inflicted not in combat but in a car accident. Still 85 kept up its gallant if increasingly hopeless struggle and on 19 May its pilots experienced their most hectic day since the start of the German assault.

During the 19th, 85 Squadron was engaged in three major clashes with enemy formations. Flying Officer Count Manfred Czernin, a naturalized Pole, destroyed two bombers but most of 85's pilots were kept away from the Heinkels and Dorniers by swarms of Messerschmitt Bf 109s. These also shot down and killed Sergeant Little, though not before he had been seen to destroy two of their number. South African Pilot Officer Albert Lewis also shot down at least two 109s and Flying Officer Patrick Woods-Scawen downed three, as well as damaging a fourth that was crash-landed by its wounded pilot.

Squadron Leader Oliver did not lead his men into action on this date; on the previous day he had been promoted to wing commander and transferred. He was succeeded for a tragically brief period by a young man who, had fortune been more kind, might have left a record as remarkable as that of his equally ill-fated best friend.

Michael Fitzwilliam Peacock was born in South Africa but educated at Wellington College in Berkshire, where he met and formed a lasting friendship with another South African named Roger Bushell. They both subsequently became barristers in the same chambers and they both became members of 601 Squadron of the Auxiliary Air Force. This was known as the 'Millionaires Squadron' but Peacock and Bushell were far from wealthy, having to share not only a small flat but also a car and a formal dress-suit. They were, however, welcomed into 601 for their charm, their flying ability and their readiness to defend any member of their squadron, pilot or ground crew, who had earned the displeasure of the authorities. They were so successful in this role that they were themselves regarded with some disfavour and it is to the credit of all concerned that this did not have an adverse effect on their careers and both became flight lieutenants.

Of the two, Peacock was perhaps less forceful and determined but more friendly and more tolerant. He also had a keen sense of humour and there is a story that he flew to one court martial wearing his barrister's gown over his uniform and, after landing, changed his flying helmet for his barrister's wig while taxiing to dispersal. His exit from the cockpit was greeted with delighted amazement by all who saw it.

Soon after the outbreak of war, Bushell was promoted to squadron leader and sent to re-found 92 Squadron that received Spitfires in March 1940. On 23 May he was shot down over the French coast and taken prisoner, to become famous as 'Big X', the inspiration behind and organizer of the 'Great Escape' from Stalag Luft III.

Peacock remained with 601, flying Blenheims, and was awarded a DFC for his part in a raid on a German seaplane base at Borkum on 28 November 1939. In February 1940, 601 converted to Hurricanes and in May Peacock was promoted and became 85's CO. On the 20th he went in low to strafe German troops near Arras, but before he could regain sufficient height he was pounced upon by Messerschmitt Bf 109s and killed. One can only surmise what he might have achieved had he been spared, as indeed is the case with so many of the young pilots who died in the first few months of 1940.

Also on 20 May 85's Flying Officer Count Czernin destroyed a Henschel Hs 126 army co-operation aircraft and Sergeant Harold Howes destroyed two Dornier Do 17s. Howes was then shot down himself, as was Sergeant Allgood, but both survived with minor injuries. It was 85's last day of combat in France and it now prepared to withdraw to England. The rapid German advance prevented the evacuation of damaged but repairable aircraft, several of which had therefore to be destroyed on the ground. In all since 10 May, 85 had lost twenty-four Hurricanes and only three were flown back to Britain.

Also since 10 May six of 85's pilots had been killed and others wounded, yet for all the losses of men and machines, the morale of the survivors remained high. The squadron claimed a total of eighty-nine German aircraft destroyed and, although the real score was probably about sixty, this was a considerable achievement bearing in mind the adverse odds faced and takes no account of the enemy machines damaged. Still more important, and whatever may have been said later, the pilots were justly confident in the capabilities of their Hurricanes. These were, as 'Dickie' Lee told the American War Correspondent Drew Middleton: 'Bloody good. Give us enough of them and enough trained pilots and we can hold them.' There would soon be an alarming shortage of trained pilots but there was never a shortage of Hurricanes and the reasons for this emphasize the value of the type and the good sense of its designer.

When Hawkers were contemplating the creation of their new monoplane fighter, they were aware that they would be competing with Supermarine Aviation Works Limited, a firm with considerable experience in building high-speed seaplanes. It was rightly assumed therefore that Supermarine's proposed monoplane fighter, then austerely named Type 300, was likely to have a faster speed than anything Hawkers could produce at that time and have a more advanced light metal stressed-skin monocoque fuselage.

Faced with this challenge, Camm made a characteristic practical response. He would not attempt to match Supermarine by seeking the greatest possible speed or the most modern form of construction. Instead, he would obtain an acceptable performance based on the standard Hawker fabricated steel tubular structure with fabric covering, as used on the Hart and Fury; indeed the Hurricane was provisionally entitled the Fury Monoplane until so many alterations were made from the original Fury design that the name ceased to be appropriate. The 'selling point' of the Hurricane and its value for the future would be not modernity but reliability. It would be easy to produce, easy to maintain, easy to repair and very difficult to hurt.

These virtues would prove of incalculable importance. Supermarine's fighter would be the most beautiful and graceful aircraft of the Second World War. It would, from its earliest version, be some 20 mph faster and with a better rate of climb than the Hurricane. It would be capable of far more development, receiving a sequence of more powerful engines that enabled it to remain as a pure interceptor fighter throughout the war, whereas the Hurricane had ceased to be one in Britain by the end of 1941 and overseas as well eighteen months later, though its strength and versatility allowed it to perform other duties until the end of hostilities. As a final touch of glamour, the Supermarine fighter even had a wonderfully evocative name, although curiously enough one disliked by its designer: the Spitfire.

Yet its performance was attained at a high and very nearly fatal cost. A marvellous flying machine, the Spitfire was not at first a practical warplane. Nor did it help that its designer, Reginald Mitchell, died in June 1937 at the tragically early age of 42 when only the prototype had flown, leaving his assistant and successor as Supermarine's Chief Designer, Joseph Smith, to cope with all the Spitfire's practical difficulties.[1]

The Spitfire's 'teething troubles' in fact went far beyond those suffered by the Hurricane and were not just with the early Merlin engines. Its beautiful elliptical wings were not only a less steady gun platform than those of the Hurricane but have been described as 'a nightmare to manufacture'. Construction as a whole proved difficult for several years and Leo McKinstry in *Hurricane: Victor of the Battle of Britain*, reminds us that the famous aircraft factory at Castle Bromwich, Birmingham, then the largest in Europe, was built in 1938 with the promise that it would turn out 1,000 Spitfires by May 1940, yet by that date not a single one had been built there. Moreover, as Mr McKinstry further points out, at the best of times 'the Spitfire took almost twice as long to build as the Hurricane', and this despite the Hurricane being a bigger aircraft.

Had the Hurricane been subjected to anything like the delays in production that affected the Spitfire, it is the opinion of both Dr John Fozard, Camm's successor as Chief Designer at Hawkers, and test pilot Philip Lucas that, following the heavy losses in France, Fighter Command would have had no Hurricanes at all at the start of the Battle of Britain. In that case, bearing in mind that the Hawker fighters made 80 per cent of the interceptions of enemy aircraft during that battle, the Luftwaffe would have been able to gain a victory by sheer weight of numbers and Britain would have faced certain invasion and probable defeat.

Fortunately this was not the case and during 1939, a steady supply of Hurricanes was reaching the squadrons, not only from the Hawker factories but from the Hucclecote factory of Gloster Aircraft Company Limited that had become a subsidiary of Hawkers in 1934. In addition, early in 1940 Hurricanes started to reach Britain from the Canadian Car & Foundry Co. Ltd of Montreal, which had received microfilm from Hawkers containing full details of every Hurricane component. As a result, despite those cruel losses, by July 1940 Fighter Command contained twenty-seven Hurricane squadrons – as opposed to nineteen of Spitfires – and that does not include 245 (Hurricane) Squadron in Northern Ireland that provided a useful reserve of fresh pilots for the units more actively engaged.

In addition, Hurricanes could now be produced with such speed that in July Hawkers made good all their losses and even enabled a new Hurricane squadron, No. 232, to be formed on the 16th. This pattern would continue throughout the Battle of Britain. While the number of Spitfire squadrons would remain at nineteen and these found it hard to replace losses, five more new Hurricane squadrons would see combat before the battle was over.

One squadron to benefit from the speed with which new Hurricanes were leaving the factories was No. 85. As we have seen, only three came back from France but by 1 July the squadron had eighteen of them, of which fifteen were serviceable, and by 8 August when the Luftwaffe's main assault began, it had twenty-one Hurricanes ready for action. Moreover, the RAF's indispensable ground crews proved capable of keeping a greater percentage of Hurricanes serviceable than was the case with any other type of aircraft. This was a direct result of its 'old-fashioned' construction; the ground personnel found this very little different from that of the biplanes they were used to looking after. When it is added that the fabric-covered fuselage of the Hurricane enabled battle damage to be repaired far more quickly and easily than did the all-metal fuselage of the Spitfire, Camm's decision to prefer simplicity to modernity may be still further admired.

It was less easy to replace the men, but fortunately 85 had a splendid basis on which to build. Count Czernin had been posted to another Hurricane squadron, No. 17, with which he was to gain many successes, but most of the old hands would be found at 85's new base at Debden: Lee, Lewis, Woods-Scawen, Howes and particularly Allard, now a flight sergeant, rested and ready to resume his role as the squadron's finest pilot. The 'new boys' who replaced those lost in France were more of an anxiety. None of them had any experience of combat, some of them had less than ten hours' flying time on Hurricanes, and two were killed while learning how to manage these. Yet most were to show their worth and to add fresh lustre to 85's record.

A very great deal of the credit for this belonged to the officer, only 25 years of age, who arrived at Debden on 23 May to become 85's third CO in less than a week. Squadron Leader Peter Townsend's previous career with 43 (Hurricane) Squadron had shown him to be a brave, intelligent and skilful pilot, but perhaps not one likely to be an inspirational leader for he was modest and retiring and his shyness could make him appear aloof and distant: 'a grave courteous man,' as Drew Middleton describes him, 'who seemed older than his years.'

Townsend, however, did prove a magnificent leader by precept and example. He took full advantage of the lull while the Germans completed their conquest of France to get his new men into the air at every possible moment so that they could get used to handling their aircraft. He personally 'thought the Hurricane was great' and he was able to impart his confidence to his pilots. He also taught them what to expect when the Luftwaffe turned its full attention onto Britain. A good tactician and an exceptional strategist, he realized that the German fighters could do no great harm and the major danger was the bombers. He therefore told his squadron that its task was to attack enemy bombers – he was another believer in the head-on assault – engaging enemy fighters only in self-defence or if they blocked the way to the main targets.

If 85's pilots did clash with enemy fighters, Townsend emphasized that they must not try to climb or dive but should 'turn and turn again', as the Hurricane could always outmanoeuvre its opponents. Indeed, and rather ironically in view of Townsend's perfectly correct insistence on the importance of dealing with the enemy bombers, 85 would provide convincing evidence that the Hurricane was more than a match for the Bf 109 providing it could gain sufficient height to prevent its enemy diving onto it from above, and more than a match for the Bf 110 in virtually all circumstances.

When the Luftwaffe did return to the attack, 85 Squadron saw little action at first. On 8 July Flight Sergeant Allard, while on convoy patrol, sighted and shot down one more Heinkel He 111 to add to his already impressive list. Other encounters took place on later occasions, but by 11 August 85 had destroyed only two more enemy aircraft, the extraordinary Allard playing a part in downing them both. He had already been awarded a Distinguished Flying Medal, and on 17 August he would be commissioned as a pilot officer.

On the other hand, in July 85 lost two pilots and very nearly its CO. On the 11th Townsend sighted a Dornier Do 17 over the sea near Harwich. He badly damaged this and wounded three of its four-man crew, but its return fire shattered his Hurricane's engine and he was forced to bale out. He was rescued unhurt by a trawler, brought ashore at Harwich and was flying again that evening.

By this time, though, Townsend had created a magnificent 'team spirit' that united his squadron. How completely would be vividly illustrated on 18 August. Townsend had led twelve Hurricanes, as he thought, against over 100 enemy aircraft. After the battle, he found that there had really been thirteen Hurricanes in the air. 'What the devil do you mean by taking off without orders?' he demanded of his extra man. 'I'm sorry,' replied Pilot Officer James Marshall, 'but when I saw you all going off it was just too much, so I followed.'

This 18 August has been called 'The Hardest Day', though there were several, earlier and later, when both Fighter Command and the Luftwaffe made greater efforts and the former had much less success. Admittedly, the RAF did lose twenty-nine Hurricanes and six Spitfires in combat and had the losses in pilots been as high, then the day might indeed have been a disaster. Happily, a large majority of the Hurricanes either got back to base and were 'written off' afterwards, or at least remained airborne long enough to allow their pilots to take to their parachutes. Only nine Hurricane pilots died. Moreover, the RAF fighters and ground defences between them destroyed more enemy aircraft than on any other day of the battle, bar 15 August: seventy, assuming the German loss records are correct.

After the war, the 'official' figures for German losses were taken from the Luftwaffe quartermaster general's returns. Since these were used as a basis for getting replacements, it was understandably argued that no German commander would have understated his losses here. However, Francis K. Mason, who investigated the whole question very thoroughly in his *Battle Over Britain*, has demonstrated that the quartermaster general's returns do not give the whole picture and even if they did, the interpretation of them by the official British assessors would still not allow Fighter Command the full credit that was its due.

Taking the last point first, the 'official' figures do not include German losses incurred on essential 'war support flights' such as air-sea rescue missions. Nor do they include many of the enemy aircraft that returned to base only to be 'written off'. The Germans calculated their losses on a percentage basis, depending on what parts could be salvaged for future use. A 'write-off' was assessed at 60 per cent or over but the British did not appreciate this and only added 'write-offs' to the 'destroyed' list if they were reported to be 80 per cent or more.

Even more significantly, while undoubtedly exaggerated, claims were made – they were inevitable with the sheer speed of air-fighting – both *Battle Over Britain* and individual squadron histories give numerous examples of losses not being recorded in the quartermaster general's returns, although prisoners were taken and/or wreckage was examined and paraded in triumph through local villages, and/or the damage caused by the falling machine was still clearly visible fifty years later. It is clear therefore that either some of the quartermaster general's records have been mislaid or there were other channels by which losses could be reported.

Indeed, further Luftwaffe records were discovered after the publication of *Battle Over Britain* that would enable Mr Mason in his later version of *The Hawker Hurricane* to show that some German units, such as JG 54 and KG 53, did not file all their loss returns with the quartermaster general. This new information allows him to increase on 30 August the number of Heinkel He 111s shot down from seven to thirteen, probably all by Hurricanes; the number of Bf 110s from four to six, certainly all by Hurricanes; and the number of Bf 109s from twelve to sixteen, eleven of them by

Hurricanes. It is perhaps only fair to add that during the day eleven Hurricanes were also shot down or 'written off' and seven pilots killed or fatally wounded.

Bearing these points in mind, let us consider 85 Squadron's claims on 18 August. German records confirm that it shot down a Heinkel He 111 but the details of its loss show how easy it was for duplicate claims to be made in all good faith. It was first attacked by Flight Lieutenant Hamilton who left it with 'smoke pouring from the fuselage and two engines' but did not see it crash so claimed only a 'Probable', though he was convinced, not unreasonably, that it would never return to base. It was then attacked again by Pilot Officer Marshall who reported that he saw pieces break off and a dense cloud of white smoke pour from it. This so obscured his view that he crashed into the tail of the Heinkel which now finally went down. Marshall's Hurricane lost the tip of its starboard wing but carried him safely back to Debden. It was repaired, to fly and fight again.

Squadron Leader Townsend made three claims. He first engaged a Messerschmitt Bf 110 that 'heeled over spiraling vertically downwards'. Townsend was convinced he had killed the pilot – a view shared by two of his men who saw the incident – but as the 110 was not seen to crash, we will be sceptical and accept that it pulled out of its spin and survived. He then fired on a Bf 109. The Squadron Diary says that this 'spun down in flames' but Townsend's own account in his *Duel of Eagles* reports that 'a sudden spurt of white vapour turned into flame.' We may again be sceptical and suggest that he overestimated the damage he had inflicted, particularly since he had at once to turn his attention to another 109 attacking him. This he undoubtedly shot down: the pilot baled out and the 'kill' is confirmed by the German records.

Townsend's men believed they had downed two other 109s. One was described as 'diving vertically into the sea' but the 109s often escaped by diving steeply, knowing that they could accelerate faster than a Hurricane, and perhaps that was what happened here. The Squadron Diary states that the other 109 was confirmed by the pilot's cine-camera gun but no details are given so it may be that again the harm inflicted was exaggerated.

The pilots also claimed five other Bf 110s as destroyed. Flight Lieutenant Hamilton, who was no boaster as his claim for a 'Probable' only for the Heinkel confirms, sent one down 'with both engines on fire'. Sergeant Howes shot one down in flames. We will assume they attacked the same aircraft. Howes also reported that he had attacked another 110 that he saw crash into the sea. So did Sergeant 'Frank' Walker-Smith. Again, assume they were referring to the same victim. Walker-Smith then took on a second 110; this 'broke up, one of the crew baling out.' The German records confirm the loss of only one of these 110s, but however cynical one tries to be, it is hard not to feel that at least two others in fact fell and their loss, like those on 30 August, was filed elsewhere and not in the quartermaster general's returns.

Whatever the true extent of its successes, 85 paid a price for them. Pilot Officer Hemingway baled out and was rescued from the sea but 'Dickie' Lee was last seen alone pursuing three Bf 110s. Townsend called to him over the radio to come back but in vain. What happened next is unknown. Perhaps the 110s turned on him. Perhaps other enemy fighters showed up. Nothing more was heard of Lee and, as Townsend reports, 'hope faded to tragic certainty.'

There would be more hard days ahead for 85 Squadron and, indeed, for Fighter Command in general. His heavy losses on 13, 15, 16 and 18 August had convinced Göring that he must provide heavier fighter protection for his bombers. Accordingly, Luftflotte 3 transferred most of its Bf 109s to Kesselring's Luftflotte 2 which would henceforth carry out the majority of daylight raids. Moreover, these would be directed against really valuable targets. Luftwaffe Intelligence had so far been woeful and attacks had been wasted on training aircraft and Bomber or Coastal Command bases but now Göring's airmen, by using their eyes and their brains, had discovered, though not fully realized, the significance of the RAF's vital sector stations.

These were the bases that had operational command of the RAF's fighters. They usually controlled three squadrons and were responsible for liaison with the radar chain. In Park's No. 11 Group there were seven of them: Biggin Hill and Kenley just south of London; Hornchurch, North Weald and Northolt just north of

London; Debden in Essex; and Tangmere in Sussex. It was on these that Kesselring launched the main part of his assault. If he could knock them out, No. 11 Group would be paralysed.

As mentioned earlier, on 19 August 85 changed places with 111 at Croydon. This was not a sector station but it was not neglected either and Townsend's men would see constant action when the new German tactics commenced on 24 August. Their time of trial started in the early hours of the 24th, when a night raid destroyed one of their aircraft and damaged two more.[2]

Early next morning they would attempt to engage a strong force of bombers above Dover, only to have to scatter when fired on themselves by the AA defences. One of them was then attacked by a 109 but out-turned this and shot it down. The airman in question, it comes as no surprise to learn, was Pilot Officer Allard. On the 26th 85 was able to get at a formation of Dornier Do 17s without interference, shooting down two or three before the escorting 109s could intervene. When these did join in the fight, they brought down Pilot Officer Hemingway but he escaped by parachute.

On the 28th, perhaps heartened by a visit from Prime Minister Winston Churchill, 85 shot down six Messerschmitt Bf 109s without loss. The Squadron Diary and Townsend's *Duel of Eagles* both make it clear that all the 'kills' were confirmed on the ground and by signals from No. 11 Group. That only four can be located in enemy records suggests that this was another occasion when one of the enemy units involved reported losses through channels other than the quartermaster general's returns. Whatever the true total, the episode makes it clear that Hurricanes were quite able to deal with the finest fighters then available to the Luftwaffe.

Next day, the 29th, was less satisfactory for 85. That afternoon, it was attacked by a large force of 109s. Two Hurricanes were lost but both pilots baled out safely. Townsend downed one enemy fighter. Flight Lieutenant Hamilton shot down a second one, but that evening he himself was killed in combat. On the 30th the squadron scattered a formation of Heinkel He 111s escorted by Messerschmitt Bf 110s. Both Allard and Woods-Scawen definitely destroyed 110s and some of those Heinkels and 110s that formed part of the revised figures for enemy losses on this day may also have fallen to 85's guns.

One Hurricane went down but Pilot Officer Marshall baled out.

Soon after midday on 31 August the Luftwaffe paid 85 the compliment of sending its finest unit to raid Croydon. The Hurricanes were just taking off when bombs from Erprobungsgruppe 210's Messerschmitt Bf 110s crashed into their airfield. All got off safely but were promptly attacked from above by 109s and 110s. The pilots believed they inflicted losses on these but Townsend was forced to bale out with a wound in his foot and Pilot Officer Worrall, after definitely downing a 110, also had to take to his parachute.

With Townsend in hospital having part of his big toe removed, Flying Officer Woods-Scawen became 85's temporary and unofficial CO. He led it into two more battles on the 31st, one in the late afternoon and another in the evening. On both occasions he shot down a 109 and his men added four or five more 109s in total during the two actions, bringing 85's official – if no doubt exaggerated – 'score' for August alone to forty-four.

No Hurricane was lost in the evening combat on the 31st but one did crash-land and was 'written off' as a result of the fighting in the late afternoon. Pilot Officer William Hodgson, a New Zealander, had already won the nickname of 'Ace' but nothing that he did can have matched the skill and quiet, unselfish courage that he showed on this occasion. He had just shot down a 109 when another one attacked him, its cannon shells setting his engine on fire. He prepared to bale out but then realized he was over a thickly-populated area that contained the Thameshaven oil tanks. Rather than allow his blazing Hurricane to crash in such an area, he determined to land it in open country where it would do no damage. Side-slipping violently to keep the flames under control, he finally located a large field, only to discover at the last minute that this contained anti-glider obstacles. He somehow managed to avoid these, made a successful 'wheels-up' landing and escaped without injury.

On 1 September, however, 85 Squadron's luck ran out, its pilots' reactions no doubt fatally slowed by constant strain and exhaustion. A clash with Bf 109s in the morning did nothing to help this, though Allard and Sergeant Goodman shot down enemy fighters. That afternoon 85 engaged a formation of Dornier Do 17s and although none are reported lost in the 'official' German records we know that at least three were in fact downed since members of their crews were taken prisoner. Then, however, a wave of Bf 109s and Bf 110s fell on 85 from above. Allard had shot down one of the Dorniers but then had to land at a forward airfield with engine trouble. While his Hurricane was being serviced, it was hit and destroyed in an air-raid.

At least Allard was unhurt. The same was not true for four other pilots, their fate described dispassionately in the Squadron Diary but made almost unbearable by the portraits of them in Townsend's *Duel of Eagles*. Flying Officer Woods-Scawen – 'little Patrick, who smiled with his eyes' – 'was posted missing'; his body was found almost a week later, 'his parachute unopened'. The parachute of Sergeant Booth – 'a tall quiet youth' – caught fire and 'he suffered a broken back, leg and arms'; he died six and a half months later. Sergeant Ellis – 'the cock-sparrow' – 'was also killed in this fight.' Flying Officer 'Gus' Gowers – 'to whom life was a huge joke' – 'baled out with severe burns on hands and wounds in hands and foot'; he survived and even found some amusement in his removal for treatment to a mental hospital.

By the end of the day, 85 Squadron, without a CO, without any flight commanders, with only seven aircraft still serviceable and with its surviving pilots exhausted, was clearly in no condition to continue the fight. On 3 September it left Croydon and was soon to transfer to Church Fenton in the north of England. Yet the resistance that it and other Fighter Command squadrons had made since 24 August would have momentous results. By this time, the attacks on the sector stations had given the Luftwaffe the upper hand. Fighter Command's defence system was starting to unravel and the number of its trained pilots had fallen desperately low. Unfortunately for the German cause, the progress being made was too slow and too undramatic for the theatrical Göring who, moreover, had other matters to consider.

On the night of 24/25 August, some bombers that had lost their way accidentally hit the centre of London, contrary to Hitler's express instructions. The following night Bomber Command retaliated with a raid on Berlin and repeated this twice more before the month was out. The damage done was minimal but the German public was stunned; Göring, who had loudly boasted that this would never happen, was greatly embarrassed; and a furious Hitler revoked his prohibition against bombing London.

That, of course, did not mean that London must be bombed and had Göring been an able officer, he would have allowed nothing to deflect him from his raids on the sector stations. On the contrary, he eagerly embraced the opportunity for a spectacular demonstration. On 3 September at a council of war with his Luftflotten chiefs, he announced his decision to direct future daylight attacks against London. This, he believed, might break Britain's will to resist and would in any case force Dowding to commit a last reserve of fighters that Göring thought was being deliberately held back. On 7 September Göring began his daylight assault on London and thereby lost the battle and, as it transpired, the war.

Meanwhile, 85 was reluctantly settling down to its role as a 'Class C' squadron, with some of its finest and longest-serving pilots going to strengthen other Hurricane units. Sergeant Howes, for instance, went to 605 Squadron, gaining further successes until he was killed in a flying accident in late December. Pilot Officer Lewis similarly added to his achievements with 85 while serving with 249 Squadron, until he was shot down and badly burned on 28 September. He recovered and would later command 261 (Hurricane) Squadron entrusted with the defence of the great Royal Navy base at Trincomalee in Ceylon.

The squadron did still fly daylight patrols and on one on 27 October, Marshall, now a flight lieutenant, shot down a Heinkel He 111. In the main, however, the last few days of October were spent in preparing the squadron for night operations and in November it returned to No. 11 Group as a night-fighter unit. It would continue in this role until May 1944; an appropriate duty for a squadron with a motto translating as: 'We hunt by night and day.' Its earliest experiences, though, were not happy ones. From November 1940 to January 1941, it flew more hours at night than any other squadron but lost several aircraft in accidents caused by bad weather and did not gain a victory until 25 February 1941 when Peter Townsend, back on duty albeit still limping, shot down a Dornier Do 17 that had considerately, if extremely foolishly, kept its navigation lights on.

Also in late February 1941, 85 began to receive Douglas Havocs, twin-engined aircraft fitted with Airborne Interception (AI) radar. The change was soon to cost the squadron and the RAF dearly. On 3 March Flight Lieutenant Allard – he had been promoted in the previous September – took off from Debden, where 85 was now once more based, in one of the new Havocs, carrying as passengers 'Ace' Hodgson and 'Frank' Walker-Smith whom he was taking to a Maintenance Unit where they could collect more Havocs. His aircraft had not been ready for him because one of its nose panels had come loose, so Allard had impatiently seized a screwdriver from the rigger and fastened this down himself. As the Havoc took off, the panel broke away and smashed into the rudder. The Havoc swung sideways, then turned over, crashed and burst into flames, killing all three pilots.

In April 85 converted entirely to Havocs and by the end of July, its three remaining ex-Hurricane pilots – Townsend, Marshall and Hemingway – had all departed. Marshall and Hemingway went to other Havoc units[3] but Townsend received a series of staff appointments and promotions. In February 1944 Group Captain Townsend was appointed an equerry to King George VI who was delighted to welcome a Battle of Britain veteran and, Townsend felt, treated him more like a guest than an aide. Townsend, for his part, proved capable, tactful and loyal and his three months' trial period was quickly extended.

Townsend was also charming, attractive and undeniably good-looking and he won the admiration of the king's vivacious younger daughter, Princess Margaret. They became good friends but no more, since Townsend was married with two sons. Later, however, after the king's death and the breakdown of Townsend's marriage through no fault of his own, their relationship deepened and a tremendous storm arose over the possibility of the new queen's sister marrying a man who had been party to a divorce, even though the innocent party. There is no need to pursue the story further; suffice to say that both the pilot and the princess were subsequently married, but not to each other. Townsend was the lucky one, for his marriage was happy and lasting. That of the princess, by a somewhat vicious irony, ended in divorce. Far more pleasing to relate is an incident from their earlier acquaintance that added a delightful footnote to the story of the Hawker Hurricane.

Hurricane PZ865, a Mark IIC, was the last of its type to be built. On its completion in late July 1944, Hawker Aircraft Limited bought it back from the Air Ministry to appear at a farewell ceremony at Langley. On 27 July it was demonstrated in masterly fashion before a large audience by 'George' Bulman, who came out of retirement for the purpose. PZ865 remained with Hawkers until 29 March 1972, when it was presented to the RAF's Battle of Britain Memorial Flight. Much earlier, however, in May 1950 it was decided to enter 'The Last of the Many', as it was proudly named, in a number of air races. In these it was sponsored by Princess Margaret and flown by her friend Group Captain Townsend.

It is often said, somewhat apologetically, that the Hurricane lacked glamour. Certainly its virtues – strength, reliability, adaptability, versatility, ease of production and ease of maintenance – are severely practical ones. Yet the story of this last Hurricane, entered in air races by the daughter of the reigning monarch and flown by that monarch's equerry, surely holds a touch of glamour, and PZ865, with its drab wartime camouflage replaced by Hawkers' racing livery of royal blue with gold stripes, was surely the most beautiful Hurricane of them all.

Notes

1. In January 1954, the then President of the Royal Aeronautical Society, Sir William Farren, would declare that Mitchell 'made the Spitfire possible' but Smith was 'the man who made the Spitfire'.
2. Townsend tells us it was reported that someone on the ground was signalling to the enemy. This would seem most unlikely, were it not for a later incident. On 1 September Sergeant Goodman shot down a 109 with only the guns on his Hurricane's port wing firing. It was discovered that the air lines to the four starboard guns had been blocked by having matches forced into them. The person responsible was never discovered.
3. Marshall became a squadron leader but was killed in another Havoc crash in April 1942. Hemingway survived the war and eventually retired as a group captain.

Chapter 4

County of Gloucester 501 Squadron

Plenty of other Hurricane squadrons endured the hard days of late August and early September 1940 and it may cause some surprise to remark that several of them were not Royal Air Force squadrons. This may be thought to be a reference to the Polish and Czech Hurricane squadrons but in fact these were considered to be RAF units and their original squadron and flight commanders were British. The Royal Canadian Air Force's No. 1 Squadron, also equipped with Hurricanes, was, by definition, not then a unit of the Royal Air Force but it was later treated as such and renumbered 401. Yet throughout the Battle of Britain, Dowding commanded fourteen squadrons – two of Blenheims, six of Spitfires, six of Hurricanes – that were not part of the Royal Air Force, and the reason for this was that they belonged to the Auxiliary Air Force which did not even gain the prefix 'Royal' until 1949.

The Auxiliary Air Force had come into being in October 1925, on the urging of Lord Trenchard. Its squadrons were made up of volunteers who had professions or businesses outside the services but were prepared to give up holidays, weekends and after-work hours for the pleasure of being able to fly, often at considerable personal expense. They were affiliated to cities or counties, drew their membership from local areas and were based within them, close to the homes of their personnel. Their standards were high and the loyalty they aroused was intense.

To confuse the issue still further, a third organization came into existence in July 1936. This was the Royal Air Force Volunteer Reserve that was formed to train both flying and ground personnel who would be ready in the event of war. When this became inevitable, however, the three organizations merged. The men of the Volunteer Reserve were posted to both 'regular' and Auxiliary squadrons to bring them up to their required wartime strength. The Auxiliary pilots simply donned RAF uniforms, if sometimes with interesting variations.

Later, suggestions would be made that the pilots of the 'Weekend Air Force', as the Auxiliaries were collectively called, were none too popular; that on the one hand, the professional pilots considered them too frivolous and too interested in matters not directly connected with the service, while on the other, the Volunteer Reserve pilots, all of them initially sergeants, found them snobbish and unwelcoming. Many of these stories were nonsense, all of them were exaggerated and none of them survived long in wartime conditions. No such criticisms, in any case, could have been made of the first Auxiliary unit to receive Hurricanes.

This was No. 501 (County of Gloucester) Squadron. It had become an Auxiliary squadron on 1 May 1936[1] and was then a bomber unit flying Hawker Harts and Hawker Hinds, but in late 1938 it was changed to the fighter role. It took delivery of its Hurricanes in March 1939 and was for some time not just the first but the only Auxiliary squadron so equipped.

Squadron Leader Montague Clube, who became 501's CO in December 1938, worked hard to ensure that his pilots were proficient in the use of their Hurricanes. He was also aware that he would receive half-a-dozen sergeant pilots in the event of hostilities, but far from resenting this he welcomed the prospect, asking only that they should be experienced in flying modern fighters.

Hostilities would not be long in coming, but for several months 501 flew only convoy protection patrols, first over the Bristol Channel from its base at Filton and later over the English Channel from its base at Tangmere. It saw no action and had its most exciting experience late in 1939 when Squadron Leader Clube suffered the embarrassment of crashing while attempting to land.

Happily he was uninjured and his Hurricane was subsequently repaired.

It would take the German blitzkrieg of 10 May 1940 to change 501's fortunes and give its pilots the opportunity to show their mettle. The assault did not come as a total surprise to the Allies since there had been increased enemy aerial activity on the previous day and the RAF's photographic reconnaissance missions had revealed ominous signs of a build-up of enemy land forces. Some Hurricane squadrons, including 501, had therefore been given warning of a possible move. These circumstances would introduce one of 501's best pilots and indeed its future Commanding Officer.

Flying Officer Eustace 'Gus' Holden had previously flown Hurricanes with 56 Squadron but in early May was transferred to 501. He was allowed a brief leave before reporting to his new unit but on learning what was going on, he cancelled his own leave and hurried to Tangmere. He was at the controls of one of the sixteen 501 Hurricanes that, on the afternoon of 10 May, flew to Bétheniville near Reims to support 1 and 73 (Hurricane) Squadrons in the Advanced Air Striking Force. Thus 501 was the first Auxiliary Hurricane squadron to be sent to France, although 607 and 615 Squadrons in the Air Component were then in the process of receiving Hurricanes in place of their Gladiators and on 12 May another Auxiliary Hurricane squadron, No. 504 (County of Nottingham), flew from England also to join the Air Component.

The pilots found 501's new base singularly unattractive. It was a typical French grass airfield, with no facilities and no accommodation until the squadron had put up some tents. Despite this, the pilots were delighted at the prospect of engaging enemy aircraft and would soon have the opportunity to do so. Pilot Officer Kenneth Lee bore the nickname of 'Hawkeye', apparently originally because he had slightly drooping eyelids that resembled those of a bird of prey. It would prove a highly appropriate designation, however, as Lee would become noted for his ability to be the first to spot German warplanes. On 10 May he sighted a formation of Heinkel He 111s. He attacked one that he left losing height with an engine smoking, though he did not see it crash. This, 501's first successful interception, was soon followed by its first 'kill': Flying

Officer Pickup encountered a lone Dornier Do 17 and shot it down in flames.

Tragically, 501 also suffered its first casualties, and not in combat either. Its remaining personnel were carried to Bétheniville in a pair of Bombay transports but the pilot of one of them misjudged his height when attempting to land and crashed. The squadron lost three reserve pilots and six ground crew killed outright or fatally injured, while several others received injuries that were less serious.

During the next couple of days, 501 demonstrated beyond argument that an Auxiliary squadron was in no way inferior to any in the 'regular' Royal Air Force. On 11 May it believed it had destroyed six enemy warplanes, although it may have rather overestimated the extent of its successes. It suffered no losses, even though 'Gus' Holden was attacked by a whole formation of Messerschmitt Bf 109s while on a lone patrol. His Hurricane's wing was damaged but he escaped by diving steeply and making off at very low level. He reached his airfield safely and by next morning his damaged aircraft had been repaired by 501's loyal ground crews.

On 12 May a series of actions took place throughout the day, in which 501's pilots, probably optimistically, thought that they had downed about a dozen German bombers. This time, however, 501 paid for its achievements. In the morning, several Heinkel He 111s were destroyed but Flying Officer Rayner, after being seen to account for one of them, was hit by return fire, crashed and died.

In the afternoon 'Hawkeye' Lee again lived up to his name, being the first to sight a formation of Dornier Do 17s that he promptly attacked single-handed. He shot down one of them, the destruction of which was confirmed by French AA gunners, but was then caught in the crossfire of several other bombers and his Hurricane struck by thirty-seven bullets, in spite of which Lee was able to return safely. His colleagues were less fortunate, for as they attempted to engage the Dorniers as well, they were attacked from above by the escorting Messerschmitt Bf 110s. Flying Officer Malfroy escaped by parachute but Flying Officer Smith was killed.

Although other pilots were sent out to France to replace 501's casualties, they were usually inexperienced and compelled to learn their trade in the most difficult circumstances. One of them, Pilot

Officer John Gibson, had previously only flown biplanes and, it is said, had never so much as seen a Hurricane. Happily, the myth that the Hurricane was fearsome and dangerous had long been replaced by the more accurate assessment that it was easy to fly and very forgiving. After Gibson had been shown the layout of the unfamiliar cockpit, therefore, Squadron Leader Clube quietly suggested that he should 'have a little ride' in a Hurricane. Gibson took off, flew and landed, all perfectly. He would become one of the squadron's best pilots and one of its flight commanders during the Battle of Britain.

That, though, lay in the future. In May 1940, the thirteenth day proved 501's most important one, for it was then that its finest airman came to the fore. Sergeant James 'Ginger' Lacey, like Geoffrey Allard, was a red-haired, sharp-eyed, quick-witted Yorkshireman who was a very good pilot indeed. He was also a very experienced pilot, having been an instructor at a flying club prior to the war. Moreover, he was a member of the Volunteer Reserve who had come straight to 501 on the outbreak of war and he had already flown Hurricanes while on temporary attachment to No. 1 Squadron. Yet on 11 and 12 May, he had been airborne five times in all but had recorded no successes.

That all changed on the 13th. Lacey was one member of a section detailed for a dawn patrol but engine trouble delayed him and the other Hurricanes took off without him. Lacey's engine then decided to start, so he followed them. He was still alone, however, when he encountered a solitary Heinkel He 111 escorted by a single Messerschmitt Bf 109. According to Richard Townshend Bickers in his biography *Ginger Lacey, Fighter Pilot*, the first thought of 501's future leading 'ace' was to 'yearn for his flight commander' to tell him what to do. We may legitimately doubt this. 'Ginger' Lacey had a keen if somewhat peculiar sense of humour, a carefully-calculated nonchalance, a pronounced lack of respect for authority, and a point to make.

In the early days of the war, the RAF's obsession with formation-flying and formation attacks had led to a squadron's sergeant pilots being left out of briefings; it was considered that their job was simply to follow their flight or section commander on patrol or into action. This foolish practice was naturally not appreciated but it did not survive the experience gained in combat conditions and the NCOs were soon to be fully briefed, at first by their flight or section commander, then at the same time as the officer pilots. It is particularly doubtful if it lasted long in 501, since Squadron Leader Clube early adopted the practice of entrusting formations to senior NCOs; Lacey either forgot or omitted to tell his biographer that the dawn patrol on 13 May was led not by a flight commander but by Flight Sergeant McKay. Indeed, before another week had passed, Lacey would personally be leading a section and he would later declare that: 'There was little difference in status between officers and NCO pilots.'

In any case, it did not take Lacey long to work out what he was supposed to do on 13 May. He first attacked the 109, which disintegrated in a spectacular explosion, then sent the Heinkel down minus one wing and trailing smoke and flames. French AA gunners confirmed both his successes. Furthermore, Lacey's morning had only just started, for he had hardly had time to refuel and rearm before he was ordered off again as part of another patrol, this one led by Flight Lieutenant Griffiths. It encountered a formation of Messerschmitt Bf 110s, three of which were shot down by Griffiths, 'Hawkeye' Lee and Lacey, his third victory before breakfast. Lacey was then attacked by several other 110s but escaped by some dramatic manoeuvres that, reports his biographer, 'an aircraft less sturdy than the Hurricane could not have survived without having its wings ripped off.' The Hurricane and its pilot did survive and the French rewarded Lacey with a Croix de Guerre.

On 14 May 501 made successful interceptions of formations of Heinkel He 111s and Dornier Do 17s, several of which were thought to have been destroyed. On the 15th 501 undoubtedly shot down two Dorniers, one of which crashed in flames, while the pilot of the other one baled out and was taken to Bétheniville, where his arrogant attitude did much to convince 501's pilots that they were fighting in a worthy cause. Interestingly, what particularly disgusted them was the contempt he showed for the ground crews, whom he considered unmilitary; further evidence, if any were needed, of the close bond the pilots had with the men who looked after their aircraft.

By this time, though, 501 not only had to face the German Air

Force but was threatened by the relentless advance of the German army. Accordingly, it retreated to a series of alternative bases, first in the vicinity of Paris but later moving ever further westward. Over the next ten days, it had few encounters with enemy aircraft. After one of these, Pilot Officer Sylvester was reported missing, having been hit first by the gunner of a Dornier he had attacked and then by anti-aircraft fire. It later transpired that he was able to make a forced landing and he rejoined 501, just in time to take part in the squadron's most successful aerial battle.

This took place on 27 May, on which date 501 moved to a grass airfield near Rouen with the delightful name of Boos. The Hurricanes had only just landed when Boos was bombed by Heinkel He 111s but miraculously all escaped damage. That afternoon, their pilots gained an ample revenge when thirteen of them, led by 'Gus' Holden, encountered twenty-four Heinkels escorted by twenty Bf 110s. The 110s were probably short of fuel, for when the Hurricanes attacked they turned away, though not before one had been severely damaged by Sylvester and Sergeant Farnes. Then 501 went for the Heinkels, urged on by Holden's command to 'select one and kill it'. The pilots reported eleven Heinkels destroyed and three more probably destroyed, although no doubt there were some duplicated claims in that total. Among those who at least helped to destroy a Heinkel were Holden, Lacey, Lee, John Gibson, now an experienced Hurricane pilot, and two very inexperienced Hurricane pilots, Pilot Officer Hewitt and Sergeant Lewis, both of whom were taking part in their first combat. The Hurricanes suffered only minor damage in this action and all returned safely.

Sadly, the remaining days of May and the first part of June painted a different picture. During this time, 501 was mainly engaged in protecting those British soldiers who had not been trapped at Dunkirk as they retreated westward and were subsequently evacuated. It did gain a number of successes against Heinkels and Bf 110s on 5 June and against Dorniers on the 6th, but Pilot Officers Claydon and Hulse were killed in action and John Gibson, although destroying two enemy aircraft and damaging others, was shot down twice, crash-landing on 30 May and baling out safely on 10 June.

Also on 10 June, 'Hawkeye' Lee somehow managed to bale out when his Hurricane exploded during an engagement with a group of Heinkels, but he hit his machine's tailplane and injuries to his leg kept him off the squadron's strength for some time. On the previous day, an unlucky accident temporarily deprived 501 of the services of 'Ginger' Lacey as well. He attempted to land his damaged aircraft in what seemed a suitable field but it proved to be a swamp. His Hurricane turned upside down, causing injuries to his head and trapping him in his cockpit for about an hour while rising water threatened to drown him. Luckily, French farm workers had seen his plight and eventually cut him free.

Finally, on 16 June, 501 was moved to Jersey in the Channel Islands, from which it covered the evacuation of British troops from Cherbourg. On the 18th, it left for Croydon, bringing back eight valuable Hurricanes to add to Fighter Command's strength as it made ready to fight the Battle of Britain. Squadron Leader Clube, who had been 501's CO since it first became part of Fighter Command, now left it on his promotion to wing commander. His place was taken by Squadron Leader Henry Hogan who had not previously flown Hurricanes in action but quickly proved he was well capable of doing so.

He would have plenty of opportunities. As Tony Holmes points out in *Hurricane Aces 1939-40*, other Air Component or Advanced Air Striking Force Squadrons 'were posted out of the front-line' but 501, operating at a number of different bases, 'remained in No. 11 Group' throughout the Battle of Britain.[2] This was the post of honour and of danger and Mr Holmes states that 501 'engaged the enemy on a record thirty-five days', eleven days more than any other unit.

The first of 501's thirty-five days was 11 July, the day after the Battle of Britain officially began, when three of its pilots intercepted a force of Junkers Ju 87 Stuka dive-bombers, escorted by Bf 109s, attacking a convoy. They were overcome by greatly superior numbers and lost Sergeant Dixon who baled out only to be drowned. Next day, Pilot Officer Hewitt was also killed while driving Dornier Do 17s away from another convoy.

For 501 there was then a temporary break from action until the afternoon of 20 July, when it again attempted to engage Junkers Ju

87s; before any of its pilots could open fire, they were assaulted by the escorting Messerschmitt Bf 109s. Pilot Officer Sylvester was shot down and killed but Lacey out-turned a 109, poured two bursts of fire into it and watched as it plunged down 'getting smaller and smaller' until it 'went straight into the Channel.' Next, he outmanoeuvred another 109 and crippled this. Flight Lieutenant Cox pounced on it and finished it off, and Lacey saw its dive get 'steeper and steeper' until it crashed 'almost right beside the oily patch marking the place where my first one had gone in.'

Squadron Leader Hogan, 501's new CO, also claimed to have destroyed a 109. Since he was a comparative novice, it is possible that he was mistaken but Lacey was very experienced and he clearly witnessed two Messerschmitts hit the water. That neither loss can be found in German records would seem to provide one more instance where those records are incomplete.

Further clashes occurred during the remaining days of July and 501 suffered another tragic loss when Flight Lieutenant Cox was shot down and killed by the Dover AA gunners. On the 29th, however, the squadron effectively repulsed a raid by Junkers Ju 87s, definitely destroying two and possibly damaging others.

In early August, two of 501's aircraft collided while landing in bad visibility. Happily the pilots were unhurt and at this time also, 501 received welcome reinforcements: six Polish airmen who had made their way to Britain by various means in order to renew the fight against Germany. Flying Officer Witorzenc, Pilot Officer Skalski and Sergeant Glowacki would prove to be among the squadron's most successful members but Pilot Officer Lukaszewicz would be killed in action on 12 August when 501 engaged a strongly-escorted formation of Stuka dive-bombers.

The Luftwaffe in fact delivered several raids on the 12th in preparation for Eagle Day on the 13th, on which, somewhat surprisingly, 501 played no part. By contrast, it was very much involved on the 15th, when in the morning it engaged a formation of Junkers Ju 87s heading for its own airfield at Hawkinge. This raid was effectively disrupted and 501 claimed to have destroyed at least ten Stukas. In reality, only two were shot down[3] and 501 lost two Hurricanes, though Flight Lieutenant Putt and John Gibson, now also a flight lieutenant, both baled out and were quickly back in action.

Later that day, 501 attacked a formation of Dornier Do 17s, shooting down two without loss, and on the 16th it again helped to repulse enemy raids, destroying at least one more Dornier, again without loss. It was a different story on the 18th. In the morning, early afternoon and late afternoon, 501 was in action against heavy adverse odds. In the course of the day, it shot down two Messerschmitt Bf 110s, the destruction of which was confirmed beyond doubt and may well have at least damaged several other enemy aircraft but it lost no less than seven Hurricanes. Mercifully, only two pilots were killed; five of the stricken Hurricanes managed to remain airborne at least long enough for their pilots to escape by parachute.

Of these, two were unwounded and were soon back in action. 'Hawkeye' Lee was wounded and, being well aware that German fighters had recently fired on men who had baled out, he made a dramatic 'free-fall' of over 10,000ft before opening his parachute. Pilot Officer Kozlowski, one of 501's Poles, was also wounded and it was several weeks before either of them rejoined their squadron. Flight Sergeant McKay, who escaped from a Hurricane already in flames, never did rejoin it. On recovering from burns, he was posted to another Hurricane unit, ultimately rising to the rank of flight lieutenant.[4]

Thus 18 August had deprived 501 of three pilots permanently and two others temporarily. Fortunately, 'The Hardest Day' had been even harder on the Luftwaffe, so much so that there followed a lull until the 24th, gratefully accepted by 501's remaining pilots. When the enemy returned in force on the 24th, however, the squadron was faced with a long period of desperate fighting as the Luftwaffe delivered unrelenting attacks on Fighter Command's sector stations. The Germans had also adopted new tactics and thereby made 501's task more difficult. Squadron Leader Hogan, like Peter Townsend, believed that his primary duty was to shoot down or drive back the enemy bombers but these were now being protected by an increasing number of enemy fighters.

On 24 August 501 was able to disperse a formation of Junkers Ju

88s, destroying two of them and probably damaging others before the Messerschmitt Bf 109s came to their bombers' aid. These then shot down two Hurricanes. Pilot Officer Aldridge baled out but was admitted to hospital with a broken arm, while the Polish Pilot Officer Zenker was killed. On both 28 and 29 August the 109s prevented 501 from getting at the bombers, but suffered for their successes. On the 28th the Hurricanes definitely shot down three, probably four 109s without loss; on the 29th they undoubtedly shot down two more 109s, but this time two Hurricanes also fell. Flight Lieutenant Gibson and Sergeant Green both baled out but Green went to hospital with a wounded leg and took no further part in the battle.

There were more actions on 30 and 31 August and 1 and 2 September but it is impossible to determine 501's part in the confused and complicated fighting. Also it will be recalled that for this period the German records are admittedly incomplete. On 30 August, for instance, 501 at various times broke up or drove away three bomber formations. That alone was a considerable achievement but Luftwaffe accounts seem to deny any numerical success. This, though, was the day on which later information has revealed that the Germans lost six more Heinkel He 111s and two more Messerschmitt Bf 110s than was originally believed. It seems highly likely that some of the Heinkels fell to 501's guns.

The Heinkels' gunners put up a good defence and might have gained a valuable prize had the Hurricane been a less robust aircraft. 'Ginger' Lacey was hit repeatedly but was able to return to base, landing just beside a newsreel film unit that had already been delighted by a spectacular squadron take-off that they had quite wrongly believed to have been staged for their benefit. They obtained convincing evidence of the ruggedness of the Hurricane, for Lacey's machine had eighty-seven bullet holes in it, plus a considerable number of large gashes from splinters. It was perhaps this incident that prompted Lacey to remark that the Hurricane was clearly 'made up of non-essential parts'.

At the time there was little opportunity for humour as 501's pilots, like those of many another squadron, had become physically exhausted and were under constant mental strain. Even Lacey, though outwardly untroubled and still deadly when in action, was longing for a break and unable to prevent himself from vomiting whenever the call came for the squadron to take to the air. Nor could much relief be expected from new pilots, for these were being rushed to the squadrons from the Operational Training Units (OTUs) without anything like sufficient experience to enable them to fly modern interceptors, let alone fight with them. For example, in the morning of 2 September, Pilot Officer Rose-Price joined 501. He was young, charming and eager but 501's veterans felt that his inexperience was such that he should never have been sent to a front-line squadron. He was killed that same afternoon on his first combat sortie.

Like other squadrons also, the strength of 501 was being slowly drained away. Three other Hurricanes were lost on the afternoon of 2 September, though none of the pilots was seriously hurt. On the 5th, Lacey downed a Messerschmitt Bf 109, while three others, the fates of which are unknown, 'failed to return' to their base; it is possible that some or all of these were further victims of 501 pilots. Unfortunately, Pilot Officer Skalski, having been one of those who baled out on the 2nd, had to do so again on the 5th and this time went to hospital with serious burns. On 6 September 501 shot down two more 109s but three more Hurricanes were destroyed and two more pilots killed.

Salvation came on Saturday, 7 September – not only for 501 but for Fighter Command as a whole – courtesy of Hermann Göring. This was the day on which he turned his Luftwaffe onto London and though the city would suffer grievously, the constant pressure on the sector stations was lifted and Fighter Command was given a chance to recover.

In the fighting on the 7th, 501 played no part and for the next week it had only the occasional encounter. On the 8th, Pilot Officer Duckenfield shot down a 109. On the 11th, the squadron dispersed a group of Dornier Do 17s; the fighter escort then counter-attacked and shot down Sergeant Pickering but he baled out safely. On the 13th, 'Ginger' Lacey attacked a lone Heinkel He 111 that was reported to have bombed Buckingham Palace. His first burst killed the rear gunner but, as he renewed his attack, another member of the crew who had pulled the dead gunner aside, opened fire on him 'at a range', he afterwards declared, 'of, literally, feet', blowing away 'the entire radiator'. The Hurricane and the Heinkel continued to exchange fire until both were ablaze. Both crashed but while the remainder of the Heinkel's crew died, the Hurricane kept on flying until its pilot could escape by parachute with only minor burns.

Fighter Command and the Luftwaffe, though neither realized it, were in fact preparing for a major confrontation on 15 September. Field Marshal Kesselring had determined on massive raids on both the morning and the afternoon in a final attempt to shatter the defences. So large was the first raid that it took time for it to assemble over the French coast, thus giving Fighter Command plenty of time to be ready for it. As the Germans crossed the coast of England, they were attacked by two Spitfire squadrons but they were able to fight these off. Then it was the turn of a pair of Hurricane squadrons: 253 and 501.

As usual, the Hurricanes selected as their primary target the 100 Dornier Do 17s forming the bomber contingent of the enemy's assault. Some of the 300 or more enemy fighters tried to prevent them and 253 became engaged with these, no losses being suffered on either side, but 501 did get at the bombers, shooting down three and damaging a fourth before the 109s could intervene. When they belatedly did so, 501 downed one of them as well but lost two of its own aircraft. Squadron Leader Hogan baled out but Pilot Officer van den Hove, a Belgian recently transferred from 43 (Hurricane) Squadron, was killed.

The pilots of 501 had made the first dent in the huge enemy formation and it finally disintegrated after being attacked by nine more Hurricane and five more Spitfire squadrons; the proportion is worth noting. As well as defeating the first wave, these squadrons did much to ensure the failure of the afternoon raid; Kesselring could not give its bombers adequate protection in view of the number of his fighters that had been lost in the morning or had suffered damage, often only minor but sufficient to keep them on the ground. Moreover, news of the morning's events had greatly raised Fighter Command's morale and reduced that of the Luftwaffe. As a result, the afternoon attackers showed less resolution than those of the morning and some bombers turned back, jettisoning their weapons, when confronted by Hurricanes.

This time the enemy advanced in three separate groups and the fighting was even more confused. Once again, 501 was closely involved. It suffered no casualties and Lacey certainly added a 109 in flames to his impressive list of victories, but it is impossible to determine just what else Hogan's men achieved. Not that it matters: the combined effort of all Fighter Command squadrons was what counted and two days later, Hitler postponed Operation SEALION, his planned invasion of Britain, 'indefinitely'. Hitler's decision meant that the Battle of Britain had been won but it had not ended. The Luftwaffe continued its daylight raids, partly because Göring still hoped that British morale might collapse – though the events of 15 September had surely shown that this could not be expected – and partly with the intention of inflicting damage on the country's military potential. This was a much more reasonable objective and could hardly fail to inflict losses on squadrons like 501 that had been so long in the front line.

Thus in air battles on 17, 18 and 19 September, 501 lost Sergeant Egan and a total of four Hurricanes without being able to show much in return. There followed a welcome period of patrols that did not result in combat but during the last four days of September, 501 was again in the thick of the fighting. It destroyed a Junkers Ju 88 and two Messerschmitt Bf 109s and probably damaged other enemy aircraft but five more Hurricanes were lost, two pilots were killed – one when his parachute failed to open – and a third went to hospital. On the other hand, Pilot Officer Hairs escaped from superior numbers of enemy warplanes with only a cannon-shell through one wing as a result of a dramatic high-speed stall and spin.

In October the Luftwaffe tried a new tactic, sending out Messerschmitt Bf 109s fitted with a single bomb which they dropped at random from a high altitude. Since Fighter Command had only the briefest warning and the Hurricane did not have a very fast rate of climb, it is much to the credit of 501 that its record in October was quite a bit better than that in the second half of the previous month.

Exactly what 501 achieved is difficult to determine. It was only one of several squadrons to make contact with the raiders and there is again the question of the reliability of the Luftwaffe's records. On

12 October, for instance, 501 made a number of claims against 109s that cannot be confirmed from those records. It is easy to believe that 501 may have exaggerated its successes but when one learns that two of the 109s were seen to crash into the sea, not only by the pilots but by observers on the ground, it is hard not to feel that these claims at least were justified.

During this period, the most successful member of the squadron was a 'new boy' who had the advantages of being not only a very fine airman but of being fresh and with a useful number of hours' experience flying Hurricanes, although not in combat. Pilot Officer Kenneth William Mackenzie who, by the way, was not a Scot but a fighting Ulsterman, came to 501 from 43 Squadron on 3 October. Next day, he gave advance notice of his promise when he and 'Gus' Holden intercepted a lone Junkers Ju 88 that they damaged so badly that it crashed on landing and was 'written off'.

Another successful interception was made by 501 on 5 October and on the 7th, the squadron in general and Mackenzie in particular fought a memorable action against a large group of Messerschmitt Bf 109s. Flying Officer Barry was killed but 501 shot down four 109s and a fifth was crash-landed by its wounded pilot and 'written off'. Mackenzie first attacked a 109 that had already been hit by Squadron Leader Hogan and shot it into the sea. In the process, he became separated from the rest of his squadron and while still alone sighted eight more 109s. One of these he damaged and it turned back towards France, slowly losing height. Mackenzie dived in pursuit, only to discover to his fury that he had used up all his ammunition.

'I was determined that he should not get away,' Mackenzie later stated in his autobiography *Hurricane Combat*. He signalled to the German pilot that he should 'ditch' but not surprisingly was ignored. He therefore decided to knock the Messerschmitt's tail off with his undercarriage but when he lowered this he found he lost ground, so instead he 'smashed my starboard wing tip down onto his port tail-plane.' The 109 went straight into the sea and Mackenzie's Hurricane lost 3ft of its wing. Nonetheless, it continued to fly and since the wing had luckily snapped off cleanly without damage to the aileron, Mackenzie was able to turn towards home.

Any satisfaction that Mackenzie felt at the success of his

unorthodox manoeuvre, however, quickly vanished when he was attacked by two more 109s. These pursued him almost to the cliffs at Folkestone and inflicted further damage on his aircraft. Then, mercifully, the enemy fighters, presumably short of fuel, turned back and Mackenzie, with smoke pouring from his engine, crash-landed in a convenient field. Thinking he might need to make a speedy departure from his cockpit, he had undone his harness and was flung forward into his gun-sight, splitting his jaw and smashing four teeth. The Hurricane's injuries were later repaired and it was put back into service. Mackenzie also made a quick recovery and received a Distinguished Flying Cross in recognition of a probably unique achievement.[5]

As mentioned earlier, 501 had another good day on 12 October but was less successful on the 15th when two of its Hurricanes were destroyed, Sergeant Fenemore being killed and Sergeant Jarratt wounded. On the 25th it had mixed fortunes. In the morning it shot down two 109s without loss but in the afternoon it was about to engage another 109 formation when the Czech Pilot Officer Goth, who had fallen behind and was hastening to catch up, crashed into Mackenzie so violently that their aircraft virtually disintegrated. Goth was killed. Mackenzie baled out and, like Lee before him, made a long 'free-fall' before opening his parachute in order to prevent himself from becoming a target.

In fact, it is unlikely that the 109s would have been interested in Mackenzie for they were too busy attacking 501's remaining pilots, taking full advantage of the shock and confusion caused by the accident. They shot down two more Hurricanes, though both pilots baled out, and only one enemy fighter was lost in return. There were further lesser clashes throughout the remainder of October and in these 501 did better, destroying at least two more 109s and suffering no losses. Officially, 31 October was the last day of the Battle of Britain but in reality Luftwaffe nuisance raids continued during November. On the 12th Mackenzie and Flight Lieutenant Morello shot down a lone enemy bomber, and as late as the 15th Mackenzie downed yet another Messerschmitt Bf 109.

Now 501 was at last moved from No. 11 Group to a series of bases around Bristol and Bath, where it was employed mainly on uneventful convoy patrols. Sadly, even in this quiet time, there were casualties: two pilots were killed in air accidents and a third, even more sadly, in a car crash.

There were also other less tragic departures. Squadron Leader Henry Hogan left to become a wing commander (and ultimately an air vice-marshal), his place as 501's CO being taken by 'Gus' Holden, who would also go on to become a wing commander. All 501's leading Polish pilots – Skalski, Witorzenc and Glowacki – were transferred. The last-named rose to be squadron leader and after the war, perhaps wisely, remained in the Royal Air Force and later emigrated to New Zealand. Both Skalski and Witorzenc returned to Poland – the former as a wing commander, the latter as a group captain – but their country's puppet Communist government at first allowed neither to serve in the Polish Air Force, and Skalski, the more rebellious of the two, was accused of being a spy and was under sentence of death for a time. Mercifully, more humane attitudes were eventually adopted: Witorzenc became Chairman of the Polish Airmen Society and Skalski a general of the Polish Air Force.

Some 501 pilots who had served with it for far longer than the Poles left as well. John Gibson enjoyed a varied career in the RAF which included service in the Pacific and in which he rose to be a squadron leader. After the war, he became the personal pilot of first Field Marshal Montgomery and then Marshal of the Royal Air Force Lord Tedder.

Kenneth 'Hawkeye' Lee was also sent abroad, in his case to the Middle East, where he became CO of 123 (Hurricane) Squadron in March 1943. In July, however, he was hit by AA fire when leading a low-level raid on Crete, crash-landed and was taken prisoner. He was sent to Stalag Luft III, where he assisted the preparations for the 'Great Escape' by the undramatic but essential task of dispersing the sand from the tunnel. The bulk of those who eventually used it were chosen by lot and it turned out to be lucky for Lee that he was not one of them, since fifty of those who escaped and were recaptured were murdered by the Gestapo. Lee, by contrast, remained in captivity but survived the war.

The remaining 501 pilots did not see action again until 17 April 1941 when their Hurricanes escorted Blenheims on a raid on

Cherbourg. The bombers suffered losses from AA fire but 501 had no casualties and gained some satisfaction from the thought that British aircraft were now taking the offensive. Soon afterwards, however, Spitfires began to replace 501's Hurricanes and in May it became fully operational with its new machines.

In later days, 501 would have further important successes with Hawker aircraft. In August 1944 it converted to Tempests and shortly afterwards it became the only Tempest squadron to specialize in opposing the V-1 flying bombs at night; it is believed to have destroyed nearly 100 of these. After the war, 501 flew jet aircraft but on 2 February 1957 it and all other Auxiliary units were disbanded and the Royal Auxiliary Air Force disappeared from history but not, one trusts, from memory.

Neither of 501's two most remarkable Hurricane pilots would fly its Tempests or its jet fighters. Both did fly its Spitfires for a time but by the late summer of 1941 both had been transferred elsewhere. 'Ginger' Lacey had been commissioned in January 1941 and by the time he left 501, he was a flight lieutenant. Since he was widely and rightly respected for his achievements, it seemed that a brilliant career lay ahead of him but it was not to be. Mackenzie, though personally liking Lacey, says that he was 'direct, intolerant and had a marked indifference to others.' It may be that these qualities were not considered likely to make him a good squadron leader.

In any case, it was not until 23 November 1944 that Lacey commanded a squadron: No. 17 flying Spitfires on the India/Burma front. His leadership was certainly novel. He ordered that all ranks should shave their heads to indicate solidarity with the Gurkhas who guarded No. 17's airfield. This perhaps reflected his peculiar sense of humour more than anything else and it certainly much amused the Gurkhas. He sent experienced pilots who had had slight landing accidents away for further training and refused to allow officers who were flight lieutenants but not his flight commanders to wear the badges of their rank. These actions may have indicated his own high standards but if anyone else had ordered them, it is to be wondered whether Lacey would not have been the first to label him a martinet.

Lacey remained in the RAF after the war but his disinterest in recording flying hours in his logbook 'when there are no longer any aircraft to shoot at' and even his appearance, very different from the slim, youthful-looking sergeant pilot who had flown with 501, suggest that he was one of those warriors who could not be really happy in peacetime. After leaving the service, though, he reverted to being a flying instructor in Yorkshire and perhaps this did bring him a measure of contentment.

Kenneth William Mackenzie on leaving 501 became a flight lieutenant and a Hurricane pilot again, serving on 247 Squadron, then mainly flying defensive patrols at night. Mackenzie soon showed his capability in this role, personally destroying two enemy aircraft, his first 'kills' since he had ceased to fly Hurricanes with 501. On 29 September 1941, however, he took part in a strafing attack on an enemy aerodrome at Lannion in Brittany, was badly hit by AA fire, was forced to 'ditch' and became a prisoner of war.

It was not to be expected that Mackenzie would be a good prisoner and he made several unsuccessful attempts to escape, was transferred from camp to camp and finally ended up in the notorious Stalag Luft III, though in the East Compound not the North Compound from which the 'Great Escape' was made. By this time Mackenzie, who could not speak German, was convinced that there was no possibility of his making a 'normal' escape. He therefore decided to feign madness in order to get himself repatriated. In *Hurricane Combat*, infuriatingly, he relates only that he put on an act with the collaboration of the camp's medical officer. It appears, however, that he pretended to have had a nervous breakdown and practised an alarming twitch and a severe stammer that he would later find difficult to lose.

Whatever the details, Mackenzie's deception worked and he was returned to England in October 1944, to be known henceforth as 'Mad Mac'. Whether this was due solely to his method of escaping from captivity or was also influenced by memories of his knocking down the 109 with his Hurricane's wing is disputed. He remained in service with the RAF after the war, becoming a wing commander. On retirement, he took up the post of deputy commander of the Zambian Air Force. According to old 501 acquaintances who knew about his role, he 'was' the Zambian Air Force.

Both Lacey and Mackenzie considered that the most worthwhile part of their careers was not just their time with 501 Squadron but their time on Hurricanes with 501 Squadron. Mackenzie declares that he flew the Hurricane and the Spitfire and he 'liked them both but preferred the Hurricane.' Perhaps inevitably, remembering his exploits, this was chiefly because of the Hurricane's 'ruggedness'. 'Ginger' Lacey's opinion was equally clear but more subtle. As Britain's highest-scoring 'ace' at the end of 1940, his verdict on Britain's two great fighters of that momentous year, if not the final one, is surely the most interesting: 'I'd rather fly in a Spitfire but fight in a Hurricane.'

Notes

1. It had previously been a unit of the RAF's Special Reserve as from June 1929 and since May 1930 had been known as 501 (City of Bristol) Squadron.

2. On 4 July 501 moved to Middle Wallop, north-east of Salisbury. This was later included in No. 10 Group but that did not happen until early August and 501 had returned to the south-east on 26 July. It subsequently operated from Gravesend, Hawkinge and Kenley.

3. While doubts have rightly been cast on the completeness of the German records, it is right to say that RAF – and Auxiliary Air Force – pilots did on several occasions undeniably overestimate the number of Stukas destroyed. It is suggested that the Ju 87s, when trapped, would attempt to escape by going into a power dive. Since Britain had no dive-bombers with which comparisons could be made, it was natural for Fighter Command's airmen to believe that they had fatally disabled the Stukas in question or perhaps killed their pilots.

4. McKay survived the war but Messrs Shores and Williams provide a tragic footnote to his career in their *Aces High*: 'It is understood that following the death of his wife, to whom he was devoted, he took his own life on 30 September 1959.'

5. There are several instances during the Battle of Britain where British fighters were reported to have rammed German aircraft. It seems, though, that apart from Mackenzie's exploit, these were either accidental collisions or cases where the fighter pilot had pressed home his attack to very close range and had been caught in the blast when his target exploded.

Chapter 5

First in All Things
1 Squadron

For 85, 501 and many other Hurricane squadrons, their exploits in the Battle of Britain are regarded as their highest achievements. This is both inevitable and right, because it was this battle that justified the existence of the Hurricane and the foresight of its creator. If the Hurricane had done nothing else, it would still deserve to rank among the most important warplanes of all time. In fact, of course, it did a great deal more and we will meet famous Hurricane squadrons that took no part in the Battle of Britain. In the case of the squadron about to be discussed, it did play a creditable part in that battle but no one has ever disputed that its 'finest hours' came both earlier and later.

The first connection of No. 1 Squadron of the Royal Air Force with Hawker fighters came in February 1932 when it received Hawker Furies. With these it became famous for its brilliant aerobatics, at which it was rivalled only by 43 Squadron, also based at Tangmere and also flying Furies. The good-natured but intense determination of each of these squadrons to better the performance of the other one provided the high points of many an Air Force Display and Air Defence Exercise.

At the time of the Munich Crisis, Squadron Leader Bertram supposedly told his pilots that the only way their Furies were likely to destroy German aircraft was by ramming them. Even so, no great welcome awaited the arrival at Tangmere of a new Hawker aircraft.

The Hurricane was regarded with some distaste and unkindly described as 'a single-seat troop carrier'. Officially the first Hurricanes started to reach Tangmere in October 1938 but it is clear that No. 1 remained basically a Fury squadron until February 1939 and it was only then that the new Hawker fighters were flown by all its pilots including, incidentally, a certain Sergeant James 'Ginger' Lacey of the Volunteer Reserve, with No. 1 on temporary attachment.

Within a matter of weeks, it became obvious that 1 Squadron's pilots would need to become proficient at flying Hurricanes without delay. In March 1939, in flagrant defiance of Hitler's explicit promises at Munich, Germany swallowed up Czechoslovakia and it was horribly clear that Nazi aggression could only be checked by armed force. Since it was realized that Poland would be Germany's next target, Britain and France undertook to go to her aid should she be threatened. From that moment in practice war was inevitable and 1 Squadron spent the summer in intensive training for action by day and night. There were the usual accidents as the pilots got used to their new machines and these included the death of the capable and popular Flight Lieutenant Hemmings who became disorientated, dived down a searchlight beam and crashed into the South Downs at 400 mph.

The squadron had been warned that if or, more realistically, when war came, it would be sent to France and on 8 September it duly left Tangmere, originally for an airfield near Le Havre where it was to form part of the Air Component. A series of moves to other airfields followed, and finally on 9 October No. 1 took up residence at Vassincourt 50 miles east of Reims where, together with 73 (Hurricane) Squadron, it formed 67 Wing, the fighter contingent of the Advanced Air Striking Force.

The transfer to France had been led by Squadron Leader Patrick Halahan who had succeeded Bertram as CO in April 1939. Halahan was nicknamed 'the Bull' and this was entirely appropriate for he was a sturdy, broad-shouldered, powerful man who was generally considered as hard mentally as he was physically. He was difficult to get to know and was far from tolerant. He disliked reporters and banned them from contact with his pilots. He was not fond of his

French allies with the exception of Lieutenant Jean-François Demozay, who had been attached to No. 1 as liaison officer and interpreter, and he was intensely hostile towards the Germans. When the squadron entertained Unteroffizier Arno Frankenberger, a Dornier pilot who had put up a most gallant fight before being shot down and taken prisoner, Halahan expressed regret that he had allowed this. Frankenberger proved so pleasant that No. 1's pilots began to wonder if the enemy was as bad as had been painted; they changed their minds later after seeing the Luftwaffe mercilessly machine-gun helpless refugees.

Indeed, it might be hard to find Halahan likeable were it not for his steadfast concern for his squadron. He would not be found at the head of his men in the air all that often and this seems to have caused some resentment, particularly among those who joined the squadron later. He believed, however, that he could look after their interests better by dealing with the squadron's liaison and administrative affairs and taking up his pilots' concerns with the authorities. He insisted, for instance, on back-armour being installed in the Hurricanes in France, as was already being done in those in Britain. It appears that his superiors appreciated his views, for he was at one time 'grounded' as being too valuable to lose and only released from this restriction after the start of the blitzkrieg.

Halahan was fortunate in being able to entrust combat leadership to two exceptionally able flight commanders. Peter 'Johnny' Walker and Peter Prosser Hanks possessed great tactical skill, having an uncanny knack of knowing when to engage the enemy and when not to engage. They were aided by Halahan's determination to instil in his squadron the need for teamwork. This became a matter of pride and extended beyond the pilots; it was a saying in 1 Squadron that each Hurricane had a crew of three: its fitter who looked after its engine, its rigger who took care of its airframe and its pilot who brought it into action.

As far as team spirit among the pilots was concerned, it is only necessary to mention an incident at the end of March 1940. In the early days of the war there was less interest in the Messerschmitt Bf 109 than in the Bf 110 since it was known that the 110 was regarded with particular favour by Göring and was flown by specially-selected pilots. Air Marshal Barratt, the Commander-in-Chief of the British Air Forces in France, had therefore promised a dinner in Paris for the first pilot to down one. On 29 March the prize was claimed when three of No. 1's Hurricanes engaged nine Bf 110s. It was believed that two of these had been damaged and one was certainly destroyed by Flight Lieutenant 'Johnny' Walker; it was confirmed on the ground and later in German records. Walker duly dined with Barratt at Maxims but rather daringly insisted that the 110 had been 'brought down by teamwork' and the other members of his section – Flying Officer Stratton and Sergeant Clowes – should be invited as well. The air marshal generously complied.

This team spirit was all the more commendable in view of the fact that throughout its time as a Hurricane squadron, No. 1 included several pilots who were not British. Halahan, for instance, came from the Irish Republic, as did Flying Officer Kilmartin who was posted to No. 1 in November 1939. Flying Officer Stratton was a New Zealander; Flying Officer Mark Henry 'Hilly' Brown, who had joined the RAF on learning of the rapid expansion of the Luftwaffe, was a Canadian; and Flying Officer 'Pussy' Palmer, the man who shot down Arno Frankenberger, was an American.

Then there was the Australian contingent. Flying Officer Paul Richey kept a very detailed diary of his time with 1 Squadron and later expanded it into a superb book entitled simply *Fighter Pilot*. In this he describes himself as 'Irish-Australian'. Flying Officer Billy Drake – 'Billy' was the name with which he was christened, not a nickname or abbreviation – has stated that he was 'half-Australian'. Finally there was Flying Officer Leslie Clisby, an aggressive, reckless and rather ferocious character who once landed alongside a Heinkel He 111 that he had forced down in a field and, waving a large revolver, captured its crew, who he handed over to French troops. He could never have been mistaken for anything other than wholly Australian, even without his strong accent and his insistence on wearing a somewhat tattered Royal Australian Air Force uniform.

On the other hand, Flight Lieutenants Walker and Hanks, whose role in 1 Squadron's successes was crucial, were both English. So was Pilot Officer 'Boy' Mould who, on 30 October 1939, shot down a Dornier Do 17 reconnaissance aircraft to record the first 'kill', not just by No. 1 but by any Hurricane squadron in France. The Hurricane units rarely encountered enemy aircraft at this time, so there was considerable excitement in 1 Squadron when on 23 November it had a hand in the destruction of two more Dorniers and a Heinkel He 111.

It is clear that Squadron Leader Halahan was making operational flights at this time because he and 'Hilly' Brown shot down one of the Dorniers in flames. The other Dornier was the one flown by Arno Frankenberger. This was first attacked by 'Pussy' Palmer who left it losing height with one engine on fire. The navigator and rear gunner baled out and Palmer could see Frankenberger slumped over the controls. As Palmer flew past, however, Frankenberger ceased feigning death and put thirty-four bullets into the Hurricane, an episode that convinced Halahan of the need to have back-armour fitted to his machines. Another pair of No. 1's Hurricanes then shot down the Dornier but its gallant pilot, as we saw, survived to be entertained in the victors' mess.

Palmer, it may be added, was able to put down safely in a field. This was something that the Hurricane's strength, in particular its wide undercarriage, enabled it to do with comparative ease, thereby preserving a number of valuable lives. An even greater example of the Hurricane's reliability occurred on the same day during No. 1's destruction of the Heinkel He 111. A group of French fighters rushed in to assist and one crashed into the tail of the Hurricane flown by Sergeant Arthur 'Taffy' Clowes. The Frenchman baled out but Clowes flew his Hurricane back to Vassincourt despite its having lost one elevator and most of its rudder. He then had to land at 120 mph to maintain control and the Hurricane tipped up on its nose. Yet Clowes, though understandably shaken, was unhurt and his aircraft was repaired on site; an illustration of both the damage a Hurricane could sustain and the ease with which it could be made ready to fly and fight again.

Winter weather brought an end to such encounters, but they were resumed in March 1940 when 1 Squadron destroyed a Dornier Do 17 on the 2nd and a Heinkel He 111 on the 3rd. Unfortunately, return fire from the Dornier inflicted the squadron's first fatal casualty of the war, Pilot Officer Mitchell being brought down and killed. The 29th of the month saw No. l's first clash with Messerschmitt Bf 109s, Paul Richey damaging one so badly that it crash-landed with a wounded pilot at the controls. Later the same day, No. l's first action with Messerschmitt Bf 110s resulted in one being downed by 'Johnny' Walker, as already described.

Throughout April, 1 Squadron had several fights not only with reconnaissance machines but with 109s and 110s. It enjoyed a number of successes but exactly how many is impossible to determine. When German records fail to admit the loss of more than one aircraft seen to fall in flames and confirmed by the French on the ground, it is difficult to deny that, as in the Battle of Britain, they are simply incomplete. Equally there were undoubtedly cases where the damage inflicted on the enemy was overestimated and Christopher Shores points out in his *Fledgling Eagles* that when 109s dived away steeply, they poured out a 'thick exhaust trail' that could easily lead to over-optimism. Of course, if the 109s were going flat-out back to Germany, they scarcely considered themselves superior to the Hurricanes and the confidence of the RAF pilots was increased by an incident in early May.

On 2 May a 109 was forced down near Amiens and captured intact. Next day 1 Squadron's pilots inspected it and it was flown by 'Hilly' Brown in a mock combat with the Hurricane of Prosser Hanks that appeared to most spectators to be terrifyingly realistic. It was accepted by 1 Squadron that the 109 was faster at most altitudes and had a better rate of climb. It was also praised for its excellent rearward vision, though this would no longer be the case during the Battle of Britain by which time additional armour-plate had been fitted behind the pilot's head.

No mention was made of armament but in fact, while the 109's two 20mm cannons and two 7-9mm machine guns packed a heavier punch than the Hurricane, this was balanced by the latter's greater steadiness as a gun platform and its greater ability to endure combat damage.

On the credit side, the Hurricane was found to be faster at ground level, a trait that would benefit its later career when it would be directed mainly against targets on the ground. Better still, it was much more manoeuvrable and could easily out-turn the 109.

Squadron Leader Halahan formally reported his conviction that 'provided Hurricanes are not surprised by 109s', then 'the balance will always be in favour of our aircraft', while Paul Richey declares: 'We loved our Hurricanes and believed them to be a match for anything the Germans could put up, especially in a dog-fight.'

So when Hitler made his move on 10 May, and despite being transferred on this same day to Berry-au-Bac, north of Reims and nearer to the German advance, 1 Squadron faced the onslaught resolutely. Squadron Leader Halahan had ordered that if possible his pilots should always engage the German fighters, on the somewhat dubious grounds that the enemy bombers would retire once they had lost their escort (which in practice they rarely did). On 10 May, however, 1 Squadron attacked Heinkel He 111s and Dornier Do 17s and inflicted losses on them. This, though, was only a preliminary to the squadron's most remarkable combat that took place on the following day.

Already on 11 May No. 1 had recorded a few successful clashes when in the late afternoon, five of its most experienced pilots – Walker, Brown, Kilmartin, Richey and Sergeant 'Frank' Soper – sighted near Sedan thirty Dornier Do 17s, escorted by fifteen Messerschmitt Bf 110s. The unpleasant odds of nine to one against were at least reduced by the hasty retirement of the Dorniers but the 110s took on the Hurricanes, still with a three to one advantage. Despite this, No. 1's airmen believed that they shot down ten 110s. Since German official records, examined after the war, state that only two 110s fell, this would seem another good moment at which to assess the evidence for the pilots' claims.

Paul Richey in *Fighter Pilot* gives a detailed and vivid account of this action. 'We went in fast in a tight bunch,' he tells us, 'each picking a 110 and manoeuvring to get on his tail.' Having done so, Richey shot his target down in flames, the pilot baling out and being taken prisoner. Looking round to check what was happening, Richey could see four more 110s going down – a sight he would never forget – but also 'three cunning chaps' who had climbed above the main battle and were ready to pounce on the Hurricanes. He therefore flew towards them, shot one down in flames, but was then attacked by the other two as well as by more 110s from below.

By this time, the other Hurricanes, having dealt out destruction but used up all their ammunition, had had no choice but to leave the scene. This meant that Richey was on his own, but he continued his single-handed fight for what watchers on the ground estimated at a quarter of an hour or more. Finally the adverse odds prevailed and the 110s shot Richey down. He took to his parachute and landed safely.

It can be seen that Richey had personally observed the destruction of six enemy aircraft and since the entire population of a nearby village had poured out to watch the fight, there were plenty of other witnesses to testify to the 110s' discomfiture. The French authorities, who were very thorough when checking enemy losses, subsequently found the wrecks of all ten of those claimed on the ground. Still more significantly, Richey, who had every reason to know, and the watching villagers agreed that his long solo battle had been fought not with thirteen 110s as would have been the case if the German records were correct, but with five 110s, all that were left of the enemy formation. In these circumstances it is difficult not to consider No. 1's claims far more reliable than any post-war assessment.

On the following day, the 12th, 1 Squadron performed its official task of protecting Allied bombers: five Battles of 12 Squadron, sent to attack the Veldwezelt and Vroenhoven bridges over the Albert Canal across which German forces were pouring. Squadron Leader Halahan, his 'grounding' order rescinded, took eight Hurricanes to the area just before the British bombers arrived so as to keep enemy fighters away from them. This they succeeded in doing but the Battles were met by a murderous concentration of AA fire. All were shot down or crash-landed, although the Veldwezelt bridge was shattered, almost certainly by the section leader, Flying Officer Garland. He and his observer, Sergeant Gray, the navigator for the strike, each received a posthumous Victoria Cross. Garland's wireless operator/gunner, Leading Aircraftman Reynolds, received no recognition but let his name be recorded alongside those of his companions.

For their part, No. 1's pilots shot down several Messerschmitt Bf 109s and two others were seen to collide when engaging 'Hilly'

Brown. Brown's Hurricane was damaged, as was that of Sergeant Soper, but both got back to base safely. Halahan force-landed and Flying Officer Raymond Lewis had to bale out, but they both survived as well and later rejoined their squadron. On the return flight, the aggressive Leslie Clisby sighted a group of Henschel army co-operation aircraft and shot down two or three of these as well.

Thereafter, 1 Squadron, like the other Hurricane units in France, saw constant action and took a steady toll of its enemies. On 14 May, for instance, it clashed with formations of Heinkel He 111s escorted by 110s and of Junkers Ju 87 Stukas escorted by 109s, gaining successes against all of these. Next morning, another fierce battle with 110s resulted in the destruction of at least six of these that were confirmed by the French on the ground and possibly more. Paul Richey again downed two 110s but was again shot down himself and once again escaped safely by parachute.

Other members of the squadron were less lucky. On 13 May Billy Drake shot down a Dornier Do 17 – confirmed by British army units – only to be attacked from behind and brought down by Bf 110s. He baled out, was fired on as he descended by parachute though fortunately without result, and ended up in hospital where shell splinters had to be removed from his back without anaesthetic since the hospital in question had been overwhelmed by the need to cope with swarms of refugees.

Worse was to come on the afternoon of the 15th. A force of some thirty Messerschmitt Bf 110s had flown overhead and although no orders to scramble had been given, a 1 Squadron fitter begged Flight Lieutenant Hanks to take his six Hurricanes in pursuit. Against his own inclinations and perhaps over-confident after No. 1's recent successes, Hanks complied. The 110s turned on his outnumbered flight and while the No. 1 pilots believed they had inflicted losses on their enemies, three Hurricanes failed to return to Berry-au-Bac and 'Boy' Mould only managed to escape after some dramatic manoeuvring among treetops. Hanks had baled out safely but Leslie Clisby and Flying Officer Lorimer were dead.

On the following day, the German advance forced 1 Squadron to leave Berry-au-Bac in some haste and for the next month it kept moving to a succession of airfields until it finally reached north-western France where it covered the evacuation of the remainder of the BEF. The squadron's last major clash with the Luftwaffe came on 19 May when it sighted an unescorted formation of Heinkel He 111s and recorded several successes. Paul Richey was again well to the fore. He shot down one Heinkel for certain and probably two more but was then badly wounded in the neck by return fire. He managed to make a forced landing and was taken to hospital in Paris.

Normally, however, it was the light 'flak' with the German ground forces that proved most dangerous to the squadron during these latter days. This brought down three of its members at various times, all of them becoming prisoners of war. There were still occasional encounters with enemy aircraft, of course, and that No. 1 did not suffer heavier losses was again due to the extraordinary strength of its Hurricanes.

Thus on 17 May Sergeant 'Frank' Soper had a fight with Messerschmitt Bf 110s, downing two of them in flames but being badly shot up in return. His Hurricane was hit by three cannon shells and thirty bullets that damaged an aileron and all its controls, yet he was able to fly it back to his base where it had to be 'written off' as unrepairable. On 4 June Pilot Officer 'Pat' Hancock damaged a Heinkel He 111 but his Hurricane was also hit and injuries to its elevators made it difficult to control. Consequently, when Hancock landed, he crashed into a parked Blenheim, fortunately unoccupied, and is said to have 'cut it in half'. His Hurricane suffered further severe damage but its pilot was unhurt.

The squadron flew its last operational mission in France on 17 June, though in tragic circumstances. At St Nazaire, heavy clouds enabled Heinkel He 111s to evade a section of No. 1's Hurricanes and sink the troopship *Lancastria* with 5,000 men on board, over half of whom were lost. Some belated revenge was obtained when Sergeant George Berry shot down the bomber responsible.

This horrible catastrophe overshadowed but should not be allowed to conceal the achievements of No. 1 Squadron. Since 10 May, it believed it had downed 129 German aircraft, 114 of them in the ten days from 10 to 19 May. Michael Shaw, in his history of the squadron, *Twice Vertical*,[1] estimates that they brought down eighty-seven during the earlier period and ten or eleven more later. It may well be that even these reduced figures include exaggerated or duplicated claims but equally there may have been other successes of which the details are unknown since No. 1's own records were lost in France and the German records, as we have seen, are not complete.

In any event, when one considers that only two of the squadron's pilots were killed during this period, No. 1's record is quite outstanding and would never be equalled. It was fittingly acknowledged in a unique mass award of decorations announced in the *London Gazette* on 14 June: the Distinguished Flying Cross to Halahan, Walker, Hanks, Brown, Kilmartin, Mould, Stratton, Palmer, Richey and Clisby; the Distinguished Flying Medal to Soper, Berry and Clowes. Of these, the most surprising is the award to Clisby, not because it was not well-deserved but because normally only the Victoria Cross could be awarded posthumously. For once this rule was waived, possibly because the recommendation had been made prior to Clisby's death, possibly because at this time he was reported only as 'Missing'. In either case, it seems only appropriate that he should thus be associated with his fellow pilots, all members of the same exceptional team.

On the same 17 June that No. 1 fought its last action in France, the bulk of the squadron was evacuated from La Rochelle, leaving only the pilots to fly its remaining twelve Hurricanes and enough ground crews to keep them serviced. On the 18th the Hurricanes set off to Tangmere. Lieutenant Demozay, No. 1's faithful liaison officer/interpreter, packed the ground crews into an old Bombay transport and flew it to Britain. Here, under the *nom-de-guerre* of 'Moses Morlaix' – to avoid reprisals against his family; Morlaix is a town in Brittany – he would rejoin No. 1 in a more active role.

Other members of the squadron returned to Britain by diverse individual routes. 'Hilly' Brown, now a flight lieutenant, had been forced to bale out on 14 June but managed to get to Brest, where he caught a ship home. The squadron's wounded, Drake and Richey, were flown back. Brown rejoined No. 1 at Tangmere but the other two were sent at first to Operational Training Units where they could pass on the knowledge they had acquired. Both would later see active service and would renew their acquaintance with the

Hurricane in circumstances illustrating other aspects of the Hawker fighter's history.

In October 1941 Billy Drake would take command of 128 (Hurricane) Squadron. This was based in West Africa at Hastings, Sierra Leone, an example of the many different areas in which the Hurricane served: here we might mention Iraq, Iran, Iceland, Madagascar and the Atlantic, Arctic and Indian Oceans. Later Drake would move to the Middle East where, as CO of 112 (Kittyhawk) Squadron, he would be credited with an impressive list of victories. He would retire from the RAF as a group captain.

Paul Richey, while never becoming a fighter 'ace' of the calibre of Drake, proved an equally capable fighter leader, first of squadrons – he was the officer whom 'Bee' Beamont succeeded as CO of 609 (Typhoon) Squadron – and later as a wing commander in Burma. Here, during the second half of 1943, he was in charge of 165 Wing containing 79 and 146 Squadrons with Hurricane Mark II fighters and Richey correctly felt that these were becoming outdated as interceptors.[2] In December, however, he took over 189 Wing and before he had to return to Britain early in 1944 on account of ill-health, he had presided over a fundamental change that was taking place in the employment of the Hurricane. The two squadrons in 189 Wing, 34 and 42, were equipped with Hurricane fighter-bombers and it was in this ground-attack role that the Hurricanes in Burma were to prove outstanding.

Most of 1 Squadron's longest-serving pilots had returned to Britain earlier than Brown or Drake or Richey, specifically on 24 May after 'Bull' Halahan had twice protested that the exhaustion of his veterans was such that if the fighting in France continued at the same pace, they would all be killed within a week. Rather to his surprise, his request was granted.

After a brief period of welcome rest, Halahan and his men were sent to Operational Training Units and later dispersed to bring the benefit of their experience to various other Hurricane squadrons. Kilmartin, who had come to No. 1 from 43, rejoined 43 and later went to 128 Squadron where he succeeded Drake as CO. Walker became CO of 253 (Hurricane) Squadron. Hanks went first to 257, then became CO of 56 Squadron. Stratton remained for a long time at OTUs but flew Hurricanes with 213 Squadron in the Middle East in March 1943 and in November became CO of 134 (Hurricane) Squadron and took it to Burma where he led it until May 1944. All of them survived the war: Kilmartin as a wing commander, Walker and Hanks as group captains. Stratton was also a wing commander when hostilities ceased but prior to that he had transferred to the Royal New Zealand Air Force and ended his career as Chief of the Air Staff with the rank of air vice-marshal.

Other stories ended less happily. Sergeant Soper was commissioned and in June 1941 joined 257 (Hurricane) Squadron as a flight lieutenant, becoming its CO in September. On 5 October, however, he was hit by return fire from a Junkers Ju 88 and killed. 'Pussy' Palmer also became a squadron leader but died in combat on 27 October 1942, flying a Spitfire. 'Boy' Mould took command of 185 (Hurricane) Squadron, a new unit formed in Malta in May 1941. He led this in several successful interceptions of enemy raiders and also on a number of effective ground attacks on targets in Sicily but on 1 October 1941 he too was killed in action.

'Bull' Halahan also had an unhappy connection with Malta. On 27 April 1941, by now a wing commander, 'the Bull' was on board HM aircraft carrier *Ark Royal*, there supervising the launch of twenty-four Hurricanes to the island-fortress as reinforcements for its then sole fighter squadron, No. 261. All except one arrived safely and Halahan was sent to Malta himself to act as Fighter Controller. Sadly, in June, the pilots of 249 Squadron, who had flown to Malta in late May to relieve 261, became involved in a riotous drinking spree that got out of hand. Halahan, who had accompanied them, took full responsibility and was transferred forthwith to the Middle East. Here it seems that his rather belligerent attitude earned him more enemies, a promised promotion to group captain failed to materialize and he retired from the RAF in November 1943.

Halahan's successor as 1 Squadron's CO was Squadron Leader David Pemberton who knew No. 1 well, having been Chief Operations Officer at 67 Wing. His task was far from easy, for his squadron was soon to move to Northolt where it was likely to be in the thick of the action when the German assault was launched. Moreover, of the original body of highly-experienced pilots who had followed Halahan to France, there remained only 'Hilly' Brown, Flying Officer Peter Matthews and Sergeants Berry and Clowes, and Berry was to be killed in action on 1 September. Nonetheless, Pemberton was able to maintain No. 1's team spirit, not least by his sterling personal example: in August alone, he would fly sixty-six sorties.

Like most Hurricane squadrons, No. 1 saw little action in July. On the 19th, a section of its Hurricanes engaged a Heinkel He 111 that was believed to have been damaged, but Pilot Officer Browne was hit by return fire and crash-landed. His aircraft was 'written off' but, as so often, the pilot was unhurt. On the 25th, No. 1 had better fortune when Pilot Officer Goodman shot down a Messerschmitt Bf 109.

In August the fighting intensified but 1 Squadron had little luck at first. On the 11th, Pilot Officer Davey was killed in a battle with Bf 110s and on the 15th the squadron, attempting to intercept the redoubtable Erprobungsgruppe 210, was attacked while still climbing and lost three Hurricanes and two pilots. That evening the Hurricanes of 111 Squadron would exact a terrible revenge for No. 1's sufferings but this was not known to Pemberton's men who, of course, were unaware of the identity of their attackers.

Over the next few days matters improved slightly. On the 16th No. 1 repulsed large enemy raids, Squadron Leader Pemberton and Pilot Officer Goodman each destroyed a Heinkel He 111 and probably other German aircraft were at least damaged. The squadron lost one Hurricane, apparently to 'friendly' AA fire, but Pilot Officer Elkington baled out. On the 18th the squadron again repelled enemy raiders, Pemberton downed a Messerschmitt Bf 109 and his men may have inflicted further damage.

Minor actions were fought later in the month and Sergeant Merchant had mixed fortunes on its last two days. On the 30th he destroyed a Heinkel He 111 but next day, his Hurricane was set on fire in a fight with Bf 110s. Merchant could not at first get his cockpit hood open and although he eventually managed to bale out, he was taken to hospital suffering from burns. Then No. 1's misfortunes were resumed and in the first three days of September three of its pilots were killed, including Sergeant Berry as mentioned earlier.

On 6 September, 1 Squadron had an encounter that held particular significance for a Hurricane unit. The Luftwaffe had decided to make every effort to bomb Hawkers' Brooklands factory that produced half the total output of Hurricanes during 1940. The first attempt on 4 September was thwarted by the Hurricanes of 253 Squadron that shot down six Bf 110s without loss and so shook the survivors that they bombed the nearby Vickers works instead. The next and last attempt on the Hawker factory was made on the 6th. This time it was No. 1 that intercepted the raiding Bf 110s, two of which it shot down for the loss of one Hurricane, from which Pilot Officer Goodman baled out safely. Only minor damage was caused to the Brooklands works and this had no effect on Hurricane production.

A few days later, 1 Squadron was withdrawn to the Midlands. It was high time, for once again exhaustion was beginning to reduce effectiveness. During October, No. 1 would have the occasional battle with enemy bombers, shooting down two but losing Sergeant Warren and having two Hurricanes crash on landing, fortunately without injury to the pilots. Then on 3 November, Squadron Leader Pemberton crashed shortly after take-off and was killed. It is reported that he had tried to do a slow roll, which seems incredible because not only was there no reason for this but Pemberton, like Halahan before him, had always been scathingly contemptuous of such demonstrations. Perhaps the strain on him had been even greater than supposed and he had had some kind of seizure or heart attack and simply lost control. In any case, it was a dreadful postscript to the Battle of Britain.

Flight Lieutenant 'Hilly' Brown was now deservedly promoted and took charge of the squadron he had first joined as a pilot officer in 1937. This sequence of promotions in the same unit is said to have been unique in the Royal Air Force, though Sergeant 'Taffy' Clowes had risen almost equally rapidly; he had been commissioned in September and was now a flight lieutenant, as was Peter Matthews. Brown, it may be recalled, was a Canadian and it was rather appropriate that he should become 1 Squadron's CO at this particular time since several pilots from outside the United Kingdom joined it in late 1940 and the first half of 1941.

In two cases, in fact, the pilots in question rejoined No. 1. Flying Officer Raymond Lewis, who, like Brown, was Canadian, had fought with it in France and had since been 'rested' as an instructor in an Operational Training Unit. Jean-François Demozay, No. 1's French liaison officer/interpreter, had also come from an OTU where he had been learning to fly modern fighters; he proved singularly proficient and would receive rapid promotion to flight lieutenant. Mention might also be made of Pilot Officer Raymond, a New Zealander who would also soon become a flight lieutenant, Pilot Officer Maranz from the United States and Flight Sergeant Blair from South Africa.

By far the largest contingent of recruits, however, came from central Europe. If 501 was famous for its Poles, 1 Squadron was famous for its Czechs. At different times twenty of them flew Hurricanes with No. 1, the name of Sergeant Karel Kuttelwascher being particularly worthy of notice. Finally there was Pilot Officer Romas Marcinkus, quiet, serious and rather formal, who had reached Britain by way of Poland, France and North Africa to become the only Lithuanian to fight with the RAF.

On 15 December 1940, 1 Squadron returned to Northolt and on New Year's Day 1941 began a new phase of its career when three Hurricanes flown by Clowes, Lewis and Pilot Officer 'Tony' Kershaw strafed enemy positions between Calais and Boulogne for some twenty minutes, unhindered by enemy fighters. On 4 January No. 1 moved to Kenley and it would later move to other bases in the London area from which it continued to fly offensive missions across the Channel. These took two forms. Raids by small numbers of Hurricanes, like that on 1 January, were mysteriously known as 'Rhubarbs', while 'Circuses' were larger operations in which British bombers, usually Blenheims, attacked German installations with a fighter escort.

The pilots of 1 Squadron did not greatly enjoy 'Circuses' but they took some satisfaction from 'Rhubarbs', particularly one on 7 April when they strafed some Bf 109s on the ground. According to Air Marshal Sir Peter Wykeham in his *Fighter Command*, Hurricanes were 'invaluable' in this role and No. 1's appreciation of its aircraft was increased by the arrival in late February of Mark IIAs. The

Squadron Diary confirms that: 'There were no adverse criticisms.' There were certainly none from Demozay or Kuttelwascher, both of whom used IIAs to shoot down Bf 109s at this time, and in April Hurricane IIBs with their armament of twelve machine guns also reached the squadron.

Sadly, though, the days when 1 Squadron achieved its successes with very few fatal casualties were gone for ever and during these early months of 1941, three Hurricanes were shot down. The Czech pilot Sergeant Prihoda escaped by parachute but Flying Officer Lewis and Pilot Officer Kershaw were not so fortunate. Both baled out but Kershaw's parachute did not open in time; Lewis was never seen again and presumably drowned. Also at this time Sergeant Stocken was killed in an accident in the squadron's Miles Magister trainer and communications aircraft.

At the end of April, 1 Squadron's three remaining pilots from the Battle of France days – Brown, Clowes and Matthews – were all posted, as was Demozay not long afterwards. All four of them would see later service on Hurricanes. 'Hilly' Brown was promoted to wing commander and went to Malta. On 12 November 1941, he led a section of 249's Hurricanes to strafe an airfield in Sicily but was killed by AA fire. The Italians buried him with full military honours. Clowes commanded 79 (Hurricane) Squadron and later became a wing commander. Matthews served with 73 Squadron and eventually rose to be group captain. Demozay went to 242 Squadron and he too became a wing commander but was killed in a flying accident in December 1945.

Command of No. 1 now passed to Squadron Leader Richard Brooker who had flown Hurricanes with 56 Squadron during the Battle of Britain. He was soon to lead No. 1 to its greatest success since the Battle of France. It had flown several night patrols, so far without result, but on the night of 10/11 May the Luftwaffe, encouraged by good weather and a full moon that promised unlimited visibility, decided to deliver what would be its last major raid on London.

Unfortunately for the raiders, the weather and the moon provided equally good opportunities for No. 1 and other night-fighter squadrons. It is believed that some thirty German aircraft were brought down. Of these, 1 Squadron was credited with the destruction of seven Heinkel He 111s and one Junkers Ju 88. The Czech Sergeant Dygryn in three separate sorties destroyed two of the Heinkels and the Ju 88. The squadron's satisfaction, however, was marred by the death of another Czech, Pilot Officer Behal, who may have been hit by 'friendly' AA fire.[3] Squadron Leader Brooker, who had himself downed a Heinkel, was awarded a Distinguished Flying Cross; he took pains to point out that this should be treated as an acknowledgement of the achievements of his whole squadron.

Then it was back to 'Rhubarbs' and 'Circuses'. During the remainder of May and throughout June, there were frequent encounters with enemy warplanes in the course of which No. 1, in addition to a number of 'damaged' claims, believed it had destroyed one luckless Heinkel He 59 seaplane, one Messerschmitt Bf 110 and a dozen Bf 109s, at least three of the latter being 109Fs, an improvement on the 109E that had been the Luftwaffe's main weapon in 1940. Once more, though, No. 1 did not escape unscathed. During this time four Hurricanes and three pilots were lost in combat and another Hurricane and pilot in a flying accident, and the squadron's most depressing period lay just ahead.

It would seem that No. 1's great night success had not been forgotten, for on 2 July it was transferred to Tangmere and shortly afterwards was re-equipped with Hurricane IICs armed with four 20mm cannons for the role of a night-fighter squadron. It would continue in this role through the winter of 1941/42 but had no further victories and lost four pilots as a result of flying accidents.

Squadron Leader Brooker, to his credit, succeeded in preserving his men's morale. Perhaps, though, he was not too displeased to be transferred in November 1941, despite being called on to undertake a still more harrowing task. In January 1942 he went to the Far East where the Allies were reeling under a Japanese onslaught for which they were quite unprepared. Brooker took command of 232 (Hurricane) Squadron and fought a valiant, if hopeless, delaying action until early March, first in defence of Singapore, then in Sumatra and finally in Java, personally downing three enemy aircraft and earning a Bar to his DFC. On his return to Britain, he was promoted and from January 1945 commanded 122 (Tempest) Wing during the fighting leading up to and including the crossing of the Rhine. He was killed in action on 16 April 1945.

Brooker was replaced as 1 Squadron's chief by a still more remarkable character. James MacLachlan had flown Battle bombers in France and Hurricanes in the Battle of Britain before he won fame as a flight commander with 261 (Hurricane) Squadron in Malta. He arrived there on 17 November 1940 after a nightmare flight from HM Carrier *Argus*. The twelve Hurricanes coming as reinforcements had been sent off too far away from Malta as a result of a perceived threat from the Italian Fleet and only four, including MacLachlan's, reached their destination before their fuel ran out.

Once in Malta, however, MacLachlan quickly proved his worth. Among his exploits were a couple of sorties on the night of 8/9 February 1941 when he shot down one Junkers Ju 88 and so damaged another that it returned to base only to be 'written off'. He therefore might seem very suitable to command No. 1's night operations. In fact, it was surprising that he could lead a squadron at all. On 16 February 1941 he had been shot down by 109s and, as he nonchalantly announced in his Combat Report, had had his 'left arm written off by cannon shell'. It had to be amputated at the elbow.

That would normally have been the end of MacLachlan's career as a fighter pilot, but he had other ideas. Incredibly, in just over a fortnight he had slipped out of hospital and flown a Magister (one-handed). On returning to England, he visited Queen Mary's Hospital, Roehampton, specialists in fitting artificial limbs. Here he 'explained the layout of a Hurricane' and in due course received a new arm ending in a three-pronged adjustable claw with which he could control the engine-throttle. He then set out to persuade his superiors to allow his return to operations. Impressed by his resolution, and perhaps recalling the example of Douglas Bader, they complied with his request.

It had been intended that MacLachlan should lead No. 1 on those night-intruder missions once favoured by 'Widge' Gleed, but before he could do so his squadron was called on for a very different and dangerous mission. During the night of 11/12 February 1942, the German battle-cruisers *Scharnhorst* and *Gneisenau* and heavy cruiser

Prinz Eugen made a dash from Brest to Germany through the English Channel. They caught the defences so completely by surprise that they passed right through the Straits of Dover without interference. Later both the battle-cruisers were damaged by mines but sadly, no real harm was done by a series of belated but very courageous attacks by the Royal Navy, the Royal Air Force and the Fleet Air Arm.

One of these attacks was made by six Hurricane IICs from 1 Squadron. They were directed against the destroyers escorting the major German warships and were divided into three sections, each of which engaged a different vessel. The pilots involved were Flight Lieutenant Raymond and Pilot Officer Sweeting who together formed Red Section; Kuttelwascher, now commissioned as a pilot officer and Pilot Officer Halbeard (Yellow Section); and Pilot Officer Marcinkus and Flight Sergeant Blair (White Section); a typical No. 1 combination of nationalities: two British, one New Zealander, one South African, one Czech and one Lithuanian.

All six Hurricanes shelled enemy destroyers with their 20mm cannons and though they could not hope to inflict more than token damage, they did kill a few wretched German seamen. The squadron's period of ill luck was not yet over, however. Only four Hurricanes got back to Tangmere and Pilot Officer Sweeting, who had defied the guns of the German navy, was killed four days later when No. 1's Magister inexplicably crashed. Of the pilots who did not return, Blair had died instantly when his aircraft was hit by the big guns of his target, while the fate of Marcinkus, though delayed, was perhaps the saddest of all.

The Royal Air Force's only Lithuanian pilot had been compelled to 'ditch' close to the enemy-occupied coast, was taken prisoner and was sent to Stalag Luft III. Here he took part in the 'Great Escape', partnering Flight Lieutenant Gilbert 'Tim' Walenn, the head of the 'forgers department' that prepared false identity documents for the escapers. Walenn was pretending to be another Lithuanian, rather to the amusement of Marcinkus who pointed out that he could not speak a word of the language; Walenn agreed but doubted if any German interrogator would be able to either. Their intention was to make for Danzig where they could board a ship for neutral Sweden and considering that Marcinkus knew the area well and could speak fluent German, their chances were considered high and they were awarded early places in the tunnel: ten and eleven.

On their way to Danzig, Marcinkus and Walenn teamed up with two other officers who had been Walenn's room-mates. This was natural but perhaps unwise, for in the uproar that followed news of the mass break-out a group of four healthy young men was likely to arouse suspicions and Walenn was not an ideal travelling companion, being noticeably good-looking and sporting a huge bushy 'RAF-type' moustache. The four were recaptured near Danzig and murdered by the Gestapo. Marcinkus was 33 years old.

Meanwhile 1 Squadron had embarked on its night-intruder operations, the first of them on 1 April 1942. In contrast to the teamwork that had been such a feature of No. 1's activities in earlier days, these missions were very much individual affairs as single Hurricane IICs, carrying two 45-gallon drop-tanks to provide extra fuel, prowled over enemy-occupied territory looking for targets of opportunity. On 1 April only two experienced pilots went out. Squadron Leader MacLachlan returned without having sighted an enemy but Kuttelwascher, who was now a flight lieutenant, began what was to be an extraordinary sequence of successes at night by shooting down one Junkers Ju 88 and damaging another.

For the next three months, members of 1 Squadron set out to look for trouble every night when the weather was suitable and the moon was bright. On 26 June Pilot Officer Perrin, finding no targets over Holland, flew as far east as Düsseldorf in search of prey, although sadly his determination went unrewarded.

As well as seeking out enemy warplanes, No. 1 also indulged in 'train-busting', destroying at least seventeen locomotives, Flight Sergeant Bland alone wrecking five of them on 1 May.

Normally, however, No. 1's main quarry was German bombers that it caught over their own aerodromes either setting out on or, more usually, returning from raids of their own. So proficient in this role was No. 1 – and other night-intruder Hurricane squadrons to a lesser extent – that the Germans diverted a proportion of their own night-fighter strength to deal with them rather than with the heavy attacks the RAF was now mounting. On 30 May the first 'thousand bomber raid' was made on Cologne and although 1 Squadron encountered – and damaged – only a single enemy aircraft, its diversionary effects seem to have been considerable, judging by congratulatory signals received from the Secretary of State for Air, Sir Archibald Sinclair, and Bomber Command's formidable Air Marshal Harris.

It might be added that the Luftwaffe's attempts to interfere with No. 1's activities proved singularly unsuccessful. The only occasion on which one of the Hurricanes was attacked by a German night-fighter came on the night of 26/27 April. Kuttelwascher had just shot down a Dornier Do 217, an improvement on the old Do 17, when he came under fire from a Junkers Ju 88. He outmanoeuvred this and damaged it, though he did not see it crash. By contrast, in the early hours of 1 June Sergeant Pearson sighted a Junkers Ju 88 night-fighter about to land at its base and promptly shot it down.

Pearson was one of only four No. 1 pilots who destroyed enemy aircraft on a night-intruder raid. Another was Flight Sergeant English who, by the way, was not of English nationality but a Canadian. On the night after Pearson's success, English downed a Dornier Do 217, only to lose his own life in a flying accident on 3 June. It must also be recorded that during this period three other Hurricanes and one other pilot were lost as the result of accidents and it seems probable that two more pilots who did not return from night-intruder sorties also met with accidents since the enemy never made any claim for their destruction. Saddest of all, on 4 June Joseph Dygryn, now a warrant officer, also died. He had temporarily left No. 1 for a Czech Hurricane squadron, No. 310, in September 1941, but had returned in May and was on his first night-intruder mission when he was shot down by AA fire over Le Havre.

Despite this high casualty list, 1 Squadron undoubtedly had the better of its night-intruder actions. As well as its attacks on trains and other targets on the ground, it destroyed twenty-two German aircraft at night and damaged thirteen others.

Squadron Leader MacLachlan shot down five enemy warplanes, including two – a Dornier Do 217 and a Heinkel He 111 – in one night on 3/4 May. The outstanding achievement of any No. 1 pilot or indeed of any Hurricane pilot at night was that of Flight

Lieutenant Karel Kuttelwascher who made fifteen of the squadron's 'kills'. His most remarkable success came on the night of 4/5 May. Sighting six Heinkel He 111s orbiting their airfield at St André, he joined the circle and in four minutes sent three of them down in flames. Then the lights on the airfield went out, AA guns began firing wildly and Kuttelwascher wisely retired from the scene.

On the night of 1/2 July, 1 Squadron flew its last night-intruder sorties. It ended these missions as it had begun them, successfully, two Dornier Do 217s being destroyed, both by the amazing Kuttelwascher, and three more damaged. The squadron then 'stood down' from operations and shortly afterwards retired to Acklington in Northumberland where it gave up its Hurricanes for Typhoons and both its night-intruder 'aces' left it.

MacLachlan would later fly Mustangs on low-level sorties over France but on 18 July 1943 he was hit, apparently by small-arms fire, and, as he was too low to bale out, he tried to crash-land. Sadly, the Mustang smashed into a wood and MacLachlan received injuries from which he died some days later. Kuttelwascher went on to fly Mosquitoes at night but despite their having Airborne Interception radar, he never as much as sighted another German aircraft. Clearly he had been born to be a Hurricane pilot.

The end of the Second World War did not end 1 Squadron's association with Hawkers. Before the war it had flown Hawker Furies. During the war it flew Hawker Hurricanes and Typhoons. After the war it would fly Hawker Hunters from 1955 to 1969 and then they would be replaced by a very different Hawker fighter. This was the Hawker P.1127 vertical take-off and landing 'jump jet' that completed its trials during 1960 and 1961 for which, incidentally, Hawkers' own Hurricane PZ865 acted as 'chase plane'. Designed by Ralph Hooper, then a project engineer, under the general supervision and with the steadfast support of Sir Sydney Camm, the P.1127, after improvements and developments, became the Hawker Siddeley Kestrel and this in turn the famous Hawker Siddeley Harrier that No. 1 was the first squadron to receive in the summer of 1969.

Just as after their beautiful Furies, No. 1's pilots had at first been none too pleased with their Hurricanes, so after their elegant

Hunters, their Harriers, according to Michael Shaw in *Twice Vertical*, 'seemed at first sight to be almost deformed.' Once more, though, the squadron's airmen were to win fame with an aircraft that they had initially not appreciated.

This would come in the Falklands War in the summer of 1982, when six Harriers of 1 Squadron under Wing Commander Squire, later reinforced by four more, all hastily adapted for shipboard use, served on HM Carrier *Hermes* and later on landing-strips in the vicinity of San Carlos in the Falklands. Though not employed as interceptor fighters, a task performed – brilliantly – by the Royal Navy's own Sea Harriers, they carried out reconnaissance flights and close support duties, making attacks with bombs and rockets on troop positions, gun batteries, fuel dumps and enemy aircraft on the ground. Although three Harriers were brought down by AA fire and one was 'written off' in a take-off accident, no aircraft was lost to enemy warplanes and no pilot lost his life. History had indeed repeated itself. Whether flying Hurricanes in France in 1940 or Harriers in the Falklands in 1982, the pilots of 1 Squadron had lived up to their proud motto: 'First in All Things.'

Notes

1. The reason for this title was that when No. 1 was formed on 13 April 1912, it was equipped with airships and did not receive aeroplanes until May 1914. On 4 August 1969, at which time Michael Shaw was one of its members with the rank of flight lieutenant, No. 1 became the first RAF squadron to be equipped with the Hawker Siddeley Harrier vertical take-off fighter.

2. It is only right, however, to relate that much of Richey's criticism was directed towards the tactics being adopted against the Japanese fighters. In his *Air War for Burma*, Christopher Shores sets out a long report by Richey to the effect that the Hurricane was faster and stronger and had greater fire-power than its opponents, but that they were more manoeuvrable so had the advantage in a dogfight. He also quotes Japanese pilots whose views were the same and who admit that the Hurricane, if properly handled, could inflict 'deadly damage'.

3. The very great sacrifices made by those pilots from the German-occupied countries who chose to fly and fight with the Royal Air Force should never be forgotten. Of the twenty Czechs who joined 1 Squadron, for example, seven were killed serving with the squadron – Behal was the first; ironically Dygryn would be the last – and four more died in later operations with other RAF units.

Chapter 6

The Fighting Cocks
43 Squadron

When No. 1 Squadron left for France on 8 September 1939, it was sent on its way by a radio message from its base at Tangmere, wishing it 'Good-bye and good luck from 43 Squadron.' The good wishes were sincere, for 1 and 43 were firm friends. They had also, however, been keen rivals, especially in aerobatic displays when both had flown Hawker Furies, and 43's pilots were undoubtedly rather envious. They would much have preferred to accompany No. 1 to France where they anticipated there would be more chance of seeing action.

The badge of 43 Squadron was a gamecock, derived from the fact that it flew Gloster Gamecocks after the First World War. This had resulted in its pilots receiving the semi-official nickname of 'the Fighting Cocks', except in No. 1 Squadron where they were rudely referred to as 'the Chicken Farmers'. They had received their Furies in May 1931 – the first RAF squadron to do so – but in late November 1938 the first Hurricanes arrived; the last Furies left in early February 1939. The squadron at once started training with its new machines both by day and by night and it is with tragic inevitability that we learn of the death of Flying Officer Rotherham in an aerial accident on 22 April 1939.

Ironically, despite not going to France, 43 was the first Hurricane squadron to fire its guns in anger, although only at an escaped barrage balloon. This took place on 8 September and Flying Officer

Kilmartin, who as we saw would soon join No. 1 in France, required 1,200 rounds to destroy it. Over the next fortnight, 43 shot down half-a-dozen other balloons, including three in one day on 17 September. Then in late October, Squadron Leader George Lott succeeded Squadron Leader Bain as 43's CO and in mid-November led his men to Acklington in Northumberland. Here on 18 January 1940, they suffered their first wartime losses when Sergeants Steeley and Mullinger collided in the course of a mock dogfight, both being killed.

After that, 43's fortunes began to improve. On 30 January Flight Lieutenant Hull and Sergeant Carey, while on a convoy protection patrol, intercepted a Heinkel He 111 and shot it into the sea. They were subsequently awarded a Distinguished Flying Cross and a Distinguished Flying Medal respectively.

This was 43's first victory of the Second World War and it could not have been gained by a more suitable pair of pilots. Both Hull and Carey were small men, both had joined 43 in 1938 and both had been members of 43's Fury aerobatics team. In background and temperament, however, they were very different. Frank Carey – his name really was 'Frank', not 'Francis' – was a Londoner who had begun his RAF career as an aircraft apprentice, qualifying first as a rigger and later as a fitter – the former with 43 Squadron – before applying for training as a pilot. His first posting after qualifying was to 43, where he quickly showed great ability but he was a quiet and retiring man and although he would become one of the greatest of all Hurricane pilots, he never lost his genuine modesty.

By contrast, Caesar Hull, a Rhodesian-born South African, was a complete extrovert of unfailing good humour and inexhaustible energy, both of which proved infectious. Hull's fellow flight commander was Peter Townsend who, as mentioned earlier, was basically shy and reluctant to attract attention to himself but Hull persuaded Townsend to be his (Hull's) regular partner in performances of a Latin-American 'dance' that surged all over the room and is said to have resembled 'a sort of combination wrestling match and steeplechase.'[1] Hull was a brilliant pilot whose eagerness to get at the enemy was undisguised, but whose excitement at his victories was tempered by shock at the realization that he had killed fellow airmen. Not that his friends remembered his skill as well as they did his strangely hoarse chuckle and the gleam of his big white teeth when he smiled. When the news of his death was received, many wept unashamedly.

On 3 February 43 Squadron recorded another 'first' when a section led by Townsend engaged a Heinkel He 111. Fatally struck, the bomber turned inland to find somewhere to put down. Townsend called off the attack and watched as the Heinkel crash-landed in farmland near Whitby. It was the first enemy raider to come down in England (as distinct from in Scotland or in the sea). It was also the first opportunity 43 had had of checking the effectiveness of the Hurricane's fire-power. This proved horribly obvious. The Heinkel left a trail of blood behind it as it came in low. Of its crew, two were killed and a third so badly wounded that he had to have a leg amputated. Only the pilot was unhurt. The war in the air was still gentlemanly at this time and 43 sent a wreath to the dead crewmen's funeral, while Townsend visited the injured gunner in hospital to give him some oranges – then a rare treat – and a packet of cigarettes.

Also on 3 February, a second Heinkel was shot down by Carey and Sergeant Peter Ottewill – this one went into the sea – while two more were damaged. On the 9th, 43 Squadron had a further clash with a Heinkel, during which it seems that Flying Officer Carswell's Hurricane was hit in the engine, forcing him to 'ditch'. He was quickly rescued by a nearby vessel but the North Sea in winter is a very hostile environment and it would be some three months before he rejoined his squadron. The Heinkel responsible was hit by Sergeant James Hallowes, destined to be another leading Fighting Cock and although he received no credit for his victory, Intelligence later revealed that his target failed to return to base. There was no argument about 43's next success. On 22 February Peter Townsend attacked a Heinkel that went into a steep dive; both its wings were torn off on the way down and the fuselage plunged vertically into the sea.

On the previous day, or more precisely night, there had been an incident that was not in combat but definitely deserves mention. The Fighting Cocks seem to have been determined to emphasize the ruggedness of the Hurricane and one of them certainly did so on this occasion. Flying Officer John Simpson suffered engine failure when taking off on a night patrol. His Hurricane crashed through a haystack and a telephone pole into a wood of larch trees, of which it demolished thirty-six. Simpson broke his nose and one cheekbone but was able to walk away from the crash.

Peter Townsend's victory was the last one gained by 43 Squadron while at Acklington, since four days later it moved to Wick in the far north-east of Scotland. Here, in company with the Hurricanes of 111 and 605 Squadrons, it defended the Royal Navy base at Scapa Flow and here it remained until 31 May when it returned to Tangmere. This meant that its pilots, much to their regret, missed the savage fighting that immediately followed the German blitzkrieg but they did not avoid all action for during their time at Wick they destroyed eight more enemy bombers, two of them being 'shared' with Hurricanes from 605.

The squadron had its best day on 8 April. As dusk was falling, its pilots intercepted a raid by Heinkel He 111s and brought down four of them. One of these was attacked by Sergeant Hallowes, was badly damaged and had two crewmen killed. The pilot decided to 'ditch', mistook the flare-path at Wick that had been lit up to guide home the Hurricanes for lights at a seaplane base and crash-landed on 43's own airfield. The two remaining German airmen threw out a dinghy, removed their flying boots so as to be able to swim more easily and dived out onto dry land! There is even a story that they then got into their dinghy and began rowing but this should be considered apocryphal.

What is not in doubt is that the captured airmen insisted that they had been shot down by a Spitfire, of which there were none within miles. Townsend, in his *Duel of Eagles*, calls this 'Spitfire Snobbery' and Douglas Bader, who ranked the Hurricane as his favourite fighter, echoes this 'splendid phrase' in his *Fight for the Sky*. The Luftwaffe fighter pilots had more respect for the Spitfire because of its greater speed but their attitude becomes surprising considering the successes enjoyed by Hurricanes against Messerschmitt Bf 109s, examples of which have already been described, and ridiculous when it becomes clear that they frequently failed to distinguish between

Hurricanes and Spitfires, as did the crew of the Heinkel at Wick, for instance. It may be added that Dennis 'Hurricane' David reports in his autobiography that in fact many German bomber crews told him that 'the Hurricane was the aircraft they dreaded.' This is not surprising because the steadiness of the Hurricane as a gun platform and the strength that enabled it to endure return fire made it an ideal butcher of bombers.

Oddly enough, though, this prejudice against the Hawker fighter still exists. It is not often found outside Britain.[2] It is not found in aviation histories, as witness the very title of Leo McKinstry's *Hurricane: Victor of the Battle of Britain*. It is not even found among Spitfire test pilots, one of the most important of whom, Jeffrey Quill, is quoted in Edward Bishop's *Hurricane*, saying that 'it took both of these great aeroplanes to win' the Battle of Britain and that in 1940, even the Spitfire's superiority of performance was only 'marginal'.

Yet much of the British public still seems to cherish its 'Spitfire Snobbery'. If reference is made to the summer of 1940, it is of course the 'Spitfire summer'. If a historical novelist or a mystery writer chooses the Battle of Britain for a background, his or her characters are of course Spitfire pilots. It would seem that whatever Shakespeare's Juliet may have said, there is a very great deal in a wonderfully evocative name.

Not that the pilots of 43 Squadron were worried about such matters when they returned to Tangmere on 31 May 1940. Their confidence in their Hurricanes was complete and they looked forward to a chance of some 'real' action. Their strength, however, had been much reduced. They had suffered only one fatal casualty while at Wick when on 16 April, Flying Officer Folkes crashed into the sea on a convoy patrol in driving rain and poor visibility, leaving only a patch of oil, some debris and, strangely, a map to mark the spot. Other pilots, though, had been posted away: Caesar Hull had gone to 263 (Gladiator) Squadron to see action against the Luftwaffe in Norway; Frank Carey had been commissioned and joined No. 3 (Hurricane) Squadron to see action in France; and Peter Townsend had been promoted to squadron leader and, as we have seen, taken command of 85 (Hurricane) Squadron in England.

It was hardly to be expected that the loss of men of the calibre of Hull, Carey and Townsend would not be felt and while the remaining Fighting Cocks had by now gained considerable experience, they must have been shaken by the very large number of enemy aircraft that they would encounter when Squadron Leader Lott led them over the beaches of Dunkirk on 1 June. The CO was particularly anxious to do well, for as Richard Collier relates in *The Sands of Dunkirk*, he had just learned that he had been awarded a DFC and his 'resolution was both modest and urgent: he must do something to earn it.' He would have his chance when 43 engaged a swarm of Messerschmitt Bf 109s and Bf 110s. After evading a number of attacks, he was able to hit a 110 that dived into clouds, pouring out black smoke. Lott did not see it crash, so claimed only a 'Damaged' and he found that 'his hands were shaking on the stick, his flying overalls drenched in sweat' but his DFC 'seemed less embarrassing now.'

Faced with odds of about seven to one, 43 lost two of its Hurricanes. Sergeant Gough was killed but Flying Officer Carswell, on his first operational sortie after his return to his squadron, escaped by parachute and was able to get home aboard a British destroyer. In return it seems that 43 may have downed as many as seven 109s and two 110s and damaged others. Sergeant Hallowes was 43's most successful pilot, having shot down two 109s in flames and a 110 with its tail blasted off, while Sergeant Ottewill had also destroyed a pair of 109s.

The conclusion of the Dunkirk evacuation did not end the squadron's missions over France and on one such on 7 June, it would suffer severely. It was intended to refuel and rearm at Boos airfield but on the way there it was ambushed by 109s that shot down four Hurricanes in short order, two of the pilots being killed. Flight Lieutenant Rowland, on his first operational sortie with 43, was able to crash-land and subsequently make his way home, but a wound in the foot from a cannon-shell put him into hospital. The fourth Hurricane hit was that of the redoubtable Sergeant Hallowes. As his cockpit filled with smoke, he prepared to bale out, only to see a 109 overshoot him. Dropping back into his seat, Hallowes shot this down and then did take to his parachute. He also eventually returned to

England where his action was rewarded with a Distinguished Flying Medal.

Having duly refuelled and rearmed at Boos, Lott took his men into the air again, intending to act as an escort for some Blenheims, but the squadron again encountered a mass of enemy fighters. John Simpson, now a flight lieutenant, shot down a Bf 109 and then hit another that spun down and crashed into a Bf 110, both aircraft falling in 'a sort of embrace of flames'. Simpson, somewhat unfeelingly, described this as 'a wonderful sight'. Sergeant Ottewill, who had downed a 109 in 43's earlier clash, downed another one this time but then had to bale out of a Hurricane that was in flames and two other Hurricanes were also lost. All the pilots managed to make their way home but Ottewill, who had been badly burned, never returned to operational flying although he remained in the RAF, eventually becoming a group captain.

These losses did not leave 43 particularly well-prepared for the Battle of Britain and the situation was not improved by two flying accidents later in June, Sergeant Pratt being killed and Pilot Officer James ending up in hospital. The Fighting Cocks were, however, greatly cheered by the arrival of Frank Carey, whose prowess in France had been rewarded with a DFC and Bar and from which he returned in an old Bombay, having been shot down by the rear gunner of a Dornier Do 17 and reported 'missing'. He would be appointed one of 43's flight commanders and added immeasurably to its strength in the coming conflict.

That conflict would come sooner for 43 than for most Fighter Command squadrons. Officially the Battle of Britain began on 10 July but, as Squadron Leader Lott would remark sardonically, 'nobody had told the Germans' and 43's first encounter came on the 7th when three of its Hurricanes attacked a Dornier Do 17, so damaging it that it got back over the Channel only to crash in France and be 'written off'. Its return fire presumably hit the engine of Pilot Officer Cruttenden's Hurricane, for as he returned to base, it caught fire and he was forced to bale out, which he did safely. It seems, though, that he had been understandably shaken by his experience as two days later he crashed on landing, though he once more emerged unscathed.

Also on 9 July, 43 had a more sizeable clash when Lott led Frank Carey and Sergeant Jack Mills – 'Jack' was his real name – against six Junkers Ju 87s escorted by six Messerschmitt Bf 110s. On their approach, the Stukas hastily retired. The 110s stayed to fight it out but Lott's men shot down two of them and badly damaged a third that returned to base without its gunner who had baled out, presumably believing his aircraft was doomed. Unfortunately, Lott's own Hurricane was also severely damaged and he was hit in the face by splinters from its shattered windscreen. Lott had pushed up his goggles on first sighting the enemy aircraft in order to identify them better, and as a result he was blinded in his right eye. Despite his injuries, he was able to fly his battered machine to within 3 miles of his base before having to bale out. This he did safely but his career as 43's CO was over.[3]

Lott was replaced by Squadron Leader John 'Tubby' Badger who had served with 43 prior to the war and was to lead it during the first two months of the 'official' Battle of Britain. The remainder of July was not a particularly happy time for the Fighting Cocks for they lost three pilots in action – two of these baled out but were drowned – a fourth died in an accident and John Simpson went to hospital, having baled out with a bullet wound in the leg, hit the roof of a house and a garden fence and finally landed in a cucumber frame, breaking his collar bone. In return, the Fighting Cocks destroyed a Heinkel He 111, a Junkers Ju 88 and a Messerschmitt Bf 109, but the Luftwaffe could afford these losses and its leaders could be well satisfied with its early attempts to whittle down the strength of Fighter Command.

By early August, Göring was ready to begin his destruction of Fighter Command. He would start with Eagle Day on the 13th. He also made heavy preliminary raids on the 11th and 12th and as a kind of dress-rehearsal on the 8th, he sent a series of exceptionally large formations against convoys in the Channel. This day would prove the last for many weeks on which it is possible to disentangle the efforts of individual squadrons, so it provides a good opportunity to assess the value of the Hawker Hurricane.

As usual, it was Hurricanes that bore the brunt of the fighting on 8 August and, as usual, it was Hurricanes that suffered the heaviest losses: eleven in all, together with nine of their pilots, compared with three Spitfires and all their pilots and one Blenheim. The Luftwaffe lost twenty-seven warplanes destroyed or damaged beyond repair. Spitfires accounted for four of these, the fate of a reconnaissance Heinkel He 111 is unknown, and Hurricanes were responsible for all the rest: ten Messerschmitt Bf 109s, nine Junkers Ju 87s, two Messerschmitt Bf 110s and one Heinkel He 59 seaplane. It was a major achievement. The Fighting Cocks naturally played their part in that achievement, although at a cost. Confronted by an enormous formation of Junkers Ju 87s, escorted by 110s and 109s, the squadron damaged three of the Stukas but was then engaged by the 109s, which shot down three Hurricanes. Two of the pilots were killed but Pilot Officer Upton baled out. Flight Lieutenant 'Tom' Dalton-Morgan downed one enemy fighter, while Sergeant Hallowes destroyed a second one and damaged a third so badly that it returned home only to be 'written off'. Moreover, while 43 kept the 109s occupied, the Hurricanes of 145 Squadron had a clear path to the Ju 87s, destroying at least five of these.

Further minor clashes occurred over the next few days. On 12 August Frank Carey attacked a Junkers Ju 88. He claimed only a 'Probable' but German records confirm that it failed to return to its base. On Eagle Day, 43 was again faced with heavy odds, losing two Hurricanes but both their pilots escaping by parachute. Sergeant Mills gained some revenge by downing a 109 and it appears that 43 may have had at least a share in the destruction of a Ju 88 and damage to two more. On the 14th 43 shot down two Heinkel He 111s but lost Sergeant Montgomery, and it enjoyed a surprisingly quiet day on the 15th, its only action coming when it sighted and brought down a solitary Ju 88. Its pilots were not to know that its two greatest days of the battle were not far away.

Although 15 August had resulted in the Luftwaffe's highest losses in the whole battle, its chiefs consoled themselves with the hope that it would have placed such a strain on the defenders that they would be unable to cope with another day of similar pressure. The 16th therefore saw further massive raids, one of which by twelve Junkers Ju 87s of Stukageschwader 2 was directed against 43's base, Tangmere. At the last moment a Spitfire squadron intervened and shot down one dive-bomber before it was driven off by the escorting 109s. Another dive-bomber fell to anti-aircraft fire but the remaining ten devastated the airfield and destroyed or damaged seven Hurricanes – four of them from 43 – two Spitfires, seven Blenheims and one Beaufighter on the ground.

However, they had little time in which to relish their success before 43's avenging Hurricanes, which luckily had been away from Tangmere on patrol, made one of those lethal head-on charges for which the Hawker fighter had become famous. The escorting 109s, grappling with the Spitfires, could intercept only one unlucky pilot, Sergeant Crisp; he baled out but sustained a broken leg that put him off 43's strength. The Stukas fought desperately and to their great credit damaged two Hurricanes that had to crash-land, one being 'written off' but neither pilot being hurt. It seems that every Hurricane pilot present hit a Stuka. There were numerous duplicated claims but 43 really did down seven dive-bombers and badly damaged the other three. The remaining Hurricanes then landed between bomb-craters and their pilots completed the discomfiture of the surviving enemy airmen by making them help to repair the damage they had caused.

Ironically, it was the Luftwaffe that was now exhausted, so much so that despite fine weather on the 17th, only a few reconnaissance machines crossed the Channel. One of these, a Dornier Do 17, was sighted at low level by Sergeant Hallowes who dived down on it from 30,000ft. As Andy Saunders reports in his *No. 43 'Fighting Cocks' Squadron*:

> At 12,000ft. a terrific vibration set up in the Hurricane and Hallowes noted that the ASI (air speed indicator) was off the clock at over 400 mph. Fabric was tearing from the ailerons and control surfaces, and fighting with the controls, Hallowes managed to pull out at 5,000ft.

He returned safely to Tangmere where representatives from Hawkers 'inspected the damaged airframe and concluded that a speed of 620 mph had been reached.' Undaunted by this experience, Hallowes was back in action next day, 18 August, as indeed was 43

Squadron as a whole, and to some purpose. The Hardest Day again saw the squadron in action against Junkers Ju 87s, this time from StG 77, that were attacking the radar station at Poling. The Hurricanes dived after the diving Stukas and thereby escaped the attention of the escorting 109s which remained at a high altitude and did not intervene. There were again a number of duplicated claims but five dive-bombers were destroyed or damaged beyond repair, plus two others with lesser damage. Hallowes was at least partially responsible for the loss of three of them.

Only one of 43's Hurricanes suffered damage in this action. Frank Carey was hit by return fire and wounded in the knee but his aircraft provided another extraordinary example of the Hurricane's ability to accept punishment. Its extensive injuries included having the rudder and one elevator shot off, leaving Carey, as he later remarked, with 'only about three-quarters of an aircraft to control'. Nonetheless, he was able to return to base, where he came under fortunately inaccurate fire from AA gunners who had not recognized the Hurricane's 'odd' silhouette. Carey, who eventually crash-landed, suffered no injury but his wounded knee required hospital treatment that put him off 43's strength for a time.

The successes gained by 43 on both 16 and 18 August would help to bring about immense consequences. The losses of Stukas and their obvious vulnerability could be accepted no longer, and the main result of the Hardest Day was that almost a quarter of the Luftwaffe's bomber strength was withdrawn from the front line and took no further part in the battle.

There would be several far harder days for 43 Squadron, as there would for all the defenders in the next phase of the battle. The Germans' new strategy of targeting the sector stations and new tactics of packing large numbers of fighters closely around their bombers soon began to take its toll. During the rest of August, 43 downed four or five Heinkel He 111s and a Messerschmitt Bf 109 but it lost six Hurricanes. Three of the airmen were unhurt but Pilot Officer North went to hospital on the 26th with wounds in arm, shoulder and face; Sergeant Noble was killed on the 30th; and on that same day 43 lost its leader in horrific circumstances. Squadron Leader Badger was wounded but baled out safely, only to land in some tall trees. A branch broke off and impaled him, inflicting ghastly injuries to which he succumbed ten long months later.

As Badger's successor, the Fighting Cocks welcomed back an old friend. Caesar Hull had had a remarkable career with 263's Gladiators in Norway, culminating in the destruction of four enemy aircraft, all confirmed in the German records, on 26 May. On the 27th, however, he was shot down himself and wounded in head and knee. He was brought back to Britain in a Sunderland flying-boat, recovered from his injuries, was promoted to squadron leader and now on 1 September, he returned to lead 43. He was soon back in action, for on the 2nd his squadron was engaged in a frantic clash with Bf 109s. It appears that four of these were shot down but three Hurricanes also fell. Flying Officer Carswell and the Belgian Pilot Officer Du Vivier both baled out but both were wounded: Carswell's operational career was over and Du Vivier, on recovery, would be posted to 229 (Hurricane) Squadron and would only rejoin 43 after the battle.

Sadly, on 2 September, the Fighting Cocks lost a fine pilot whose spirit epitomizes that of Britain's defenders. Pilot Officer Anthony Woods-Scawen had fought with 43 Squadron from the earliest days of the war. In the fighting over France or in the Battle of Britain he had had to bale out a total of four times and each time the same parachute had saved his life. By now his eyesight, always poor, was deteriorating badly but when apologizing to his flight sergeant for bringing back a badly shot-up Hurricane, he pleaded: 'Don't breathe a word or they might whip me off Ops.' On 2 September he baled out once again but this time too low and there was no time for his lucky parachute to open. Less than twenty-four hours earlier his elder brother Patrick had died fighting with 85 Squadron when his parachute had also failed to open.

One of the enemy fighters shot down on 2 September had fallen to a pilot who had had a particularly close relationship with the Hurricane. Flight Lieutenant 'Dick' Reynell was an Australian who had been a member of 43 prior to the war but had become a test pilot at Hawkers in September 1938. It was perhaps not a good omen that he was called to take up the task of testing production Hurricanes before their delivery to the RAF. This had previously been carried out by test pilot John Hindmarsh, but he had been killed in a

Hurricane that crashed on 6 September for no reason that anyone could discover.

Reynell, however, performed this duty without mishap. In addition, from July 1939 to May 1940, he made several first trial flights: in L1669, a Hurricane fitted with a Volkes Multi-Vee tropical filter over the carburettor air intake, intended to protect the Merlin engine on Hurricanes destined for the Middle East from harmful dust or sand particles; in P3462, a Hurricane equipped with additional fuel tanks; and in P2640, a Hurricane adapted to carry four 20mm cannons, thus paving the way for the Hurricane IIC. Yet perhaps his finest moment had been the breathtaking display of aerobatics that he gave in the old prototype K5083 at the Brussels Exhibition in July 1939. This was so thrilling that when the last Hurricane PZ865 appeared at its farewell ceremony, as previously described, it carried an 'honours board' recalling the Hurricane's exploits and this included not only Dunkirk, Narvik, the Battle of France, the Battle of Britain, Russia, Malta, Iran, Africa, Burma, Sicily, Italy and Normandy, but also the Brussels Exhibition of 1939.

In late August 1940, Reynell volunteered to rejoin 43 so as to be able to advise Hawkers on the Hurricane's performance in combat. He arrived at Tangmere on the evening of the 26th and, as we have seen, would personally demonstrate the Hurricane's ability to shoot down 109s on 2 September. He would also be able to give encouraging reports of 43's encounters on 4, 5 and 6 September. In none of these did it suffer any losses and on the 4th, it had its most successful day for some time, shooting down four Messerschmitt Bf 110s and so damaging a fifth that it got back across the Channel and promptly crashed. On the 5th a 109 was destroyed by a 43 sergeant pilot with the appropriate name of 'Alex' Hurry, while on the 6th two more 109s fell to the guns of the Fighting Cocks.

On 7 September Göring turned on London and Fighter Command's fortunes changed for the better. Regrettably, those of 43 Squadron changed for the worse. Late that afternoon, it engaged a massive formation of Heinkel He 111s and Messerschmitt Bf 109s. Hull ordered a section of three Hurricanes to 'do what you can to upset the fighters' but they were swamped by sheer weight of numbers and Sergeant Deller was forced to bale out, which he did safely. The rest of the squadron obeyed Hull's order to 'sail in and smash' the bombers. The German unit involved, KG1, did lose two Heinkels but whether these fell to 43 it is not possible to discover. Then the 109s descended on the Hurricanes. Reynell was cut off from the rest of the squadron, his Hurricane was set on fire, he baled out and his parachute did not open. Hull had tried to divert the 109s from Reynell, although it seems that he had already used up all his ammunition. He was shot down and killed as well.

It was more than even the Fighting Cocks could bear and the authorities realized this. Next day the squadron was withdrawn, first to Usworth in northern England, then at the end of the year to Drem in Scotland. 'Tom' Dalton-Morgan was promoted to squadron leader and some of 43's 'old hands' returned from other units or from hospital to assist him, temporarily at least, in carrying out day and night patrols and preparing new pilots for operations. Sadly, many were clearly not ready for this: three of them died in accidents, two others were injured and a number of 43's aircraft were 'written off'.

During this period, several of 43's best pilots left for service elsewhere. John Simpson attacked a Junkers Ju 88 on 30 November; it got back across the Channel but then crash-landed. In December, though, he was promoted and went to command 245 (Hurricane) Squadron. He later became a wing commander but in 1949 his life ended in tragedy when he shot himself in Hyde Park. James Hallowes also left. He had been commissioned in September and he too would become a wing commander but happily he survived the war and for many years thereafter.

Perhaps 43's biggest loss was Frank Carey. He also went to 245 Squadron at first but in August 1941 he became the CO of a newly-formed Hurricane squadron, No. 135. This became operational in October and soon afterwards was sent to Burma. Here Carey showed himself to be a brilliant tactician as well as a brilliant pilot. Like Paul Richey later, he emphasized that although Hurricanes could outmanoeuvre German fighters, they could not outmanoeuvre Japanese ones. Therefore his pilots should use their Hurricanes' superior speed and better ceiling to attack enemy warplanes from above and then dive away steeply and rapidly, knowing that the

A new kind of fighter. For several months 111 Squadron at Northolt was the only RAF unit to be equipped with modern monoplane fighters. To onlookers, its Hurricanes were 'a revelation' but 'a somewhat chilling glimpse of the future.'

Early 111 Hurricanes.
nearest aircraft, L1550, was
of the first four received by
in December 1

L1555, the aircraft that Gillan,
aided by a considerable tail
wind, flew from Turnhouse, ne
Edinburgh, to Northolt at an
average speed of 408.75 mph o
10 February 1938.

Sir Sydney Camm, Chief Designer at Hawker
Aircraft Limited and creator of the Hurricane.

John Gillan, the first man to command a Hurricane
squadron.

the early months of 1940, 111 Squadron was stationed at Wick in the far north of Scotland where it helped protect the British Home Fleet's main base at Scapa Flow.

uadron Leader (later Air Commodore) John
ompson commanded 111 during its time at
ck and later during the Battle of Britain.

Servicing two types of Hurricane on the
strength of 87 Squadron.
Right: A later Mark IIC receives shells for
its 20mm cannons.
Below: A Mark I has its machine guns tested
at the time of the Battle of Britain.

A pair of 87's Hurricane IIC night-fight

Early Hurricane Is of 85 Squadron, a unit that was re-form
in June 1938 from members of 87 Squadr

A pair of 87 Squadron pilots who gained fame not only in war but in peacetime as well. *Left*: Roland 'Bee' Beam
who became a brilliant test pilot and the first British pilot to fly faster than the speed of sound. *Right*: Dennis
'Hurricane' David who ensured the safety of hundreds of Hungarian refugees at the time of the 1956 uprising.

One of 85's Hurricane night-fighters. Squadron Leader Peter Townsend gained 85's first night victory, a Dornier Do 17, on 25 February 1941.

Left: Hurricanes of 85 Squadron in France, easily identified from the hexagon emblem on the tail of the nearest aircraft.

The last Hurricane PZ865 in Hawkers' livery of royal blue with gold stripes. Group Captain Peter Townsend flew this in a number of post-war air races.

ree 85 pilots who fought in the Battle of France and the Battle of Britain. *From left to right*: Geoffrey rd, 'the Pride of 85', rose from sergeant to flight lieutenant but was killed in an accident in a Douglas oc on 3 March 1941; Flight Lieutenant 'Dickie' Lee, the godson of Lord Trenchard, who was killed in n on 18 August 1940; South African Pilot Officer Lewis who survived the war as a squadron leader.

Early Hurricane of 501, the first Auxiliary Air Force squadron to receive modern monoplane fighters.

This mishap when landing must have been embarrassing for 501's Squadron Leader Clube but he was unhurt and his Hurricane was later repaired.

Three of 501's finest. *Left*: Squadron Leader Henry Hogan had not previously flown a Hurricane in action when he became 501's CO at the start of the Battle of Britain but he would serve it well. He would later to the rank of air vice-marshal. *Below left*: Pilot Officer John Gibson had never even seen a Hurricane before he joined 501 in France but quickly proved his worth and would become one of its flight commanders during the Battle of Britain. *Below right*: Flying Officer Eustace 'Gus' Holden cancelled his leave to join 501 when it flew to France. He would later command the squadron, and enjoy other leaves later.

Hurricanes of 501 Squadron take off from Hawkinge on 15 August 1940, the day the Luftwaffe called 'Black Thursday'.

Below: Pilot Officer Kenneth William MacKenzie examining his damaged Hurricane after the combat that earned him a DFC. It had lost 3ft of its starboard wing, with which MacKenzie had knocked off the tail of a Messerschmitt Bf 109.

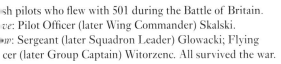

sh pilots who flew with 501 during the Battle of Britain. *ve*: Pilot Officer (later Wing Commander) Skalski. *w*: Sergeant (later Squadron Leader) Glowacki; Flying cer (later Group Captain) Witorzenc. All survived the war.

A Hurricane of 1 Squadron being refuelled at Vassincourt.

Pilots of 1 Squadron examining a machine gun from a Dornier Do 17 that the squadron had shot down in November 1939. *From left to right*: Flying Officer Paul Richey, author of *Fighter Pilot*; Squadron Leader Patrick 'Bull' Halahan; Sergeant Arthur 'Taffy' Clowes, who would later be a 1 Squadron flight command Flight Lieutenant Peter 'Johnny' Walker.

Hurricanes of 1 Squadron at their base at Vassincourt, France.

Peter Prosser Hanks, 1 Squadron's other flight commander at the time it went to France.

Mark Henry 'Hilly' Brown, the Canadian who joined 1 Squadron in 1937 as a pilot officer and left it in 1941 as a squadron leader.

[Squ]adron Leader James Maclachlan, who was 1 [Sq]uadron's last CO during the time when it was a [Hu]rricane unit. He had previously lost an arm in [com]bat over Malta and the emblem on the nose of his [Hu]rricane adequately expresses his defiant reaction.

Squadron Leader Richard Brooker, who succeeded Brown as 1 Squadron's CO and led it to its great success on the night of 10/11 May 1941.

[Hur]ricane IICs of 1 Squadron [flyin]g above their base at [Tan]gmere. It was [in] Mark IICs that the [squa]dron carried out [n]ight-intruder missions.

A 43 Squadron Hurricane at Tangmere just prior to the outbreak of the Second World War.

'Tom' Dalton–Morgan was a 43 flight commander during the Battle of Britain and later its CO and night-fighter expert.

Frank Carey was a sergeant pilot in 43 Squadron when war was declared and later one of its flight commanders during the Battle of Britain. He would become one of the greatest of all Hurricane pilots.

'Dick' Reynell was a Hawkers tes pilot who joined 43 Squadron in late August 1940 to assess the Hurricane's ability in combat. He was killed in action on 7 Septemb

The last Hurricane PZ865 with its 'honours board' of Hurricane achievements. The second entry from the left reads 'Brussels Exhibition', the scene of Reynell's most memorable pre-war triumph as a test pilot.

oy' Du Vivier, 43's lgian CO, who led his uadron into action at the e of the Dieppe raid.

rricane Mark IIB of 43 Squadron. It was with this version, armed with lve machine guns, that 43 flew most of its night-fighter missions.

rricane Mark IIC of 43 Squadron at Maison Blanche.

Above: Flight Lieutenant 'Freddy' Lister of 43 Squadron, who earned a DFC at Dieppe. He is seen here at Maison Blanche, Algeria, where 43 had become the first RAF unit to land in Vichy French North Africa.

Above: A 43 Squadron survivor. This Hurricane Mark I, L1592, can be found in the Science Museum, London. It is known as a 615 Squadron machine and indeed flew with 615 during the Battle of Britain. Previously, however, it had fought with 43 Squadron in the air battles over Dunkirk.

Left: Sergeant Alfred Marshall, the most successful 73 pilot during the squadron's early days in the Middle East.

Right: Flight Sergeant 'Bob' Laing, the first 73 pilot to land on Crete. After a brief but eventful stay, he left Crete in a Hurricane flown by Flying Officer George Goodman, who was sitting on his lap.

Below: The first RAF pilot to be credited with five victories was New Zealand Flying Officer Edgar 'Cobber' Kain of 73 Squadron. He is seen here examining the wreckage of a Dornier Do 17 that he had shot down in November 1939.

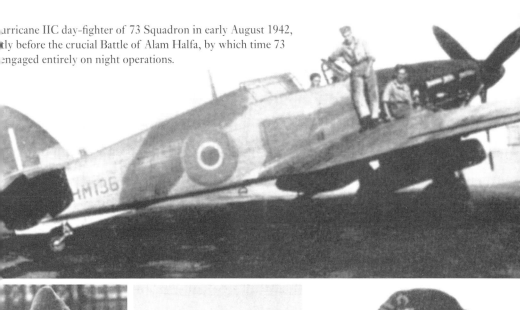

...urricane IIC day-fighter of 73 Squadron in early August 1942,
...tly before the crucial Battle of Alam Halfa, by which time 73
...engaged entirely on night operations.

...nt Sergeant Donald Beard,
...quadron's most successful
...t-intruder pilot.

Night-fighter Hurricanes of 73
Squadron over the desert.

Squadron Leader James 'Jas' Storrar
had fought with 73 Squadron as a flying
officer in defence of Tobruk and was
still flying Hurricanes in June 1944.

...urricane of the Air Delivery Letter Service, as used by Storrar and others to fly high-priority
...atches to and from the Normandy battlefront.

Flying Officer Charles Dyson of 33 Squadron may have gained a record number of victories on one sortie but his feat is the subject of much dispute.

'Pat' Pattle, 33's quiet but brilliant So African CO and the top-scoring RAF of any nationality in the Second Worl

Sergeant George Genders destroyed a Messerschmitt Bf 109 on 15 April 1941 in his first combat in a 33 Hurricane.

Vernon Woodward was one of 33's most successful pilots and for a time the top-scoring Canadian in the RAF.

Early Hurricane delivered to 33 Squadron by the Takorac supply route.

Lance Wade fought with 33 Squadron in desert for almost a year, becoming one of its flight commanders and the top-scorin American pilot in the RAF.

Flying Officer John Lapsley of 80 Squadron whose Hurricane provided admirable protection for Britain's Mediterranean Fleet. He would become an air marshal.

last Hurricane left in the Hurricane Unit, Crete. It was n out of the island in the late afternoon of 19 May by quadron's Sergeant Maurice Bennett.

250lb bomb carried by the Hurricane IIC (one under wing). This was the weapon used by 80 Squadron ng the Battle of El Alamein.

Flying Officer Peter Wykeham-Barnes of 80 Squadron who gained the Hurricane's first victories in North Africa. He later became an air marshal but dropped the name of 'Barnes'.

ie's Battleship.' This Hurricane I, L1669, was the first to be fitted with a tropical air-filter. At the start stilities with Italy, it was entrusted to 80 Squadron which, on the instructions of Air Commodore shaw, flew it to and from several landing-grounds to convince the enemy that modern fighters were hing Egypt.

Tank-buster. A 6 Squadron Hurricane IID armed with
40mm anti-tank guns attacking German armour in Tu...

Rocketeer. A 6 Squa...
Hurricane IV landing a...
airfield in Gr...

A 6 Squadron Hurricane IV in Yugoslavia. Both this and the previous aircraft carry four rockets under on...
wing and an auxiliary fuel tank under the other. This was the combination usually adopted by 6 Squadro...
its operations in Italy and the Balkans.

Japanese pilots could not pursue without the risk of their aircrafts' wings tearing off. As first the CO of 135 and later as the leader of 267 Wing, of which 135 was one unit together with 17 and 136 (Hurricane) Squadrons, Carey certainly proved his point. The number of his 'kills' was impressive and included three Japanese fighters in one day on 26 February 1942, and he was later promoted again to group captain.

In contrast to Simpson, Hallowes and Carey, the Belgian 'Roy' Du Vivier – his real name was 'Leroy' – remained with 43 for some time after his return at the end of 1940, and in April 1941 was promoted to flight lieutenant. It was also in April that 43 received Hurricane IIBs with their twelve machine guns (plus a handful of the older IIAs) and turned its attention to night-fighting.

As usual, night operations resulted in several mishaps, two Hurricanes having to crash-land with injuries to the pilots, while the Australian Sergeant Hayley got lost and, unable to find his way back to base before his fuel was exhausted, was compelled to bale out, happily without injury. Despite this, May 1941 proved 43's best month since the Battle of Britain. It shot down five Junkers Ju 88s at night, plus two more in daylight, and received a message of congratulation from the War Cabinet.

Squadron Leader Dalton-Morgan had been responsible for three of the night 'kills' and he would confirm his reputation as a night-fighter 'ace' during the next couple of months. On the night of 8/9 June, he shot down another Ju 88 that had been flying at very low level over the sea, having spotted its shadow on moonlight reflected in the water. He destroyed a Heinkel He 111 on the night of 11/12 July and then on 24 July, he and Pilot Officer David Bourne made a daylight interception of a Ju 88. As Dalton-Morgan closed in on this, his engine faltered and white smoke filled the cockpit. Nevertheless, he made three attacks and crippled the enemy aircraft before his engine stopped altogether; Bourne quickly finished it off. Meanwhile Dalton-Morgan, too low to bale out, 'ditched' and, like Kenneth Mackenzie, lost some front teeth when he hit the gun-sight. He took to his dinghy and was picked up by a Royal Navy vessel.

Even in midsummer, the North Sea was not a pleasant place in which to be cast adrift in a dinghy and Dalton-Morgan spent some time in hospital recovering from exposure, after which he was granted a month's leave. During his absence, his squadron saw little action but lost David Bourne and Sergeant Welling in accidents. On 2 October Dalton-Morgan raised his men's spirits by downing a Junkers Ju 88, his sixth victory at night, but on 4 October the Fighting Cocks came south to Acklington and the move marked the start of a very depressing period that at least serves to remind us of how dangerous flying in wartime could be.

Misfortune first struck on 12 October, when the Hurricanes of Flight Lieutenant Alexander Hutchison and Sergeant John Turner collided during combat practice. The sergeant was killed but Hutchison was able to force-land with only minor injuries. Before 1941 was over, three more pilots died in accidents and two other Hurricanes had to 'ditch', although their pilots survived. One of the men lost was Pilot Officer Hukam Chaud Mehta, a Hindu whose presence once again illustrates the wide range of nationalities of the men who flew the Hawker Hurricane.

In January 1942 Dalton-Morgan left the Fighting Cocks, ultimately to become a group captain, and 'Roy' Du Vivier was promoted to squadron leader and took over as 43's CO. It could not have been easy to replace a popular and highly-respected leader but Du Vivier did his best to motivate his men and certainly set them a fine example when on 25 April he attacked a Junkers Ju 88 and, though hit by return fire that sent splinters into his face and neck, he shot it into the sea where it exploded. Less encouraging was the fact that during April and May, accidents cost the squadron a further five Hurricanes and three pilots including Flight Lieutenant Hutchison.

In mid-June 43 moved back to Tangmere and in July, like No. 1 before it, commenced night-intruder sorties with its Hurricanes, several of which were now Mark IICs with their four 20mm cannons. Sad to relate, however, 43 did not enjoy the same success as its old rivals; no enemy aircraft were downed, though a few trains were shot up, and two pilots were lost, apparently in accidents since they were not claimed by the enemy.

On 19 August 43 turned to daylight intruder missions, for one day only. This was Operation JUBILEE, the raid on Dieppe. The Fighting Cocks flew four sorties during the day, the first of which was a very low-level strike by twelve Hurricanes against gun positions on the coast and in buildings around the harbour, made just before the soldiers came ashore. The area was very heavily defended and although 43 scored many hits, it had to fly through an intense and accurate barrage of anti-aircraft fire from every form of light and heavy gun. The Squadron Diary, with maddening reticence, reports flatly that of the twelve Hurricanes making this attack, 'only five came back untouched. Flight Sergeant Wik is missing from this operation. Pilot Officer Snell was missing after being heard to say over his R/T that he was baling out but later he was picked up by air/sea rescue and was unhurt.'

If two Hurricanes were lost and five were untouched, however, that means that five were damaged and many of these, in the true 43 tradition, gave further examples of the Hurricane's astonishing ability to survive fearful injuries. The Squadron Diary, for instance, does not even mention that the Hurricane flown by Pilot Officer Edward Trenchard-Smith was hit by a cannon shell that blew off half the fin and rudder. Despite this, the Australian airman continued his attack and got back safely to Tangmere where 'the tail section just fell apart.' He was to be known henceforth by the nickname of 'Tail-less Ted'.

Even the Squadron Diary does record that the Hurricane IIC of Flight Lieutenant 'Freddy' Lister 'had the underside of one wing' – the port wing, in fact – 'badly shot up by a cannon shell.' A more graphic description is given in James Beedle's *43 Squadron*[4]: 'The panels above the cannons blown off; a four-foot square hole in the trailing edge took in the aileron up to its inboard hinge, and the outermost cannon, wrenched from its by no means slender mounting, was askew, damaging the front spar and buckling the leading edge.' Yet the battered Hurricane carried Lister back to Tangmere. Experiments on the return flight had shown him that he could only maintain level flight at high speed and the state of the wing indicated that it would be most unwise to attempt to lower the flaps. Such was Lister's confidence in his Hurricane, however, that he never thought of baling out and he crash-landed with his airspeed indicator showing 210 mph. He emerged from the cockpit 'quite unhurt but a little stunned by his good fortune.'

The Fighting Cocks flew three more missions on 19 August. The first of these was a search for E-boats (German Motor Torpedo Boats) supposed to be threatening the landing area, but it seems that this report was inaccurate for none were sighted. The remaining sorties were more successful, being made against enemy strongpoints or gun positions. They met less opposition from flak and when on the last one some Focke-Wulf Fw 190s, the latest German fighters, attacked the squadron, its pilots used their Hurricanes' manoeuvrability to such good effect that only Sergeant Bierer's machine was hit and this suffered only minor damage. 'Freddy' Lister flew on all the squadron's later sorties and earned a DFC. 'No bad effort after that kind of landing,' concludes James Beedle, 'and no slight recommendation for the Hurricane either.'

After Operation JUBILEE, 43 was rested and in October its pilots were shipped to Gibraltar, arriving on 5 November, ready to participate in Operation TORCH, the landings in Vichy French North Africa. 'Roy' Du Vivier had been promoted to wing commander so 43 had a new CO, Squadron Leader Michael Rook who had flown Hurricanes first with 504 Squadron in the Battle of Britain and subsequently with 134 Squadron that, together with 81 (Hurricane) Squadron, had served in North Russia during September and October 1941. It was generally felt that he did well to get into a Hurricane at all, since he was reckoned to be the tallest pilot in the RAF.

It had been decided that 43 should form part of 323 Wing together with another Hurricane squadron, No. 253, both under Wing Commander (later Group Captain) Michael Pedley. He had accompanied Rook's men to Gibraltar and on arrival they were issued with eighteen Hurricane IICs that had been sent to Gibraltar in crates and fitted with long-range fuel tanks. These were very necessary for at first light on 8 November, two flights of nine Hurricanes each led by Pedley and Rook took off for Maison Blanche aerodrome near Algiers, though it was not known whether this would have fallen to the Allies by the time 43 reached it. If not, then the Hurricanes would be unable to land and even with their long-range tanks they would not be able to get back to Gibraltar either. It must have been a long anxious flight, especially for Wing

Commander Pedley who had only once previously flown a Hurricane.

Happily, 43's flight was uneventful, Maison Blanche proved to be in Allied hands and the Hurricanes landed safely, to gain the distinction of being the first squadron to do so in Algeria. It might be thought that the pilots would be appreciative of their machines' reliability but in fact they were not very pleased with them. The Hurricanes that had been provided at Gibraltar were somewhat elderly, hard-worked and worst of all tropical, which meant that they carried the filter first flown on a Hurricane by 'Dick' Reynell and designed to protect the engine. Since without it the engine would have had a very short life this was indispensable, but the trouble was that it hung down under the nose, creating additional drag and thus much reducing the Hurricane's speed and rate of climb. Indeed, some pilots who flew Hurricanes in both Britain and North Africa have said that the tropical ones were like carthorses compared to thoroughbreds.

On the other hand, it might be noticed that Wing Commander Pedley, who was not an experienced Hurricane pilot, was well satisfied with those now under his command. He points out that their lack of speed mattered little because there were no enemy fighters to oppose them and the Hurricanes could catch the German and Italian bombers, though in the case of the Junkers Ju 88s only with some difficulty. On the credit side, he praises their ruggedness, their ability to operate in poor conditions and especially the fire-power of their cannons that 'surpassed that of any other aircraft in the theatre.' He at least certainly did not regard them as 'second class'.[5]

Moreover, as so often, whatever their disadvantages on paper, in practice the Hurricanes proved perfectly adequate to carry out their allotted tasks. Wing Commander Pedley made the first interception of an enemy aircraft in the evening of 8 November. This was a Junkers Ju 88 and Pedley claimed only to have damaged it, but enemy records showed that it failed to return to its base. Next morning, Flying Officer Deuntzer damaged another Ju 88, though this one did manage to get back to base. That afternoon, Algiers town and harbour came under attack from a large formation of

Heinkel He 111s and Junkers Ju 88s but 43's Hurricanes are believed to have downed three of the raiders, while on the morning of the 10th, another Ju 88 was shot down in flames by Flying Officer 'Paddy' Turkington.

Meanwhile, the German occupation of Tunisia had made it imperative that the Allies advanced eastward. On 11 November a landing was made at Bougie, 120 miles from Algiers, and since Hurricanes were the only long-range fighters available, 43 was soon to be found providing this with aerial protection. The squadron enjoyed a number of successes over Bougie, Wing Commander Pedley shooting down a Junkers Ju 88 and a torpedo-bomber, 'Freddy' Lister destroying another torpedo-bomber and Flying Officer Lea downing an aged Dornier Do 17.

In addition, on 12 November Squadron Leader Rook led nine Hurricanes as escorts to twenty-seven US Dakotas that dropped two companies of British paratroopers on the airfield at Bone, 175 miles further east, just in time to thwart a formation of Junkers Ju 52 transport aircraft carrying German paratroopers intended to seize the same airfield. Later, 43 would provide cover for other parachute landings: by the Americans at Youks-les-Bains on 15 November and by the British at Depienne, only some 20 miles from Tunis, on the 29th.

Unfortunately, German reinforcements and vile weather ensured that the Allies would not get to Tunis for many months. The weather conditions reduced Maison Blanche to 'a sea of mud' but 43 continued to fly convoy-protection patrols and to guard Dakotas bringing men and supplies up to advanced Allied bases well into 1943. In February, however, Spitfires reached the squadron and by early March all its Hurricanes had left it.

All 43's former Hurricane pilots had also left it by the end of 1943. Wing Commander Pedley had already ceased to be an honorary Fighting Cock in November 1942, having moved to Philippeville where his wing's other Hurricane squadron, No. 253, was based. Some pilots inevitably became casualties of war but both Squadron Leader Rook and Flight Lieutenant 'Freddy' Lister left 43 because they had been promoted to wing commander and squadron leader respectively.

From mid-September 1943, the squadron served in Italy. The Allies had now gained such complete aerial supremacy that its Spitfires had to direct their attention almost entirely to targets on the ground. This was difficult and dangerous work, as demonstrated by a regrettably large total of fatalities resulting from accidents or anti-aircraft fire. All the same, one wonders what 43's earlier Hurricane pilots – men like Carey, Hallowes, Hull, Townsend and Dalton-Morgan – would have thought about having no German warplanes to oppose. Probably they would have considered the situation highly satisfactory but just a shade unnatural.

Notes

1. This description comes from Larry Forrester's *Fly For Your Life*, a biography of Wing Commander Robert Stanford Tuck who commanded 257 (Hurricane) Squadron in the latter part of the Battle of Britain. Hull was Tuck's best friend, which was quite a compliment since, as Mr Forrester tells us, there were very few people to whom Tuck was close.
2. There can hardly be anywhere further removed from the scene of the Royal Air Force's greatest triumph than Tucson, Arizona. Yet one of the exhibits of which its Pima Air & Space Museum is most proud has a plaque that reads: 'It was the Hurricane Mark I that bore the brunt of the Battle of Britain during the summer of 1940. Hurricanes were far more numerous than the more famous Spitfire and accounted for the majority of German aircraft shot down during the Battle.'
3. Lott would later receive a DSO in acknowledgement of his leadership of 43 Squadron and have a distinguished career in the Royal Air Force, rising to be an air vice-marshal, but because his injuries were incurred before its 'official' start, he would never receive the coveted Battle of Britain Clasp.
4. The author, James Beedle, was at this time a sergeant fitter with 43 Squadron and witnessed the return of Lister and the other pilots to Tangmere.
5. Wing Commander Pedley's views appear in *Fighters Over Tunisia* by Christopher Shores, Hans Ring and William N. Hess. It is also interesting to learn from Andy Saunders in *No. 43 'Fighting Cocks' Squadron* that two American pilots who had formerly served with 43 but had now been reclaimed by the US Army Air Force visited the squadron during its time at Maison Blanche. They were now flying Bell Airacobras and declared they would gladly exchange these for 'any old beaten-up Hurricane'.

Chapter 7

Three Hundred Plus
73 Squadron

At the time when No. 43 became the first Hurricane squadron to land in Vichy French North Africa, other Hurricane squadrons were already in action in the Mediterranean theatre and had been almost from the moment when, on 10 June 1940, Hitler's ally, the Italian dictator Benito Mussolini, had declared war on Britain and France. At first, existing fighter squadrons in the Middle East had been re-equipped with or new squadrons formed with Hurricanes, but as the danger of a German invasion receded, Hurricane squadrons from Britain were sent out. The first and for some six months the only one of these was 73 Squadron, a unit that had already acquired a considerable reputation.

The squadron had begun to receive Hurricanes to replace its Gladiators in July 1938 and had been fully re-equipped in August, although it was not operational until the early days of 1939. On the outbreak of war, it was one of the Hurricane squadrons sent to France and on 9 October, together with No. 1 Squadron, it was transferred to the Advanced Air Striking Force. Squadron Leader Brian 'Red' Knox who, like No. 1's 'Bull' Halahan, came from the Republic of Ireland, led his men to Rouvres near Verdun, an airfield that placed 73 closer to the German frontier than No. 1 at Vassincourt.

It seems that Hurricane squadrons were always fated to have a great variety of experiences, not all of them pleasant, and 73 was no exception even in the quiet months before the blitzkrieg. On 31 October, for instance, the squadron lost a Hurricane that was hit by AA fire, the pilot, Sergeant Phillips, having to bale out. Then on 6 November, 73 came close to losing one of its airmen. Pilot Officer Ayerst had pursued an enemy reconnaissance machine over the German frontier but it had eluded him. While heading for home, he sighted nine aircraft that he thought were Hurricanes and was moving to join them when he recognized them as Messerschmitt Bf 109s. They promptly attacked him but he escaped by diving to low level, then dodging through broken cloud, finally landing at a French airfield. His Hurricane had ten bullet-holes in its tailplane and was so short of fuel that the engine cut out as Ayerst finished his landing run.

On 8 November 73 did lose an airman, although, as it would transpire, only temporarily. Pilot Officer 'Dickie' Martin had also been chasing a high-flying German reconnaissance aircraft when his oxygen system failed and he 'blacked out' at 21,000ft. He recovered just in time to regain control and to make a forced landing on a nearby airfield. This, though, turned out not to be in France but in neutral Luxembourg, where Martin was interned. He needed no help from the Secret Service to return to his unit. He was allowed to take exercise walks and gradually increased the length of these until, taking advantage of a thick fog, he simply disappeared into this, ran as fast as he could and ultimately reached the French frontier.

'The Prisoner of Luxembourg', as Martin was immediately dubbed, rejoined 73 on 26 December to find that quite a lot had happened in his absence. On the same 8 November that had seen him interned, Flying Officer Edgar 'Cobber' Kain, who, by the way, was not an Australian but a New Zealander, had also pursued a German 'recce' aircraft. This was a Dornier Do 17 that spotted Kain's Hurricane and, to escape it, climbed to 27,000ft, then an unheard-of height for combat. Kain, however, was flying a machine equipped with a De Havilland variable-pitch three-bladed metal propeller that was much more efficient than the old wooden two-blade version with which the earliest Hurricanes had been equipped. This enabled him to catch up with the Dornier and set its port engine on fire. It fell away in a steep dive that ended only when it crashed to earth and exploded. Kain had followed it until his airspeed indicator recorded 450 mph, when he pulled out of the dive and landed safely.

This victory, the first for 73 Squadron, achieved much publicity since a group of war correspondents was visiting Rouvres at the time. Kain was almost bound to attract attention in any case. He was a cheerful extrovert, over 6ft tall with a mass of black hair and very bright blue eyes. He always kept the top buttons of his tunic undone so as to show off his lucky mascot, a green jade 'tiki' or Maori god that he kept on a chain round his neck. He called his aircraft 'Paddy', not in memory of a girl back home as the newspapers, of course, reported but as a tribute to the Irish fitter who had been with him since he had joined 73; another illustration of the bond between pilots and ground crews. He was also an excellent airman and a fine section leader, but one who was considered too reckless and impetuous – a 'mad devil', it was said – who used to fly patrols well over the German frontier, quite contrary to his orders.

It should be emphasized that the attention and the exaggerated stories about him greatly embarrassed Kain, who believed it was unfair to 73's other pilots. Kain felt so strongly about this that when he was on leave in London, he visited the Air Ministry and volunteered to be posted to another unit in France, a suggestion that was declined.

Kain's greatest friend in 73 was Flying Officer Newell 'Fanny' Orton, whom Kain considered to have been a more worthy recipient of the praise poured out in the newspapers. Certainly Orton was a very brave and very skilful if unspectacular pilot, but one feels that their friendship was a case of 'opposites attracting' for Orton, an Englishman born in Warwick, was quiet and retiring by nature. In one respect, however, they were very similar: Orton would have disliked any attention from the newspapers even more than Kain did.

Both Kain and Orton were in action on 23 November. This turned out to be 73's best day in 1939, with two Dornier Do 17s and two Heinkel He 111s being downed, Kain getting one of the Dorniers and Orton one of the Heinkels. The year ended badly, however, for on 22 December a section of 73's Hurricanes, attacked from above by Messerschmitt Bf 109s, lost two of its aircraft and Sergeants Perry and Winn were both killed.

All aerial activity was ended by the onset of a savage winter and although the coming of spring lifted 73's spirits, it also marked the return of the Luftwaffe. In March and April 1940, 73 had several clashes with enemy fighters and although as usual it is difficult to learn the exact details, there is no doubt that at least seven Bf 109s and three Bf 110s were either shot down or so damaged that they crash-landed. 'Fanny' Orton was responsible for the destruction or serious damage inflicted on three of the former and one of the latter, and was rewarded with a Distinguished Flying Cross.

'Cobber' Kain also earned a DFC for his actions during this period, though his reckless daring led to a number of unpleasant incidents that included on one occasion his making a forced landing with a crippled Hurricane, and on another occasion his baling out of a Hurricane in flames and being temporarily off 73's strength with twenty-one shell fragments in his leg and burns to his face and hands. Also during this period, three other Hurricanes had to make forced landings and three more were shot down, two of the pilots baling out but Pilot Officer Perry (no relation to the sergeant lost in December 1939) dying in action.

On 21 April 73 was taken into action by a new CO, Squadron Leader James More, and it was he who would be in control during the hectic days that would follow the blitzkrieg, on one of which he is reported to have flown six separate sorties. The first day of the German offensive, 10 May, was described in the Squadron Diary as one of 'ceaseless activity' in which it destroyed at least four enemy aircraft but was deprived of the services of Flight Lieutenant 'Reg' Lovett. A notoriously unlucky pilot, Lovett was hit by a cross-fire from Dornier Do 17s. His Hurricane caught fire and his hands were so badly burned that he dared not bale out for fear that he would be unable to pull the rip-cord of his parachute. By diving steeply, he was able to keep the flames under control and managed to force-land successfully but he was removed to hospital and did not rejoin 73 during its stay in France.

That stay would be made more complicated by the fact that as early as 10 May, the German pressure forced 73 to leave Rouvres for an airfield further west near Reims. This was only the first of seven moves as 73, like 1 and 501 Squadrons, steadily retreated, eventually to north-western France.

From 11 May until the 19th, 73 was in almost continuous action against huge numbers of enemy aircraft. On the 14th it engaged Junkers Ju 87 Stukas, destroying at least three of them, and it also recorded successes against Junkers Ju 88s, Heinkel He 111s, Dornier Do 17s and Messerschmitt Bf 109s and Bf 110s. How many must remain uncertain, for the British records are not complete and although there were undoubtedly many duplicated or exaggerated claims, the German records again inspire little confidence. On 15 May, for instance, during a combat between six of 73's Hurricanes and twice that number of Bf 110s, 'Fanny' Orton shot down a pair of 110s confirmed in enemy accounts but no other losses are admitted. Yet witnesses on the ground, including both British and French troops and Flying Officer Salmon of 1 Squadron who had been passing in a car, all stated that several other 110s had, in fact, fallen.

Sadly, there is no doubt whatsoever that the heavy adverse odds ensured 73 paid a high price for its successes. The Hurricane's strength did protect many of its pilots: on 11 May, for example, Squadron Leader More returned safely to his airfield in a Hurricane that had been hit by return fire from a Dornier and was so badly damaged that it had to be 'written off' as unrepairable. Even so, five of 73's men were killed and after downing his two 110s on the 15th as already described, 'Fanny' Orton's Hurricane was struck by cannon-shells that set it on fire and wounded its pilot in the shoulder. He baled out but not before he had been badly burned and he landed in a tree from which he was left dangling in his parachute harness. Flying Officer Salmon rescued him and rushed him to hospital. He was soon to be evacuated to England, receiving consolation for his wounds in the award of a Bar to his DFC.[1]

After a final encounter on 19 May in which it destroyed at least two Junkers Ju 88s and damaged others, 73 was temporarily rested from combat, and on the 21st received seven new pilots to replace its casualties. With their aid, 73 continued to down the occasional German aircraft, 'Cobber' Kain gaining his final success, a Dornier Do 17, on 27 May. By now, though, he was coming close to mental and physical collapse as a result of continuous pressure and has been described as 'nervous and preoccupied'. On 6 June he was ordered back to England to take up the post of instructor.

Tragically and wastefully, he would never pass on his experience. As he prepared to leave on 7 June, he could not resist telling those bidding him farewell that he would give 'one last beat-up, boys.' With his usual recklessness, he chose to do this in an aged Hurricane with a fixed-pitch wooden-bladed propeller – the last such on the squadron strength – that lacked the performance of the Hurricanes he had been used to flying. Roaring in at low level, he did two flick-rolls, then attempted a third. Several accounts state that his wing-tip hit the ground but Squadron Leader More later reported that the Hurricane pulled out of the final roll but had lost so much speed that it stalled and crashed, bursting into flames. Kain had presumably not strapped himself in properly, because he was hurled at least 50ft away and killed instantly.

The rest of More's men continued their fight, though encounters with the enemy became increasingly rare. The last of these was with Bf 109s on 15 June, in which Sergeant Alexander McNay was shot down. He was wounded in the shoulder but survived and was evacuated safely, rejoining 73 in July. The bulk of the squadron was also evacuated by sea two days later, while the seven remaining Hurricanes, every one of which needed repairs of some sort, were flown back to England where the squadron reformed at Church Fenton in Yorkshire and was given a chance to recover from its ordeal.

So great had that ordeal been, that 73 did not become operational again until 7 July and for some weeks it would do little more than fly uneventful patrols. The time was not wasted, though, for new pilots were carefully and thoroughly trained to fly their Hurricanes and, it is gratifying to report, without a single serious accident. The squadron's strength was also steadily built up and by 8 August it contained fifteen serviceable Hurricanes.

Much of the credit for this improved situation must go to Squadron Leader More and it seems a pity that on 8 August, he left 73 on promotion to wing commander and would not witness a great achievement by his men that came just a week later. He would eventually become a group captain but clearly never lost his thirst for action. On 22 January 1943, while stationed in Burma, he borrowed a Hurricane and joined 607 and 615 Squadrons in an attack on a

Japanese airfield. He was hit by AA fire, had to make a crash-landing and was quickly captured. He and other prisoners were later sent to Japan on the freighter *Rakuyo Maru*.[2] In the early hours of 12 September 1944, she and two other ships in the same convoy were sunk in the South China Sea by US Submarine *Sealion*. More was one of those lost.

More's successor as 73's CO was Squadron Leader Maurice Robinson and it was he who on 15 August led five of his pilots to an extremely significant interception. This was the day on which Luftflotte 5, based in Norway and Denmark, joined in the assault on Britain. Its first raid, mounted by Heinkel He 111s escorted by Messerschmitt Bf 110s – the range was too great for the more dangerous Bf 109s – inflicted minimal damage and suffered heavy casualties. Its commander, General Stumpff, was not finished, however. About fifty Junkers Ju 88s took off from Aalborg in Denmark. They would cause heavy damage to the airfield at Driffield but this did not harm Fighter Command as intended since this was in fact a bomber base.

They also paid for their limited success: they met 73's six Hurricanes and lost seven of their number shot down or damaged beyond repair. Pilot Officer Carter, who had served with 73 in France, and Sergeant McNay recovered from the wounds incurred there, both destroyed two Ju 88s and Flight Lieutenant Lovett, also fit again after his injuries in France, Pilot Officer Scott, another veteran of the days in France, and Sergeant Griffin, a 'new boy' who had joined 73 in July, all destroyed one. Only Squadron Leader Robinson was unable to record a 'kill' and he damaged another Junkers so badly that it did get back to Denmark but force-landed there. As a result of this day's actions, Luftflotte 5 was withdrawn from the conflict except for an occasional raid at night and Göring had some 150 fewer warplanes with which to fight the daylight battle.

Although 73's pilots could not know of this strategic consequence of their victory, they were naturally elated, the more so as they had not had a single Hurricane even damaged. They were not pleased to have to continue their routine patrols, particularly after Sergeant Leng was shot down by AA fire over Leeds in the early hours of 24

August, although mercifully he baled out and was unhurt. They cast envious eyes southward to where No. 11 Group was heavily engaged and were delighted when, on 5 September, they moved to Debden and a satellite airfield at Castle Camps.

However, their pleasure was dispelled that same afternoon. They engaged a large enemy formation and although they damaged a Heinkel He 111 sufficiently to cause it to force-land at its base, four Hurricanes were shot down or 'written off' after crash-landing. Squadron Leader Robinson and Flight Lieutenant Lovett were unhurt but Sergeant McNay was killed and Pilot Officer Rutter wounded and sent to hospital.

Thereafter matters improved, although 73, like No. 1, was a Hurricane squadron that recorded its greatest achievements not in the Battle of Britain but before and after. Nonetheless, on 6 September it joined with other Hurricane squadrons in opposing German raiders and at least had a hand in the fate of four Messerschmitt Bf 109s shot down or crash-landed, though Pilot Officer Eliot also went to hospital after baling out. Next day, 73 similarly played a part in the destruction of four Bf 110s but lost Flight Lieutenant Lovett killed in action. On the 11th 73, together with 17 (Hurricane) Squadron, had another combat with Bf 110s, five of which were lost in exchange for one of 73's aircraft, from which Sergeant Webster escaped by parachute.

Fighter Command's greatest victory in the Battle of Britain lay just ahead but it was preceded on 14 September by one of its worst days. On this it destroyed only eight German warplanes (though others were wrecked in accidents) and lost seven Spitfires and seven Hurricanes. The squadron hardest hit was 73 that lost five aircraft and Sergeant 'Joe' Brimble. On the 15th Pilot Officer Roy Marchand was also killed but 73 joined with 17, 257 and 504 (Hurricane) Squadrons to play a major part in smashing the massive German raids of this date. In the day's confused fighting, it is impossible to decide just what any individual squadron achieved but the total result was indisputable and two days later, Hitler postponed his invasion plans 'indefinitely'.

For 73 Squadron, the rest of the battle was very much an anti-climax. It made further successful interceptions on 23 and 27

September, though it lost four Hurricanes – but no pilots – on the former date and two more Hurricanes force-landed but in repairable condition on the latter. Its final action was fought on 11 October when it was surprised by Bf 109s that shot down one Hurricane in flames; Sergeant Plenderleith baled out but went to hospital suffering from burns.

Meanwhile, 73 was experiencing a number of changes. On 26 September Squadron Leader Robinson left, his distinguished career ultimately leading to the rank of air commodore, and was replaced by Squadron Leader Alan Murray. Then on 23 October the squadron was ordered to convert entirely to a night-fighting role. This was not a popular move with the pilots, but happily new scenes and new duties lay just ahead.

After Fighter Command had effectively ruled out any chance of an invasion of Britain, the Germans' best chance of winning the war lay in supporting their ally Italy in the Mediterranean. From Italy's then colony of Libya, they could assault Britain's main base in Egypt and from this gain control of the Suez Canal and easy access to the oil-rich lands further east. Moreover, Italy so dominated the central Mediterranean that the British would have to send most of their supplies and reinforcements some 14,000 miles round the Cape of Good Hope, whereas Axis convoys had to cover only 350 miles from the port of Messina in north Sicily to Libya's capital, Tripoli.

Fortunately for the British, 60 miles south of Sicily, right in the path of the enemy supply routes, lay the island fortress of Malta, from which aircraft, submarines and surface vessels could and did decimate Axis convoys. To avoid defeat, therefore, the British had to hold Egypt and Malta and that meant that they had to supply them with modern fighters. They were assisted in this task by another aspect of the Hurricane's reliability.

In May 1940 the Hurricanes of 46 Squadron, after being hoisted on board HM Carrier *Glorious* in somewhat undignified fashion, had flown off her decks to airfields in Norway, thus setting an example for the future.[3] On 2 August 1940, in the delightfully code-named Operation HURRY, twelve Hurricanes left the decks of HM Carrier *Argus* for Malta, where they joined the island's existing Station Fighter Flight to form 261 Squadron. On 27 November 1940 it would be 73 Squadron that would fly off an aircraft carrier on an early stage of the long journey required to supply Hurricanes to Egypt.

That journey had begun on 6 November when 73 sailed from Liverpool. The pilots and thirty-four Hurricanes fitted with tropical filters to protect their engines were taken aboard HM Carrier *Furious*, while the ground crews embarked on the cruiser *Manchester*. This carried them directly through the Mediterranean to Alexandria which they reached on 30 November, having on the way been excited witnesses to a clash between Vice-Admiral Somerville's Force H from Gibraltar and the Italian Fleet off Cape Spartivento.

Meanwhile, on 27 November 73's Hurricanes and pilots had arrived at the port of Takoradi in what was then the Gold Coast (now Ghana), where RAF personnel under Group Captain Thorold had set up a most impressive base and maintenance unit. Thorold had also created a series of staging posts all the way across Africa to Egypt for Hurricanes and other warplanes to use. By the end of July 1941, more than 300 Hurricanes had done so. By the end of October 1942, the total was over 1,500 and it was the opinion of Churchill among others that without them the British forces in Egypt would not have survived.

Not that the Takoradi route was an easy one, as 73's experiences would show. When the Hurricanes took off from *Furious*, Pilot Officer Wainwright crashed into the sea, though he was rescued and suffered only a cut chin. The other Hurricanes then had to be fitted with long-range tanks – not an easy task for, unlike the later Mark IIs, the Hurricane Is did not have special attachment points for these – before setting off on their 4,000-mile flight. The staging points were up to 650 miles apart and between them was either dense jungle or mountainous terrain where a landing would at least be extremely dangerous. The Hurricanes flew in batches, each guided by a twin-engined Blenheim, but on 1 December one of these got lost and it and the six Hurricanes it was leading had to crash-land in open country on the approach of darkness. Sergeant George Brimble was killed and all the Hurricanes were damaged, two so badly as to be unrepairable.

As a result, 73 Squadron reached Egypt with only twenty-seven

Hurricanes, not one of which was fit for combat after its gruelling trip. Happily, the squadron's ground crews, now reunited with the pilots, set to work with a will, removing long-range tanks, replacing guns that had been taken out to save weight and restoring engines and air-frames to an acceptable condition. Thanks to their efforts, twelve Hurricanes were ready for action by mid-December and all of them by the end of the month.

On 1 January 1941 No. 73 was officially declared operational as a squadron but its Hurricanes and their pilots had already seen combat, being attached temporarily to No. 274, a new Hurricane unit formed in the Middle East. These were exciting times, for in the early hours of 9 December British and Commonwealth forces attacked positions in Egypt occupied by the Italians in the previous September, and followed up their success most effectively. Assisted by a complete supremacy in the air, in just two months they overran Libya's eastern province, Cyrenaica, and virtually annihilated a much larger Italian army.

The pilots of 73 Squadron played their part in this magnificent victory, moving forward to different airfields to keep pace with the advancing soldiers; the first of a series of moves as the war in the Western Desert swayed backwards and forwards. The squadron had been reinforced prior to its departure from England with pilots from other Hurricane units, among whom we should mention Flying Officer James 'Jas' Storrar who had been so keen to join the Royal Air Force that he had falsified his age and who was credited with the destruction of eight enemy aircraft when flying with 145 Squadron in the Battle of Britain. Yet the two most successful members of 73 at this time had served with it in both the Battle of France and the Battle of Britain and although neither of them had done anything remarkable, it is clear that they had learned their trade and were ready to make good use of their experience.

Thus on 14 December, the Canadian Flight Lieutenant James Smith gained 73's first victory by shooting down a Savoia Marchetti SM 79 bomber; he then downed another on 16 December and a third on the 18th. Even more creditable were the achievements of Sergeant Alfred Marshall. On 16 December he destroyed two SM 79s and this was only a prelude to 3 January 1941, when he encountered five SM 79s attacking British warships. Italian records confirm that he shot down three of these. He believed he had damaged one of the remaining pair and it appears that he may have hit both of them since the Italians report that they both had to crash-land. On the same day Marshall, Squadron Leader Murray and Flying Officer Storrar raided an Italian landing-ground and believed that they had destroyed eight enemy aircraft.

Thereafter 73 was engaged in a variety of different activities. It had the occasional clash with Italian aircraft and on 5 January it shot down two Fiat CR 42 biplane fighters and another Savoia Marchetti SM 79, the bomber being downed yet again by Sergeant Marshall. It escorted Blenheims on bombing raids and made low-level attacks that destroyed enemy aircraft and motor transport on the ground. On 21 January, however, it had its first combat fatality in Africa when Pilot Officer Wainwright was killed in a fight with Fiat G 50 monoplane fighters. Also in January, four Hurricanes were hit by AA fire: three of them force-landed and were repaired but Sergeant Stonehouse was compelled to bale out and went to hospital with a broken leg.

On 4 February 73 intercepted a Caproni Ca 133 bomber-transport escorted by Fiat CR 42s. In the ensuing fight, Pilot Officer Millist crash-landed in the desert but he was unhurt and later was able to walk back to the British lines; his companions shot down the Caproni and one of the escorting fighters. This was the squadron's last aerial combat of the campaign, for within a week the Italians had collapsed completely. Unfortunately, it was decided that it would now be possible to render aid to Greece, a country already at war with Italy and threatened by a German invasion as well, and large military and air forces were dispatched accordingly. Even more unfortunately, this was done at the precise moment when Hitler had decided to go to the aid of his faltering ally in North Africa.

In mid-February 73 encountered German warplanes and on the 22nd, Squadron Leader Murray set a good example by downing a lone Junkers Ju 88. It had been intended that 73 would be among the units sent to Greece but in view of this new and alarming development, the plans were cancelled. Instead, 73 was strengthened, partly by Hurricanes and pilots sent up from Egypt, one of whom was 'Dickie' Martin who had been 'resting' at an Operational Training Unit and was now a flying officer, and partly by having a Free French Hurricane flight, Groupe de Chasse I, incorporated into it. It also received on temporary attachment a New Zealand airman from 274 Squadron, Pilot Officer Spence, who would soon make his mark in more ways than one.

It was just as well that 73 had gained these reinforcements, for the German Luftwaffe was quickly followed by the German Afrika Korps. On 31 March its leader, General Erwin Rommel, who had been personally selected by Hitler, launched an audacious offensive against the weakened British forces. This resulted in the recapture of the whole of Cyrenaica apart from the port of Tobruk and this was cut off and isolated on 10 April.

During this time 73 Squadron was in almost constant action, first in protecting the retreating ground troops and then, after 9 April, in protecting Tobruk from an airstrip within the port's defended perimeter. It was engaged in a variety of duties, as was well exemplified by 'Jas' Storrar on 8 April. On the same sortie he dropped messages to British forces retiring east of Derna, shot down a lone Junkers Ju 87 Stuka and sighted a Lockheed Lodestar transport that had come down in the desert. On landing to assist this, he found that it was carrying the Commander-in-Chief, Middle East, General Sir Archibald Wavell and his staff and had suffered a loss of oil pressure in one engine. He allowed oil to be drained from his Hurricane and this enabled the Lodestar to get airborne and reach British lines before it had to force-land again. Unfortunately it also prevented the Hurricane from taking off and compelled Storrar to walk 32 miles to Tobruk, travelling mainly at night in order to avoid the Axis troops surrounding it. He reached it in the early hours of 10 April.

Other 73 pilots, both before and during their time in Tobruk, made attacks on enemy motor transport. These sorties were not popular with the pilots but they caused considerable damage and on 10 April deprived the Afrika Korps of one of its leaders by wounding Major General Heinrich Kirchheim, commander of 5th Light (later 21st Panzer) Division, so badly that he had to be evacuated from Africa. On the 20th, 73 almost gained a bigger prize when three of its Hurricanes strafed Rommel's armoured control vehicle but this time only the driver was wounded, not the general.

The main task of 73, however, was opposing Axis warplanes. On 9 April the redoubtable Sergeant Marshall shot down a Junkers Ju 52 transport but its chief opponents were enemy bombers. Its Hurricanes' greatest success came on 5 April when they joined with those of 3 Squadron RAAF to rout formations of Junkers Ju 87 dive-bombers in both the early afternoon and early evening, 73 being responsible for destroying at least four Stukas. Then on 14 April 73 routed another Stuka formation, this time one attempting to clear the way for an assault by Rommel. The latter was a costly failure and 73 downed several dive-bombers and two of their escorting Fiat G 50s for good measure.

Sandstorms restricted aerial activity and provided a welcome break for a few days but on 19 April the Luftwaffe reappeared, strengthened by the arrival of Messerschmitt Bf 109s. On the 19th Pilot Officer Spence so damaged a 109 that it crash-landed and he repeated his feat two days later, this time pressing home his attack so closely that he collided with his target, though he managed to glide his injured Hurricane back to the British lines. The 109s in the desert did, however, have some distinct advantages over the Hurricanes. As mentioned earlier, the performance of the Hawker fighters was much reduced by their large engine air-filters. Those on the 109s were smaller and so less of a handicap. In addition, wind-driven sand caused so much wear on the Hurricanes' canopy Perspex that this could eventually become almost opaque and it is said that some pilots were even reduced to flying without their canopies. Similar harm was not done to the 109s since German Perspex was of a higher quality.

Despite these difficulties, 73 drove off strong formations of Stukas, escorted by 109s, on 21, 22 and the morning of 23 April and gained its final victory at Tobruk on the evening of the 23rd when Sous-Lieutenant Denis, one of the Free French pilots flying with it, shot down a 109. On the 25th the squadron was withdrawn to Egypt. Its contribution to Tobruk's defence had been vital, for it had given the defenders the opportunity to stabilize their positions and they would prove able to hold out against all Rommel's subsequent efforts. These benefits, however, had been gained at the heavy cost of twenty-eight Hurricanes lost for various reasons, seven pilots dead and three more prisoners of war. Among those killed was Flight Lieutenant James Smith who, on 14 April, was seen to shoot down two Fiat G 50s but was then shot down himself by other Italian fighters. Among those captured was Flight Lieutenant Eric Ball who had recently joined the squadron, having been one of Bader's flight commanders in 242 during the Battle of Britain. On 12 April he flew into a sandstorm and was compelled to land behind enemy lines.

There were other casualties too. Squadron Leader Murray had become ill through exhaustion and worry and on 20 April he was flown back to England – he would survive the war as a group captain – and was replaced by Squadron Leader Peter Wykeham-Barnes[4] who had previously been a flight commander with 274 Squadron. Several pilots had been injured, including on 23 April both 'Dickie' Martin who had baled out with a wounded shoulder and Sergeant Alfred Marshall who had already landed after combat when his Hurricane was strafed by Messerschmitt Bf 109s and he was hit in the head and shoulder. Both recovered from their injuries but neither returned to 73. Marshall was commissioned and had become a flight lieutenant when he was killed in November 1944, flying a Mosquito. Martin became a wing commander and survived the war and a subsequent career as a test pilot, first with Gloster Aircraft Co. Limited and later with A.V. Roe & Co. Limited.

Only four Hurricanes were still fit to fly when 73 left Tobruk for Egypt. Here other capable pilots also departed. Spence returned to 274 but was killed in action on 30 April. Storrar went to West Africa but he returned to Britain in July and we will meet him again later. The remaining airmen – rested, re-equipped and reinforced – enjoyed a comparatively easy time until late May when their attention was directed to a new theatre of operations.

The diversion of British and Commonwealth forces to Greece had not only made Rommel's task much easier but had led to far greater misfortunes in the Balkans. By the end of April, Greece had had to be evacuated and the Germans followed up with heavy air attacks on Crete. The few defending fighters were withdrawn on 19 May but it was hoped that they might be able to return. The disastrous decision was therefore taken not to obstruct Crete's main airfields so that these would then be available in such a case. Instead, on 20 May they were used by German airborne troops who, after a fierce struggle, captured the one at Maleme and into it poured reinforcements that eventually succeeded in taking the whole island.

Attempts were still made to get Hurricanes back to Crete, guided by Blenheims or Marylands. On the morning of 23 May, six of 73's pilots, led by Flying Officer George Goodman who was mentioned earlier when he was a pilot officer with No. 1 Squadron in the Battle of Britain, took off for Heraklion airfield. On their arrival at Crete, however, British warships whose crews were by now treating every aircraft as hostile, opened fire and so scattered their little formation that all except one decided to return to Egypt. Flight Sergeant 'Bob' Laing did manage to land at Heraklion, though it was still covered with wreckage from a thwarted German attack and was under small-arms fire from German troops. He received protection from a British tank, but half-an-hour later a raid by Messerschmitt Bf 110s destroyed his Hurricane on the ground, though Laing himself was unhurt.

That afternoon, Goodman again led the original five pilots, plus a replacement for Laing, to Heraklion, where they helped to drive off another air-raid before landing safely. Though they kept up patrols until nightfall, their position was clearly untenable and on learning that only limited fuel was available and no reserves of ammunition for the Hurricanes' guns, Goodman decided to return to Egypt next morning. All six Hurricanes got off safely, though two had damaged tail-wheels, and Laing was brought out with Goodman sitting on his lap. They emptied their guns into enemy troops around the airfield and then made for North Africa. Here, to complete their misfortunes, they encountered a sandstorm. The Hurricane carrying Goodman and Laing reached its base safely, as did that flown by Pilot Officer Ward, but two others had to force-land in the desert and were damaged, one beyond repair, while the remaining two presumably came down in the sea as neither they nor their pilots were ever seen again.

After this unpleasant interlude, 73's pilots resumed their duties in North Africa. A failure to relieve Tobruk in June resulted in

Churchill replacing Wavell as Commander-in-Chief, Middle East with General Sir Claude Auchinleck, formerly C-in-C, India and pouring into Egypt reinforcements of men and material originally destined for the Far East. These enabled Auchinleck's command to be built up sufficiently to become the Eighth Army at midnight on 26 September. Its supporting air arm was similarly expanded and officially became the Western Desert Air Force – although in practice the word 'Western' was rarely used – on 9 October.

In future the Desert Air Force, including of course 73, would move forward in support when Eighth Army advanced and retire, giving fighter protection, when Eighth Army retreated. It would be monotonous and no doubt meaningless to give details of all 73's activities in the course of these campaigns. It would also often be depressing, as for instance in the summer of 1941. In this, the squadron was chiefly engaged in strafing enemy aerodromes or motor vehicles. While so employed, it was very vulnerable to AA fire and attacks from above by Bf 109s and during June and July 1941 it lost ten men killed, including George Goodman, and three others prisoners of war.

By 18 November 1941, the spate of reinforcements to Egypt and the destruction wrought from Malta on the Axis supply lines to Libya had given Auchinleck such superiority that he felt able to launch the long-awaited British offensive, somewhat dramatically code-named Operation CRUSADER. After a series of complicated confused clashes with a good deal of blundering on both sides, this superiority finally forced Rommel to acknowledge defeat, and on 7 December he fell back in good order to a strong position at El Agheila on the border between Cyrenaica and Libya's western province of Tripolitania.

Though Eighth Army had received magnificent support from the Desert Air Force as a whole, 73 had played only a minor role. It had been busy reorganizing, receiving in October a new CO, Squadron Leader Derek Ward who, it will be recalled, had previously contributed much to the achievements of 87 Squadron. In addition, 73 was now receiving a mixture of Hurricane IIBs and IICs that not only had a better performance than its old Mark Is – though they too were bedevilled by poor canopy Perspex and those wretched engine-filters – but had the more powerful armament of twelve machine guns or four cannons respectively. Until the reorganization was completed, however, the bulk of the squadron remained well behind the front line and Ward could bring forward only seven aircraft to take part in the fighting.

Inevitably the pilots of these could make only a small contribution. On 27 November three of them strafed enemy landing-grounds, believing, probably optimistically, that they had destroyed or damaged many enemy warplanes. On 8 December they broke up a raid by Messerschmitt Bf 110s, two of which were shot down by Flying Officers Scade and McDougall. Both these pilots were flying Hurricane Is but next day, Flying Officer George 'Robin' Johnston was at the controls of a new Hurricane IIC when he used its cannons to good effect in destroying a Junkers Ju 88.

These successes, though minor, proved very heartening to 73 after its misfortunes of the summer and it is worthy of note that both Johnston and Scade were soon to be promoted to flight lieutenants, as was McDougall later. It was with renewed confidence that, in January 1942, the squadron as a whole moved to an airfield near Mechili in Cyrenaica, approximately midway between Tobruk and Benghazi, where it prepared to join an equally confident Eighth Army in a planned advance on Tripoli.

Never were hopes more swiftly dashed. Hitler had come to realize the effect the striking forces from Malta were having on the Axis supply lines to North Africa. At the expense of his soldiers on the Moscow front, he sent the Hurricanes' old enemies Field Marshal Kesselring and Luftflotte 2 to the Mediterranean with orders to secure those supply lines by the suppression of Malta. Kesselring duly set out to do so and as Malta was increasingly forced onto the defensive, reinforcements of men and material at last began to reach Rommel. On 21 January he launched another of his audacious offensives. This took Auchinleck, who never did or would appreciate Malta's importance, completely by surprise and by 6 February Eighth Army had lost Benghazi and Derna and was holding a line stretching south from Gazala, about 50 miles west of Tobruk. Here the front stabilized and both sides began to build up their strength for a new offensive.

Rommel's advance had caused 73 Squadron to make a rapid departure from Mechili on 3 February and it now took up station at El Adem south-east of Tobruk, where it was subjected to an air-raid two days later. For the rest of February it performed a variety of tasks, escorting Blenheims on bombing missions and fighting off attacks by enemy warplanes, losing Flight Sergeant Foster and having a number of aircraft damaged but gaining several successes. On the 9th, for instance, Squadron Leader Ward made the first 'kill' by a 73 Hurricane IIB when he destroyed a Heinkel He 111, while on the same day 'Robin' Johnston in his IIC shot down a Messerschmitt Bf 109.

Early on 10 March, 73 made its first sortie on a duty with which it would later become very familiar: night-intruder raids over enemy lines. It was not a very happy start, for Flight Sergeant Sands was shot down by AA fire, though he baled out and managed to make his way back to friendly territory three days later. Other night-intruder missions followed: Derek Ward shot down a four-engined Italian transport aircraft in the early hours of 1 May, but Pilot Officer Beaumont was killed by AA fire on the night of the 24th/25th.

On the following night, 73's pilots were again airborne but this time on the defensive, disrupting raids by Junkers Ju 88s and Fiat CR 42 biplanes carrying small bombs. Flight Lieutenant Scade and Flight Sergeant Ernest Joyce, who was destined to make quite a name for himself as a night-fighter, each destroyed a Ju 88, while Flying Officer John Selby, who was soon to be promoted to flight lieutenant, shot down a CR 42. The period of comparative quiet was over; the raids marked the start of a new offensive by Rommel. On 27 May 73 had to make another hasty retirement, this time to Gambut. Since one of its Hurricanes was still being serviced, Flight Sergeant Sands remained behind and followed the others when this had been made ready. Sadly, he never arrived and the reason for his loss is, and will probably remain, unknown.

Thereafter, 73 Squadron continued its retirement, ultimately to Burg el Arab to the east of El Alamein. It had no choice in the matter since Eighth Army was also in full retreat. By 14 June it was falling back from the Gazala Line; Tobruk was isolated by the 18th and surrendered three days later. Eighth Army then retreated all the way to the 'bottleneck' at El Alamein between the sea and the quicksands of the Qattara Depression. This was only some 70 miles from Alexandria but luckily Rommel's supply lines were now greatly over-extended and he was forced onto the defensive. He did, however, successfully resist a series of attacks by Eighth Army during July, at the end of which the fighting died down again.

During this period 73 Squadron made a number of effective interceptions both by day and at night but sadly it also often suffered heavily. A particularly dreadful incident came on 17 June. The squadron had been escorting South African Boston bombers and as it prepared to land at its base, it was attacked by Messerschmitt Bf 109s that shot down three Hurricanes. The pilots of two of these baled out but Pilot Officer Woolley was killed. Squadron Leader Ward then turned back to cover his men while they landed and he too was shot down and killed.

In all, by the end of June 73 had lost eleven Hurricanes and five pilots. During July and early August, under the leadership of 'Robin' Johnston who had been promoted to succeed Ward, it again had its successes but lost a further five Hurricanes – plus two others crash-landed – and three more pilots. It now turned entirely to operations during the hours of darkness, a role in which it would continue for most of its remaining time in North Africa.

During August 1942 Rommel was preparing for a final offensive that he hoped would carry him to the Nile. It would begin on the night of 30/31 August and would become known as the Battle of Alam Halfa. This would be the first action fought by an Eighth Army under the overall control of a new Commander-in-Chief, Middle East, General Sir Harold Alexander and the direct leadership of Lieutenant General Bernard Law Montgomery and it would decisively repel Rommel's assault.

Once again Rommel preceded his offensive with night attacks by his supporting air arm and once again 73 Squadron was there to meet these. On the night of 24/25 August, Ernest Joyce, now a warrant officer, destroyed a Junkers Ju 88 and in the early hours of the 29th, he shot down what he believed was another one. Unfortunately this was not the case. How a pilot of Joyce's experience and ability can have mistaken a single-engined Hurricane for a twin-engined Ju 88 is hard to imagine but this he undoubtedly did. As if that was not bad enough, the Hurricane that he shot down was flown by Squadron Leader Johnston.

To shoot down one's own CO must be considered tactless to say the least, but mercifully Johnston baled out, was only slightly hurt and on the night of 30/31 August when the battle began, was airborne again and himself shot down a Junkers Ju 88. Joyce was also flying and no doubt made very certain of the identity of another Ju 88 before downing this as well. His victory may have helped to obtain Johnston's forgiveness; at any rate Joyce's career did not suffer and when he left 73 later in the year, he was commissioned and by December had already become a flight lieutenant.

Johnston's men flew other night sorties during Alam Halfa, damaging at least two other enemy aircraft, and on 7 September when the battle ended, they believed they had damaged two or three more. On that date, though, they were not fighting defensively but were back on night-intruder missions. It was symbolic of the fact that the tide had turned at last and henceforward it would be Eighth Army that would be advancing.

Naturally 73, like the rest of the Desert Air Force, would assist in that advance. The squadron was now firmly committed to its night-intruder missions, normally carried out by a pair of aircraft or just a single one, for which tasks its Hurricanes were painted all-black and fitted with extra petrol tanks. It would also receive a new leader. Johnston took up other responsibilities on 1 October, and just as he had been promoted from being a flight lieutenant with 73, so one of his own flight commanders, John Selby, took his place.

It might be mentioned here that the authorities seem to have wished to keep the leadership of 73 'in the family', for when Selby in turn was posted in February 1943, the squadron was entrusted to Ronald Ellis who again was one of its flight commanders and who incidentally had previously served with 73 as a flight sergeant during its time as the defender of a besieged Tobruk. The pattern continued in July 1943, when none other than Ernest Joyce returned to 73 to succeed Ellis. Sadly, Joyce would be killed in action in June 1944, flying a Mustang, but the other three officers mentioned all survived the war; Johnston and Ellis as wing commanders, Selby as a group captain.

Although sometimes on their night-intruder sorties 73's pilots sought out enemy airfields as they had done on 7 September, most of their missions resulted in attacks on targets of opportunity on the ground, especially motor vehicles. Throughout October, in preparation for what would be the decisive British offensive at the Battle of El Alamein, 73's airmen often flew well behind the German lines. They encountered heavy flak and three of them were killed, including Flight Sergeant McPherson on 17 October. His courage and determination were respected even by his foes. As Richard Townshend Bickers records in *The Desert Air War 1939-1945*, they erected a plaque by his grave, reading (in English): 'To the memory of a brave British pilot who against intense opposition destroyed an ammunition train and in so doing lost his life.' McPherson's death had not been in vain, for the destruction of an 'ammo' train less than a week before a major battle was a serious loss to the enemy.

When the Battle of El Alamein opened late on 23 October, 73 Squadron was the very first one in action; this time not well behind enemy lines but in close support. Throughout the battle it would see action night after night. On that of the 26th/27th, Flight Sergeant Marsh and Sergeant Gadd attacked Junkers Ju 87s over their own airfield and damaged several of them, two of which crash-landed and were 'written off', while on the following night Flight Sergeant Donald Beard shot down a Junkers Ju 88. The squadron's main task, though, was strafing enemy positions, troop-carriers, supply lorries and supply dumps; its actions greatly assisted and heartened the soldiers pushing slowly but steadily forward against an enemy fighting desperately in prepared positions protected by half a million mines. These ground attacks were carried out at very low level and on 3 November another 73 pilot, Flight Lieutenant Miller, was killed by anti-aircraft fire.

On 4 November the soldiers and airmen had their reward as, for the first time in the Desert War, Rommel's troops fell back not in good order but in full retreat. As Eighth Army advanced, so did 73 Squadron: to Gambut, then El Adem, then El Magrun deep in Cyrenaica south of Benghazi. Pilots and ground crews alike were exhilarated by the change of fortune, morale is said to have been 'as high as a kite' and it was increased still further on 8 December by an encounter, minor in itself, but of immense significance to the squadron as a whole.

For once 73 was in action in the daylight hours, being sent out to intercept a raid by Junkers Ju 88s on a convoy bringing badly-needed supplies to Benghazi. When the Hurricanes approached, the Ju 88s scattered and headed for cloud cover but Pilot Officer (later Squadron Leader) Maurice Smyth correctly estimated where one of them would emerge from this and shot it into the sea, much to the delight of observers in the convoy. The members of 73 were equally pleased because this was the squadron's 300th official victory. Of course, exaggerated and duplicated past claims mean that this figure should be reduced but that is equally true of the official scores of all units of all nations. It seems fair then to suggest that they at least give a basis for comparison and to point out that the Hurricanes of 73 Squadron were credited with the greatest number of victories recorded for any single aircraft type in any RAF squadron.[5]

Nor had 73's Hurricanes finished just yet. They had several other encounters with Junkers Ju 88s throughout the rest of December and destroyed three more of them. The squadron continued moving its base forward as it kept pace with Eighth Army, first westward into Tripolitania, then after the fall of Tripoli on 23 January 1943, closer to the Libyan capital, and finally northward as Eighth Army thrust into Tunisia. The early weeks of 1943 were, however, not nearly so satisfactory. During these the squadron was used mainly for reconnaissance purposes. This left its machines vulnerable to AA fire and to prowling Messerschmitt Bf 109s. By the end of the first week of March, 73 had lost two pilots killed and two more prisoners of war.

Morale was restored in late March when 73 reverted to its night-intruder missions. On the night of the 20th, when the Battle of the Mareth Line began, 73, as at Alamein, was the first squadron over the battlefield. Flying Officer Henderson intercepted a Ju 88; he claimed only to have damaged it but enemy records show that it did not return to its base. Then after dark on the 24th, Pilot Officer Chandler also encountered a Ju 88. This time there was no question of it only being damaged: Chandler's cannons blew off half of one wing and the Junkers promptly crashed.

In early April Eighth Army moved up to assault the next line of Axis defences at the 'Gabes Gap'. As usual, 73 was there with the soldiers. On the night of the 5th/6th, it covered their final advance to their starting positions, driving off a number of enemy aircraft. After the battle had opened, it was on hand in its intruder role on the next two nights, Henderson downing a further Ju 88 on the first of these and Chandler yet another on the second one. Sadly, though, in the early hours of 11 April, Henderson was also lost in unknown circumstances.

Thereafter 73's encounters were mainly with Junkers Ju 52 transports that were originally attempting to bring supplies to their by now hopelessly surrounded troops and later trying to evacuate as many men as possible before the final surrender of the Axis forces on 13 May. As a squadron operating mainly at night, 73 took no part in the massive daylight destruction of the German aerial transports. Its pilots did, however, strafe and finish off some that had force-landed on the coast; five on the evening of 18 April and two more on that of the 19th.

Prior to this, on 15 April Pilot Officer Smyth and Flight Sergeant Beard each shot down a Ju 52 transport at night, after which Smyth was himself attacked by a Junkers Ju 88 night-fighter but outmanoeuvred this and escaped unhurt. This was the last occasion on which 73 met with any resistance and it only remains to detail its final victories at night: a Ju 52 shot down by Sergeant Thomas on 20 April; four aerial transports destroyed or damaged on 8 May; two Ju 52s downed by Beard on the night of 9/10 May; and lastly two more Ju 52s destroyed by Pilot Officer Bretherton and Warrant Officer Hewitt on the night of the 10th/11th.

So ended the two-and-a-half years when 73's Hurricanes fought in Africa but they still had one further and quite different duty to perform in the Mediterranean theatre. While part of the squadron remained in Tunisia, another part was sent to Luqa aerodrome in Malta and on the night of 9/10 July its Hurricanes accompanied the Allied airborne forces landing in Sicily as a preliminary to the main seaborne invasion early next day. The task of the Hurricanes was to attack any searchlights that might locate the gliders or the aircraft towing them. This it performed successfully and although the airborne operation as a whole was costly and unimpressive, it did capture and retain the vital Ponte Grande Bridge near Syracuse as well as causing much confusion among Sicily's defenders. Other night-intruder sorties were later flown by 73 over Sicily but already Spitfires were replacing its Hurricanes in Tunisia, and by the end of July all 73's Hurricanes had returned from Malta and the squadron had been entirely re-equipped as a Spitfire unit.

Sicily, though, was not the last invasion to concern Hurricanes flown by members, or at least former members, of 73 Squadron. On 9 June 1944 the first Allied aircraft landed and took off from a hastily-prepared airstrip in Normandy. This honour went to a Hurricane IIC of the Air Delivery Letter Service that for most of 1944 flew high-priority despatches and secret equipment to and from the battlefront and its pilot was 'Jas' Storrar, now a squadron leader. The Hurricanes were frequently deprived of their cannons to increase their performance but their flights were not without some danger as two of 73's 'old boys' discovered on 10 June.

The pilots involved were Storrar and Michael ffrench Beytagh, who had also served with 73 during the siege of Tobruk, had later flown with Storrar in West Africa and was now a squadron leader as well. During their time with 73, both had become used to emergency take-offs and this proved of value on 10 June when they landed on an airfield that was, in fact, still in German hands. They got airborne just in time to avoid death or capture and both survived the war as wing commanders. They were probably not pleased about this incident and their narrow escape but, after all, no one could possibly have imagined that Hurricanes flown by former 73 pilots would be left completely out of the fighting.

Notes

1. Orton was the first pilot to receive two DFCs for his achievements in the Second World War. On recovering from his injuries, he was promoted to flight lieutenant and posted to an Operational Training Unit as a fighter instructor. He later flew Hurricanes with 242 Squadron and while with this unit he destroyed another Messerschmitt Bf 109. He became CO of 54 (Spitfire) Squadron in July 1941 but was killed in action on 17 September.

2. All Japanese merchantmen included the word 'maru' in their names. This had been added to the names of aristocrats' sons during Japan's feudal age, so

to give it to a ship implied that this had a personality, in the same way that Europeans or Americans call a vessel not 'it' but 'she'.

3. On the evacuation of Norway, 46's ten surviving Hurricanes successfully landed on *Glorious* with bags of sand added to the rear sections of their fuselages to hold their tails down on her deck. Tragically, *Glorious* was sunk by the German battle-cruisers *Scharnhorst* and *Gneisenau* on her way home and the Hurricanes and all except two of their pilots were lost. Their exploit, however, helped to encourage the development of the Sea Hurricane that provided crucial protection for convoys to Malta and Russia.

4. This officer would later drop the name of 'Barnes' and has already been introduced as Air Marshal Sir Peter Wykeham, the author of *Fighter Command*.

5. The RAF squadron with the highest official score was 249, credited with some 350 successes. The largest proportion of these was gained by Spitfires, but until March 1942 the squadron flew Hurricanes and these were responsible for about 100 victories, including one on 16 August 1940 by a Hurricane already in flames. The pilot of this, Flight Lieutenant James Brindley Nicolson, was awarded Fighter Command's only Victoria Cross. A small part of the total was also gained by the Mustangs that replaced 249's Spitfires in September 1944.

Chapter 8

The Desert and the Balkans
33 Squadron

Among the units that were already stationed in the Middle East at the time they first received Hurricanes, it is perhaps slightly surprising to find 33 Squadron since this had once been a notable bomber unit. In February 1930 it had become the first squadron to receive the Hawker Hart. It was rightly proud of this distinction and therefore adopted a hart's head as the squadron badge. In October 1935 it had moved to Egypt and here in February 1938 it gave up its Harts, not for more modern bombers but for Gloster Gladiator fighters.

Gladiators still formed 33's equipment in June 1940 when Mussolini's declaration of war put Egypt into the front line. It and the other fighter squadrons in the Middle East were understandably anxious to receive modern monoplane interceptors but, unfortunately, it was not easy to oblige them. In June, Hurricanes were sent through France and thence via Tunisia and Malta to Egypt, but these flights were made at the very limit of the Hurricane's range, losses were heavy, only a handful reached the Middle East, and four of them were sent back to Malta to provide protection there.

In any case, these missions came to an end when France surrendered. Thereafter, Hurricanes had to be shipped to the Middle East in crates, either directly across the Mediterranean, a route that became more perilous almost daily, or round the Cape of Good Hope, which inevitably caused lengthy delays. Even so, 33 received its first Hurricanes in September and more in October, though the squadron did not attain its full wartime complement until December, by which time the Takoradi supply route that brought 73 Squadron to Egypt had got into its stride.

Not that 33 Squadron waited until it had its full strength of Hurricanes before seeking out Italian warplanes. Nor indeed did it wait until it had received any Hurricanes at all. During the early months of the war in the Western Desert, its Gladiators recorded several victories, the Canadian Flying Officer Vernon Woodward gaining particular credit. In August Squadron Leader Johnson was posted – he would shortly become a wing commander but was killed in April 1941 when the Blenheim in which he was a passenger was shot down – and it would be Squadron Leader Charles Ryley who would first command 33 as a Hurricane unit. Ryley, incidentally, had previously flown Sunderland flying-boats but seems to have had no problem in adjusting to an aircraft as reliable as the Hurricane.

On 31 October Ryley's men, then based on the airfield at Fuka, first saw action in their Hurricanes when they intercepted a raid by Savoia Marchetti SM 79 bombers escorted by Fiat CR 42 biplane fighters. They believed they had destroyed or damaged half-a-dozen enemy aircraft and there is no doubt that two of the bombers were shot down, while two others suffered such damage that they crash-landed and were 'written off' and lesser injuries were inflicted on several more. Tragically, 33 lost its first Hurricane pilot when the Canadian Flying Officer Leveille was compelled to bale out and was killed when his parachute failed to open. Flying Officer St Quintin from Southern Rhodesia force-landed but was unhurt.

The squadron's next action came on 9 December. This was the day in the early hours of which the first British offensive of the Desert War began and the soldiers of the Western Desert Force were greatly heartened by the knowledge that, though they were greatly outnumbered, their tanks, artillery and fighter aircraft were all vastly superior to those of their enemies. They were certainly given superb support by 33's Hurricanes, ranging ahead of the advancing British and Commonwealth troops, reporting the Italians' positions and movements, strafing enemy motor transport and clashing with CR 42s of which it was believed they had shot down three. That evening, however, 33 lost Second Lieutenant Fischer, a South African pilot, who failed to return from a reconnaissance mission.

On 11 December another 33 pilot did not come back from a lone patrol and was officially reported 'missing'. Happily, Flying Officer Charles Dyson was very much alive. He had emerged from cloud to find himself in an ideal position to attack a formation of six Fiat CR 42s escorting a Savoia Marchetti SM 79. He had taken these completely by surprise and claimed he had sent all six enemy biplanes down trailing smoke and flames. Almost immediately afterwards, he had encountered another group of CR 42s but after damaging one of them, he had run out of ammunition, his Hurricane was hit and he crash-landed in the desert, from which he made his way back to his squadron on foot, rejoining it on 17 December.

Dyson's story was received by his fellow pilots with incredulous amusement but they were silenced when a message was received from army sources, offering congratulations to the pilot who had 'shot down seven enemy aircraft'. The reason why Dyson's victories had been increased to seven was that apparently one of the falling Fiats had been seen to smash into the SM 79 and bring this down as well. If this report was correct, then Dyson had achieved a feat that no other RAF pilot would ever equal. However, the sceptics would claim that their attitude was justified when Italian records became available. These revealed a number of losses on 11 December, including some inflicted by other 33 pilots, and recorded the attack on a formation by a lone Hurricane but gave no indication that this had inflicted any.

There are three possible reasons for this discrepancy. One, that Dyson simply made a preposterous claim, cannot be believed. Dyson was an experienced pilot who before the war had won a Distinguished Flying Cross for actions against insurgents in Palestine and who would ultimately become a wing commander. He must have realized that a very large claim would not be well received and if not confirmed would greatly embarrass him, as indeed it did. He would serve with 33 until late April 1941 but he claimed to have destroyed only two more enemy aircraft during that time, which would indicate that he was no boaster. This is further confirmed by an incident on 13 April during the campaign in Greece. Dyson wisely refrained from attacking a huge German formation and openly and rather amusingly described how instead he 'withdrew strategically into the sun'.

Alternatively, perhaps in the confusion and excitement of combat, Dyson greatly overestimated the damage he had caused. He would not have been the only airman who did so and there would be no difficulty in accepting this explanation were it not for that army report. Since the original signal has not been traced and we know of it only at second hand, this also could have been too optimistic and generous. At the same time, its revelation that the SM 79 had also been destroyed, which was something that Dyson had never claimed or apparently known about, does suggest that the incident had been investigated by Army Intelligence and that the Italians had suffered at least some losses.

Air historians Christopher Shores and Giovanni Massimello in *A History of the Mediterranean Air War 1940-1945*[1] consider that the army report is 'unreliable' because it was received 'six or more days after the event'. The delay, though, does not seem too surprising when it is recalled that during the time in question the army was engaged in driving the Italians out of Egypt altogether and pushing on into Cyrenaica. It may even be that the delay was caused because Army Intelligence also felt at first that the story was unlikely and congratulations were only offered after it had been thoroughly checked. Certainly the doubts originally entertained in 33 Squadron must have been resolved since Dyson was shortly to be awarded a Bar to his DFC.

It would therefore not be unfair to feel that part of the confusion at least may have been caused by the Italian records not being complete. There are other instances where this could be said and a particularly informative one appears in another work by Christopher Shores, *Dust Clouds in the Middle East*. This deals with the aerial warfare in several minor campaigns including the one in what was then Italian East Africa. On 3 February 1941 Captain John Frost – his nickname inevitably was 'Jack' – a Hurricane pilot of 3 Squadron

South African Air Force disrupted a raid by Caproni Ca 133 bombers on an army camp. In an action fought 'above the heads of the exultant troops', he shot down three Ca 133s and an escorting Fiat CR 42. The Italian records confirm the loss of the three bombers but not that of the CR 42, although it was seen to crash by scores of eye-witnesses and Mr Shores reproduces a photograph taken of its wreckage.[2]

That the Italians did not conceal the loss of the more valuable bombers shows that the omission of the CR 42 from the records cannot be explained by these having been mislaid or its loss being denied for propaganda purposes. It is suggested therefore that on this and other occasions when CR 42s claimed cannot be confirmed, the reason may be that the Italian authorities were not so worried about losses of their biplane fighters since they wished to replace them with more modern aircraft as soon as possible anyway – though in practice CR 42s would be encountered as late as mid-1942 – in view of the Hurricanes' obvious superiority over them. Indeed, in January 1941 Fiat G 50 monoplane fighters would arrive in Libya, 33 having its first combat with them on the 6th when two were believed to have been shot down by Warrant Officer Goodchild.

During December 1940 and the first days of January 1941, 33 did in fact down a considerable number of Italian aircraft. Once more, though, exactly how many cannot be determined for not only were there the usual exaggerated or duplicated claims but, as just discussed, the fact that a fair number of CR 42s claimed cannot be found in official Italian sources may only mean that their loss was not recorded. The squadron suffered no further losses of its own after 11 December and whatever the true total of its 'kills', by early January it and the other Hurricane units had gained such a complete supremacy in the air that Italian moves were invariably reported and frequently attacked, while British moves were rarely detected and never disrupted. This supremacy proved decisive in ensuring that by 7 February, the British and Commonwealth land forces had captured the whole of Cyrenaica and annihilated the Italian army defending it.

This happy situation was soon to vanish with the arrival in Libya of the Luftwaffe and the Afrika Korps, but 33 was not there to meet them. On 28 October 1940 Mussolini had invaded Greece from

Albania, which he had seized in April 1939. The Greeks quickly proved more than capable of defending themselves and since they rightly believed that Hitler was not pleased by the Italian action, they showed no wish for British military aid. They did, however, very much desire assistance to cope with Italy's much larger air force and during November RAF Blenheims and Gladiators joined them in driving out the invaders and advancing in their turn into Albania.

In mid-January 1941, 33 Squadron was rested and warned to be ready for a move to Greece. On 19 February Squadron Leader Ryley led sixteen Hurricanes to Eleusis aerodrome near Athens by way of Crete, the defence of which had been taken over by Britain. The ground crews reached Greece by sea a couple of days later. There was the occasional encounter with Italian aircraft, particularly by a detachment sent to Paramythia near the Albanian frontier, but 33 was most often tasked with escorting Blenheims in attacks on Valona harbour in Albania and on Italian warships and merchant vessels. It was on one such mission on 4 March that 33 had its first casualty in the Greek campaign when Warrant Officer Goodchild was shot down and killed by Fiat G 50s.

On 13 and 14 March, the detachment at Paramythia saw combat with Italian Macchi MC 200 monoplane fighters. It helped the Gladiators of 112 Squadron to shoot down a couple of these on the 14th but lost one Hurricane, though the Rhodesian Flying Officer 'Frank' Holman, a police officer before the war, baled out safely. Meanwhile, the main body of the squadron had gone to Larissa aerodrome in east-central Greece where, on 12 March, it was joined by a new Commanding Officer, Squadron Leader Ryley having been promoted to wing commander. It is said that 33's pilots had hoped that one of their own flight commanders would take his place and were at first disappointed and somewhat indignant to receive a former flight lieutenant from a rival Hurricane squadron in Greece, No. 80.

They would soon realize how lucky they were. Squadron Leader Marmaduke Thomas St John Pattle, who wisely preferred to be known simply as 'Pat', was a South African from Butterworth, Cape Province. He was small, quiet, calm, unassuming and softly-spoken but was already recognized and respected as a superlative fighter pilot, blessed with remarkable eyesight, quick reactions, deadly marksmanship and extraordinary flying ability. In the early months of the war he had served with 80 Squadron in North Africa and had gained four victories flying Gladiators, but he was best known for an incident before the war when he had landed a Gladiator that had lost its port wheel so skilfully that it suffered only minute damage and was airborne again, with Pattle at the controls, later that same day.

It was not until 80 Squadron went to Greece in November 1940, however, that Pattle showed just what a brilliant pilot he was. By the time he took over 33, flying first Gladiators and later Hurricanes, he had shot down well over twenty Italian warplanes and received a Distinguished Flying Cross and Bar, awards made far more rarely to pilots in the Mediterranean theatre than to those stationed in Britain. As a flight commander he had also proved to be a fine tactician and when he arrived at Larissa, where he was appointed station commander as well as 33's CO, he demonstrated his ability as an organizer, arranging for the establishment of a satellite airfield and for observation posts to be sited on neighbouring hills to provide an early-warning system. Any doubters among his pilots were won over when he proved far superior to all of them in mock dogfights.

There were plenty of opportunities for such practices and for giving a number of newly-arrived pilots experience in flying Hurricanes, because the latter part of March brought little action for 33, apart from one hectic day on the 23rd. In the morning, the squadron escorted Blenheims in an attack on an airfield in Albania. It was not an easy mission, two Hurricanes being damaged by AA fire over the target and Flying Officer Charles Dyson being attacked on the return flight by Fiat G 50s and having his Hurricane seriously damaged. Fortunately the Hurricane's reliability again showed its worth: the AA victims returned safely to base and Dyson got very close to it before his engine finally ceased to function and he had to bale out, which he did without injury.

That afternoon, the Hurricanes were ordered to strafe another Albanian airfield by themselves. On the way they were engaged by Italian fighters and although they drove these off, in the excitement only Pattle and the steady, reliable Flying Officer Vernon Woodward went on to attack the airfield and damage some Italian machines on the ground. Pattle was not pleased with his pilots, for it was typical of him that nothing would distract him from carrying out a mission. It was also typical that he should have sighted a Fiat G 50 about to land on the airfield, opened fire on this and seen it roll onto its back. It was then at only 200ft but since Pattle did not see it crash, he claimed only a 'Probable'.

The squadron, though, would soon be faced with foes more formidable than the Italians. Hitler had already drawn Hungary, Rumania and Bulgaria into the Axis Pact and on 1 March had sent his troops into the last-named country, thereby threatening Greece from the north-east. On 25 March Yugoslavia also joined the Axis Pact but two days later a military coup reversed this decision and so brought about the possibility that Yugoslavia might attack the wretched Italians in Albania from the rear.

When Hitler learned what had happened, he exploded into one of his volcanic rages. On 6 April German forces, strongly supported by the Luftwaffe, crashed into both Yugoslavia and Greece. Their blitzkrieg, like that on the Low Countries and France in May 1940, was spectacularly successful; it had overrun Yugoslavia by 17 April and mainland Greece by the end of the month.

During that month, the pilots of 33 Squadron escorted Blenheims attacking, and themselves strafed German army units and raided enemy aerodromes, this time in Bulgaria. Chiefly, though, like the Hurricane pilots who faced the 1940 blitzkrieg, they were engaged in fighting off large numbers of hostile aeroplanes. Some additional Hurricanes did arrive as reinforcements from time to time, the first six on 9 April, but once more the RAF faced terrifyingly high odds.

Once more also, it is impossible to know full details of the achievements of No. 33 and the other fighter squadrons in Greece. All official records were destroyed when the British and Commonwealth forces evacuated Greece, Operations and Intelligence Summaries were usually compiled from memory long afterwards and logbooks, diaries, letters written at the time and the later reminiscences of the survivors could often be unreliable. Nor can the German accounts be trusted to give the full picture.

As was seen when dealing with the Battle of Britain, the Luftwaffe quartermaster general's returns from which the 'official' figures of German losses are taken are simply not complete. The same is true in the Mediterranean theatre and instances of 'kills' not recorded in the 'official' German returns but confirmed by witnesses on the ground or by the pilot baling out and being taken prisoner, or both, come from the Balkans, North Africa, Cyprus, Malta and the Malta convoys.

To quote just one example, on 21 March 1942 Hurricanes of 185 Squadron drove off Messerschmitt Bf 110s raiding Hal Far aerodrome in Malta. According to enemy records, only a single 110 was shot down. According to the RAF pilots, six were shot down and their version is supported expressly by experienced pilots of another squadron, watching from Hal Far, and impliedly by the Luftwaffe chiefs who never sent 110s to raid Malta in daylight again, a somewhat extreme reaction to the loss of just one of them.

Moreover, just as further Luftwaffe records later came to light revealing German casualties in the Battle of Britain not recorded in the quartermaster general's returns, so they did for the Mediterranean air battles. Christopher Shores and Hans Ring, in their *Fighters Over the Desert*, describe how on 26 June 1942, the Hurricane pilots of 213 Squadron were delighted to sight what they believed were eight Messerschmitt Bf 109s well below them. They were also somewhat surprised as 109s normally made sure they had a height advantage. They attacked at once and reported they had shot down five enemy aircraft that had been seen to hit the ground in flames. No German fighter is recorded as even being damaged at this time and, accordingly, Mr Shores and Giovanni Massimello in *A History of the Mediterranean Air War 1940-1945*[3] can only state that the affair is 'unexplained' and 'baffling'.

In fact, an explanation is given in *Fighters Over Tunisia* by Shores, Ring and William N. Hess. In an appendix recording new evidence about incidents in *Fighters Over the Desert*, we are told that 'it has subsequently become clear that additional ground-attack units of Bf 109Es were in the Desert during 1942' and one of these 'may well have been' the formation attacked by 213. If the 109s were on ground-attack duties, this would also explain why they were operating at a lower level than usual and so strongly indicates that 213's claims were correct and once more the 'official' German records are incomplete.

When one adds that during the Greek campaign, even losses reported in the records of individual German formations do not appear in the quartermaster general's returns, it seems fair to suggest that 33's pilots gained more successes in this than those for which they have received 'official' credit. They certainly shot down two or three Henschel Hs 126 army co-operation machines acting as aerial scouts for the German army, and they repelled several raids by German bombers. On 14 April, for instance, Flying Officers Woodward and Dean sighted six Junkers Ju 87 Stukas about to attack a convoy of Australian army lorries. The cheering Australians confirmed that they shot down three of these and they believed they damaged the other three.

There is also no doubt that 33's airmen proved to be considerably better fighter pilots than those of the Luftwaffe. In the incident just described, the Stukas had had an escort of 109s but these made no move to assist their charges by engaging the Hurricanes. The squadron had got off to a good start in this respect as early as 6 April. 'Pat' Pattle had led twelve Hurricanes on an offensive sweep over Bulgaria and had encountered twenty 109s. The squadron had destroyed several of these without having any Hurricane hit by a single bullet. Pattle had downed the first two 109s to fall. The other members of his section, Flying Officer 'Frank' Holman and Pilot Officer 'Bill' Winsland, both confirmed, rather sadly, that he had done so in two short bursts of fire and given them no chance of inflicting any damage themselves.

So skilfully had 33 fought that it did not lose a man until 15 April. Then, however, Larissa aerodrome was attacked by a formation of Messerschmitt Bf 109s. The Canadian Flight Lieutenant John Mackie led three Hurricanes in a desperate attempt to take off and oppose the raiders but the German fighters pounced on them while they were still climbing. Pilot Officer Charles Cheetham was shot down and killed. Mackie fired on and mortally wounded the 109 pilot responsible; he managed to bale out but died later, while his aircraft made a perfect belly-landing on its own in a nearby field.

Mackie was then brought down and killed as well but the remaining 33 pilot, Sergeant George Genders, whose first combat this was, destroyed a second 109 and subsequently landed with his Hurricane quite untouched.

By now, the British, Commonwealth and Greek armies were in full retreat and the RAF units had no choice but to follow suit. By 17 April 33 was back at Eleusis where it joined the other Hurricane squadron in Greece, No. 80. Both squadrons were placed under the tactical control of 'Pat' Pattle. He was suffering from combat fatigue and influenza, was running a very high temperature and his face has been described as 'deeply wrinkled', yet he remained indomitable. At this time he ordered Charles Dyson, who also had a fever and high temperature, off to hospital and then back to Egypt by way of Crete, but he refused to go to a sick-bed himself, feeling that it was his duty to lead his men into action and that a failure to do so would discourage and perhaps demoralize them.

There was certainly every reason for the airmen to be discouraged. Eleusis was twice strafed on 18 April and seven Hurricanes were damaged. The ground crews moved these into a hangar and by working all night made five of them fit to fly again. At dawn on the 19th, a raid by fifteen Junkers Ju 88s caught the defenders by surprise and, obviously well informed by good Intelligence work, struck unerringly at the one crucial hangar, destroying it and all seven Hurricanes.

That was only the start of two days of torment as the Luftwaffe made very determined efforts to finish off the Allied fighter force. These included another strafing attack on the 20th that destroyed two of 33's aircraft on the ground and would have destroyed several more but for the action of Aircraftsman Cyril Banks who jumped into a blazing petrol bowser and drove it away to a safe distance.

In the main, though, the Hurricane units were whittled down by sheer attrition as they battled wave after wave of enemy aircraft. During the 19th they destroyed or damaged eleven of the raiders and added several more on the morning of the 20th. During this time, however, 33 lost three more vital Hurricanes damaged beyond the repair facilities available and Flying Officer 'Frank' Holman, trying to land his crippled Hurricane in a marshy field, broke his neck when the aircraft turned a somersault. When the squadron adjutant arrived to take charge, he found that the local Greeks had laid out the body and covered it with flowers.

The culmination of the German assaults came in the late afternoon of 20 April which, by the way, was Adolf Hitler's birthday. Over 100 German aircraft attacked shipping in Piraeus Harbour near Athens. To meet them, the RAF could muster only fifteen Hurricanes – six from 33 Squadron and nine from No. 80 – all led by 33's Squadron Leader Pattle. Between them, they destroyed or damaged fifteen of the enemy but at a cost that could hardly be borne by their limited numbers.

From 33 alone, three Hurricanes were lost. Flight Sergeant Cottingham, though wounded, baled out safely, but the squadron mourned two gallant South Africans, both of whom died as a result of their complete unselfishness. The Hurricane of Flight Lieutenant 'Harry' Starrett was set on fire but since the flames seemed to be under control and knowing how precious every modern fighter was, he tried to force-land it at Eleusis. He set it down all right and it had almost come to a halt when it suddenly exploded into a mass of flames. Starrett managed to get out of his cockpit but his clothes and parachute were on fire, he was unable to throw off the latter, was horribly burned and died in hospital two days later.

An even greater loss was that of 33's inspirational leader. Although he was a very sick man, 'Pat' Pattle destroyed a total of at least seven enemy aircraft, perhaps more, in the course of 19 and 20 April. The last of them came in this fight when he spotted a Hurricane in trouble with a Bf 110 on its tail. There were other hostile machines overhead that he must have known would pounce on him but he dived to help his colleague. He shot down the 110 in flames but two others closed on him from above. It seems that Pattle was killed by their fire, for he was seen to be slumped over the controls as his Hurricane plunged down into the sea. Because his outstanding achievements took place well away from the British Isles, Pattle has rarely been accorded the respect that he deserves. His final total of victories is not known and some sources state it at over fifty but both Christopher Shores in *Air Aces* and his biographer E.C.R. Baker in *Pattle: Supreme Fighter in the Air* settle for 'at least forty'. He was surely the greatest Hurricane 'ace' of them all.

That was not quite the end of 33's activity in Greece. It continued to cover the evacuation of the army from a new base at Argos, south-west of Athens, while reinforcements and the untiring efforts of the ground crews brought the total number of Hurricanes in Greece up to twenty by 23 April. That afternoon, however, a force of about forty Bf 110s destroyed thirteen of them on the ground. Next morning, the remaining seven flew to Crete, while the other pilots of 33 and 80 Squadrons were carried to Crete in aerial transports.

On Crete, the airmen's position was perilous in the extreme. They faced a potential onslaught from over 600 German aircraft but the island's radar warning system was inadequate and there was no means of communication between pilots and ground controllers. A handful of Fleet Air Arm Fulmars from 805 Squadron and a few Gladiators from 112 had also been evacuated from Greece but the Fulmars and some of the Gladiators were soon to be destroyed on their airfields and the remaining Gladiators were 'grounded' as being too hopelessly outclassed.

That left the defence of Crete in the hands of the Hurricanes. Reinforcements of these were sent out from time to time but there were never more than sixteen on the island, not all of which were serviceable since there was a desperate shortage of spare parts. The pilots of 33 and 80 Squadrons joined forces to form the composite Hurricane Unit, Crete, but by the end of April, almost all those of No. 80 had been evacuated and in practice the Hurricane Unit, Crete became virtually just 33 Squadron.

During the first half of May, 33's pilots had a number of encounters, chiefly with Junkers Ju 88s attacking supply ships approaching the island; they shot down at least two and damaged several others. On the 13th, however, most of 33's 'old hands', by now inevitably suffering from strain and exhaustion, were evacuated and new and in many cases inexperienced pilots were flown in to replace them. The squadron was also strengthened by airmen from 112 and 805 but they were unused to flying Hurricanes and on 16 May, in clashes with Bf 109s and Bf 110s, two of the naval pilots were killed and Flight Lieutenant Fry, 112's temporary commander, had to bale out and struck his Hurricane's tailplane, suffering injuries to his chest.

Among the replacements for 33 was a new CO, Squadron Leader Edward Howell, a most experienced airman and an instructor but, curiously enough, he had never flown a Hurricane before. He was to bless its reliability when he made his first sortie in one on 14 May. He was just being shown the layout of the cockpit when a force of 109s swept in to strafe his airfield. Howell took off straight at the advancing enemy. Onlookers saw 109s flash past him on either side before he left the ground and immediately after he became airborne. As his aircraft lurched in their slipstream, Howell made a tight turn, his wingtip 'within inches of the ground'. Happily, as he would gratefully record, 'The faithful old "Hurrybus" took it without a murmur.'

Despite such handicaps as unfamiliar controls, an unadjusted rear-view mirror that prevented him from seeing behind him and a borrowed helmet that was too large for him and kept falling over his eyes, Howell out-turned his assailants, shot down one for certain and at least damaged another. He then landed safely. He would lead 33 Squadron during the remainder of its stay on Crete and would shoot down a Junkers Ju 52 transport on 16 May.

For all his efforts and those of his men, however, the Hurricane Unit, Crete would have but a short existence. By 19 May 33 had had most of its aircraft destroyed on the ground, Sergeants Hill and Ripsher had been killed in action, Sergeant Reynish had been reported missing after his Hurricane had been seen to fall in flames – though, in fact, he baled out and was pulled from the sea by a Cretan fishing boat – and only four Hurricanes remained serviceable, three of them with 33. These three and the three 'grounded' Gladiators were then flown back to Egypt to avoid further pointless loss of life.

Their pilots were the only members of 33 to get clear before, on 20 May, German paratroopers and gliders descended on Crete, which they had overrun by the end of the month. The rest of the squadron's personnel would conduct a further brave but hopeless fight, this time on the ground, and Aircraftsman Marcel Comeau who had previously fired on strafing enemy warplanes with a machine gun, proved even more dangerous to German airborne troops when armed with a rifle. Pilot Officer Dunscombe and several of 33's ground crewmen were killed in the fighting and among those taken prisoner were six pilots including Sergeant Butterick who was so badly wounded that he had to have a leg amputated, Sergeant Reynish and the 112 pilot who had flown Hurricanes with 33, Flight Lieutenant Fry. Less than half of 33's personnel were ultimately carried to safety by British warships or by Sunderlands.

Squadron Leader Howell, who had remained on Crete to help direct his men in their new role, was another of the pilots captured. On the first day of the airborne landing he was hit by machine-gun fire, badly wounded in his right arm and left shoulder and when found by a rescue party was unconscious and covered in blood. It was believed that he was dead, so he was left lying on a hillside for three days before being discovered by the enemy who removed him to hospital. He eventually made a complete recovery and even managed to escape with the aid of Greek helpers; he ultimately got back to Egypt about a year after his capture. Here he was no doubt gratified to learn that he had been promoted to wing commander and that 33 Squadron had been re-formed and had long been back in action.

Not very happily at first, however. When 33's surviving pilots returned to Egypt, they still had no new CO, so were led by Vernon Woodward, now a flight lieutenant and one of the few airmen who had served throughout the campaign in Crete. On 17 June he took 33 into its first combat since leaving Crete. It shot down a Junkers Ju 87 and a Fiat G 50 but lost Flying Officer Eric Woods, another pilot who had been a member of the squadron from its early days in North Africa.

In July, Squadron Leader James Marsden arrived to take over responsibility for 33. It was a heavy one, for in the period leading up to Operation CRUSADER, 33 gained few successes and lost twelve Hurricanes plus one more strafed on the ground, with six pilots dead and two others prisoners of war. Squadron Leader Marsden was one of those shot down while 33 was protecting a convoy heading to the assistance of the besieged garrison of Tobruk. Luckily, he was able to bale out, came down close to the convoy and was duly rescued. In addition the squadron lost the services of Vernon Woodward. He gained his final victory with 33 when he shot down a Junkers Ju 88 on 12 July, but in September he was rested and took up a post as a flying instructor before later becoming CO of 213 (Hurricane) Squadron and ultimately a wing commander.

None of these events gave 33 much encouragement for Operation CRUSADER but when this first offensive by the Eighth Army opened on 18 November, the squadron's luck changed. On the first day, it attacked Axis troop positions, motor vehicles and airfields successfully and was lucky enough to encounter only Fiat CR 42 biplanes. It believed it had shot down three of these, two of them falling to a young airman whose first victories these were but who was destined to become one of 33's greatest pilots.

Pilot Officer Lance Wade was a citizen of the United States who had joined the Royal Air Force as a volunteer in December 1940 and arrived in Egypt by way of Malta in September 1941. He quickly proved to be an outstanding airman and was known, rather dramatically, as 'The Wildcat from Texas'. He would also become a fine leader, rising to flight lieutenant by late June 1942, and many of the men who flew with him later remembered with gratitude the advice that he had given them.

Wade would have plenty of opportunities to show his worth, for 33 Squadron, flying from a variety of landing grounds, had many clashes with German and Italian aircraft during November and December 1941 and destroyed or damaged a considerable number of them. Its own temporary base was strafed on 22 November and two Hurricanes destroyed on the ground but 33 more than evened the score with a whole series of effective attacks on enemy aerodromes, though some of the machines they reported as destroyed may already have been abandoned.

Later, particularly after 7 December when Rommel began to retreat, 33 turned its attention to attacks on Axis transport, with equal success. These strikes were made regardless of heavy anti-aircraft fire and at very low level. Just how low was shown on 2 December when Sergeant Challis hit a parked Fiat CR 42 with his wing-tip, 'damaging both aircraft', although not enough in the Hurricane's case to prevent it from returning safely to its airfield. On 5 December Lance Wade attacked at such low level that when the bomber he was firing at blew up, his Hurricane was caught in the blast and he had to force-land some 25 miles behind enemy lines. A fellow 33 pilot, Sergeant Wooler, landed to assist but in the process damaged his own Hurricane so badly that it had to be abandoned. Wade and Wooler were both compelled to walk back to the British lines, which they reached safely next day.

This trick of landing in the desert to rescue a colleague was employed fairly frequently by Hurricane pilots and usually their aircraft's strength and reliability enabled them to do so successfully.[4] On 8 December, for instance, Flight Lieutenant Derrick Gould of 33 Squadron did land and take off again with Flying Officer Charles, who had force-landed after being hit by flak, sharing his Hurricane. By a cruel trick of fate, however, Charles was killed on the 16th when he came in too low and crashed into the vehicle he was strafing.

Apart from those losses already described, 33 paid for its successes at this time with five more Hurricanes down, Flying Officer Dallas missing and Flying Officer Jewell a prisoner of war. Squadron Leader Marsden might also be considered a casualty. The strain of what had been his first command had exhausted him and on 28 December he returned to Britain and Derrick Gould who, as his senior flight commander, had been taking much of the responsibility for leading 33, was deservedly promoted to squadron leader.

Gould would very soon be called upon to face another crisis. As mentioned earlier, on 21 January 1942 Rommel's troops, now bearing the inspiring name of 'Panzerarmee Afrika', commenced a brilliant counter-offensive. General Auchinleck, who was complacently planning to add the conquest of Libya's western province of Tripolitania to his gains in Cyrenaica, was caught completely by surprise and Eighth Army was bundled back to Gazala.

When the assault began, 33 Squadron was stationed at the forward airfield of Antelat, together with its old companion-in-arms, No. 112, now flying Kittyhawks. They were in a perilous situation for the enemy was advancing towards them at speed and the airfield, having been flooded by heavy rains, was largely waterlogged, leaving a strip only 500yds long and 30ft wide available for take-off. Fortunately, just enough warning was given and the ground crews of both squadrons responded magnificently. Although two Hurricanes and four Kittyhawks, lacking essential items like propellers, had to be destroyed to prevent their falling into enemy hands, each remaining aircraft was carried to the take-off area by twelve men under the wings and all got airborne safely, the last as German shells began falling on the airfield.

From its new temporary base at Msus, 33 struck back at its tormentors, making devastatingly effective attacks on Axis motor transport on both 23 and 25 January. However, the enemy columns were well defended by anti-aircraft guns and on the 23rd, Pilot Officer Edy was hit and being too low to bale out, crash-landed in the desert. Lance Wade, ignoring heavy flak, circled round several times to see if it would be possible to land and rescue Edy, but there was nowhere suitable and eventually he had to give up, leaving Edy to become a prisoner of war. On the 25th the anti-aircraft gunners claimed another victim, Sergeant Nourse being shot down and killed.

Thereafter, 33 fell back to a series of airfields east of Gazala and in early February was withdrawn from the fighting and later re-equipped with twelve Hurricane IIBs. With these it resumed its offensive sweeps but suffered losses when it encountered a new enemy trick: dummy vehicles, covered by strong anti-aircraft batteries. In all, five Hurricanes were lost, though as usual they at least protected their pilots, all of whom were able to bale out or crash-land without serious injury.

On 18 May 33 received a new CO. Squadron Leader John Proctor was a very experienced Hurricane pilot, having flown the type first with 501 Squadron in France as a sergeant pilot and then, after being commissioned, with 32 Squadron in the Battle of Britain. He did not have a pleasant welcome to the Desert War, for he was hit by flak on 21 May and had to force-land, happily without injury. It was symbolic of misfortunes to follow.

On the night of 25/26 May, 33 turned to repelling raiders in the hours of darkness, Pilot Officer Inglesby and Sergeant Belleau sharing in the destruction of a Junkers Ju 88. The raids were a prelude to a new offensive by Rommel that began next morning. The men of Eighth Army were aware of what was coming and awaited it with some confidence, having a considerable superiority in tanks, artillery and reserves. In the air the opponents were more equally balanced for Kesselring, at the cost of abandoning sustained raids on Malta, had sent strong reinforcements to North Africa. The Desert Air Force, however, delivered effective attacks on Rommel's supply lines and these were also threatened by the stubborn defence of the fortified position of Bir Hacheim at the south of the Gazala Line. Rommel therefore directed his full strength against this and its gallant garrison of Free Frenchmen was compelled to withdraw after dark on 10 June.

Rommel then struck northward to the sea, threatening to cut off the divisions in the northern part of the Gazala Line that hastily fell back along the coast road. Their lorries, bunched together, made a wonderful target for air attack, yet such was the defence provided by the Desert Air Force that just six Allied soldiers died as a result of the efforts of hostile warplanes. Sadly though, the RAF, driven from its forward airfields, could not provide similar protection to the garrison of Tobruk, against whom Kesselring hurled every Stuka that he could muster. Under cover of this 'aerial artillery', the Axis forces burst through the defensive perimeter and at dawn on 21 June, Tobruk surrendered.

Sad to relate, while other Hurricane squadrons had had considerable success against Axis aeroplanes and even more against Axis motor transport, 33 Squadron had had a most unhappy time. It gained few victories over enemy warplanes (assuming the Axis records are complete which, of course, they may well not be) and by 25 June it had lost three pilots killed and a fourth taken prisoner. It had also had seventeen Hurricanes destroyed or badly damaged, though ten of the seventeen were able to return to base despite their injuries. Even so, the pilots were no doubt grateful that on the 26th they were pulled out of the fighting in order to be re-equipped with Hurricane IICs.

They would return to the front line on 1 July, but by then the situation was very different. Heedless of the strong protests of Kesselring, who pointed out that he was having to withdraw his bombers to Sicily since Malta was again becoming a threat, Rommel, intoxicated by his success and the award of a field marshal's baton, insisted on thrusting deep into Egypt. This desperately strained his supply lines, exhausted his German troops and left his Italian units and the remains of his supporting air forces trailing well behind. When on 1 July he reached the El Alamein 'bottleneck', his advance crashed to a halt, precisely as Kesselring and others had predicted.

Rommel's impulsive action meant that when 33 resumed operations, it, like the other Desert Air Force squadrons, found few enemy aircraft to oppose for the first couple of days of July. On the 2nd, though, one 33 pilot did have a memorable experience. The New Zealander Flight Lieutenant James Hayter was attacked by a Macchi MC 202, the finest of the Italian fighters, and his Hurricane was fatally crippled. Then, however, the Macchi overshot and Hayter was able to pour a burst of fire into it. Both machines crash-landed and both pilots were unhurt but as the combat had taken place behind the British lines, the Italian pilot was taken prisoner.

By 3 July, the Germans had at last managed to get their air force up and attempted to use it to smash a way through the British defences as it had done at Tobruk. Terrific air battles took place all day and 33 played its part in thwarting the enemy's intentions, at the cost of one Hurricane, from which Sergeant Woolard baled out safely. Rommel had played his last card, for the time being at least, and it was now Eighth Army's turn to take the offensive.

In many accounts, the fighting for the remainder of July is headed 'The Stand on the Alamein Line' or something similar, thus giving the impression that Eighth Army was hanging on grimly against heavy odds. In reality, Eighth Army had an overwhelming superiority of numbers, especially of tanks, and from 4 July it was on the offensive, trying to comply with orders from General Auchinleck to 'destroy the enemy as far east as possible and not let him get away as a force in being.' In all, Auchinleck launched five offensives but all were terribly badly prepared and executed, not least because there was hardly any co-operation between army and Air Force, the headquarters of which had now been moved miles apart. It would be too depressing to describe 33's part in these failures: suffice to say that it achieved a few successes but lost fifteen Hurricanes destroyed or badly damaged in July, plus three more on 3 August, and eight of its pilots were killed.

Once more, 33 was glad to retire from the front line for a short time and when it returned to combat duty on 31 August, again a great deal had changed. Already in late July, Squadron Leader Proctor had been transferred, ultimately to become a wing commander, and had been succeeded by Squadron Leader James Finnis. More importantly, Rommel was no longer on the defensive but back on the attack, having received reinforcements that brought the numbers of the two armies closer than they had ever been before or would ever be again. Fortunately, Alexander and Montgomery were now in the Middle East, had given Eighth Army a new attitude and new tactics and restored its co-operation with the Desert Air Force.

Consequently, the Desert Air Force played a large part in the crushing defeat of the Axis army at the Battle of Alam Halfa, by fighting off the Axis air forces and by striking at the Axis motor transport, especially petrol bowsers. The satisfaction naturally felt by 33's pilots was increased by a greatly reduced casualty list of just three Hurricanes lost. Pilot Officer Dibbs had been killed but both Sergeant Belleau and Flight Sergeant Belec had baled out, in Belec's case after colliding with a Messerschmitt Bf 109 on 4 September. Presumably the 109 was lost as well. The Luftwaffe records do not confirm this but since according to them it was not even damaged, this can only be another instance of the records being incomplete.

Montgomery now had to drive Rommel back. This was no easy task, as Auchinleck had discovered in July and he had had greater odds in his favour and, unlike Montgomery, no fixed positions or extensive minefields to worry about. On the other hand, unlike Auchinleck, Montgomery made full use of his supporting airmen and from 7 September when Alam Halfa ended to 23 October in the late evening of which the Battle of El Alamein began, the Desert Air Force was preparing the way with sorties to report on and if possible 'soften up' enemy defences.

Of course, 33 was one of the squadrons involved but was perhaps not helped by being deprived of its finest pilot in mid-September. Lance Wade, now a flight lieutenant, was transferred and would later resume his career as a fighter pilot elsewhere. He would score more victories, rise to wing commander and be awarded three DFCs, only to be killed in Italy on 12 January 1944 when the light aircraft he was flying – well behind the British lines – went into an uncontrollable spin. As a final tribute, he received the very rare honour of a posthumous Distinguished Service Order.

These preliminary missions were usually carried out at extremely low level where 33's Hurricanes were very vulnerable to AA guns and attacks from above by enemy fighters. The squadron suffered only one casualty in September, when Sergeant Douglas crash-landed on the 11th and was put off its strength with wounds and burns. On 9 October, though, 33 had a dreadful day, losing Flight Sergeant Learmonth killed and three other pilots prisoners of war. Nonetheless, it kept up the pressure, its last combat before Eighth Army's offensive began, taking place on the morning of 23 October. In this action, Sergeant Pointon was shot down but baled out and was later able to make his way back to base, while Pilot Officer Peterson balanced the books by downing a Messerschmitt Bf 109.

During the course of the battle, 33 Squadron would strafe enemy positions, lorries, troop-carriers and petrol bowsers, inflicting very heavy losses. It would also engage formations of enemy aircraft attempting to assault the Allied ground troops. On at least two occasions, in company with other Hurricane squadrons, it attacked groups of Junkers Ju 87s so fiercely that they not only scattered but unloaded their bombs onto their own soldiers. Again the low-level missions were extremely dangerous and 33 had seven pilots killed in the course of the battle, among them Pilot Officer Peterson who, tragically, was shot down by Allied AA fire as he engaged a Stuka formation at which the gunners were already firing.

On 4 November 1942, Eighth Army finally broke through the enemy defences and began an advance that eventually reached Tunisia. It was accompanied by the Desert Air Force that harried the retreating enemy by constant attacks on troops and transport, though not without some sad losses such as that on 18 November of Squadron Leader Mannix, a former flight lieutenant of 127 (Hurricane) Squadron who had recently been promoted to lead No. 33.[5] At the end of the momentous year 1942, however, 33 ceased to take part in the advance and instead was charged with the defence of Benghazi and of Allied convoys in the Mediterranean. On 12 February 1943 Sergeant McKillop had a fierce clash with a Junkers Ju 88 over one such convoy, shooting it down but being hit by return fire and forced to bale out. He was rescued safely by one of the vessels he had protected.

In late February 1943, the squadron did move forward again to take over the defence of Tripoli. It also began to receive Spitfires to reinforce its Hurricanes. The Hawker fighters, though, continued to fly protective patrols over convoys for several months to come and as late as May 1943 proved their worth in this role by downing a Junkers Ju 88 and a Heinkel He 111 shadowing and attacking a convoy respectively.

The squadron would later record victories with its Spitfires and, from February 1945 onwards, with the Tempests that replaced them. It ended the war not far behind 73 Squadron with an official score of just under 300 successes, exaggerated of course, but impressive all the same. Unlike 73, it had not achieved virtually every victory with one type of fighter, but those of its Spitfires, of its Tempests and, in earlier days, of its Gladiators, all put together did not equal those gained by its Hawker Hurricanes.

Notes

1. Volume One: *North Africa June 1940–January 1942* with Russell Guest.
2. Christopher Shores can speak with great authority on the air war in East Africa since the Italians paid him the high but well-deserved compliment of asking him to join General Corrado Ricci in writing their *Official History* of this. Incidentally, one of the witnesses on the ground who confirmed the destruction of the CR 42 was George Adamson, the naturalist and conservationist of *Born Free* fame.
3. Volume Two: *North African Desert February 1942–March 1943* with Russell Guest, Frank Olynyk and Winifred Bock.
4. The first time this had happened in the desert had been on 15 May 1941, when Captain Quirk of 1 Squadron South African Air Force had earned a DSO by landing behind enemy lines to rescue his colleague Lieutenant Burger who had been shot down by AA fire. The first time it had happened in any theatre had been on 15 March 1941 in the East African campaign, when Lieutenant Kershaw of 3 Squadron South African Air Force had also been awarded a DSO for rescuing Captain 'Jack' Frost in almost exactly the same circumstances.
5. The squadron was then entrusted to Squadron Leader (later Wing Commander) Norris, who in turn was succeeded in February 1943 by Squadron Leader (later Wing Commander) May.

Chapter 9

Air Attack, Ground Attack
80 Squadron

Of all the squadrons that flew Hurricanes in the Mediterranean theatre, however, the very first to do so was No. 80, though not as a full squadron. At the time of the Italian entry into the war in June 1940, No. 80 was based in Egypt, commanded by Squadron Leader Carter Jonas and equipped with Gloster Gladiators. To these were quickly added a pair of Hurricanes but one of them was incapable of being committed to combat.

The Hurricane in question was L1669 that had been the first Hurricane flown – by 'Dick' Reynell in July 1939 – with a protective engine air-filter. It had then been sent to the Sudan in order to test the effectiveness of this installation and when hostilities with Italy commenced, it was at Khartoum. It would soon be sent to Egypt and added to the strength of 80 Squadron but as its guns had long since been rendered inoperative by the harsh environment, it could not play an active fighter role. At this time the commander of No. 202 Group, the RAF units in the Western Desert, was Air Commodore Raymond Collishaw, a Canadian who had been a fighter 'ace' in the First World War, and he ordered L1669 to be flown from landing-ground to landing-ground in the hope that the Italians would learn of these activities and believe that large numbers of modern fighters were reaching Egypt.

Whether the Hurricane, nicknamed 'Collie's Battleship' by the delighted RAF personnel, successfully bluffed the enemy is not known for certain but it seems very likely, for Italy's Regia Aeronautica showed little willingness to venture over the British lines. Their reluctance may well have been increased by the presence of another Hurricane that had been shipped out to Egypt shortly before Mussolini's declaration of war. This aircraft, P2638, had the great advantage of mounting eight machine guns in full working order. It was entrusted to Flying Officer Peter Wykeham-Barnes and on 19 June he shot down a pair of Fiat CR 42 biplane fighters to record both his own first victories and the first by the Hawker Hurricane in North Africa.

During the remainder of June, 80 Squadron received more Hurricanes, sent out by way of France, Tunisia and Malta, and was able to form a whole flight of these. It also, on 5 July, received a new CO. Squadron Leader Jonas was promoted to wing commander and posted to Malta and his successor, Squadron Leader Patrick Dunn, divided his strength, bringing his Gladiators forward close behind the British front line but moving his Hurricanes to Amiriya near Alexandria, where they guarded Admiral Sir Andrew Cunningham's Mediterranean Fleet. On 17 August Flying Officer John Lapsley provided admirable protection against a formation of Savoia Marchetti SM 79 bombers, shooting down three of them, all confirmed in enemy records.

Mention of Wykeham-Barnes, Dunn and Lapsley in quick succession prompts the reflection that 80 Squadron could boast a remarkable array of pilots who would render immense services to the Royal Air Force in years to come. All three would have their abilities recognized by a knighthood; all three would rise to the rank of air marshal. It seems rather unfair that the squadron would so quickly lose the benefit of all that talent.

By mid-August 1940, Hurricanes were starting to reach the Middle East in greater numbers and it was decided to form them into a new squadron, No. 274. Dunn was appointed its CO and on 19 August it was given 80 Squadron's Hurricanes, including L1669 for training purposes, and 80 Squadron's experienced Hurricane pilots, among them Wykeham-Barnes, Lapsley and an airman who had not yet claimed a victory but was one of 80's most remarkable characters.

Pilot Officer Ernest Michelson Mason invariably attracted attention. He possessed a heavy black beard, supposedly the only one in the RAF at this time, though it would be copied later. He received the nickname of 'Imshi', Arabic for 'go away' or 'scram', an injunction that he would roar ferociously at any unfortunates attempting to persuade him to purchase their wares. He had a fondness for driving a large motorcycle and a captured Italian light tank round his aerodrome or, when in a less aggressive mood, for demonstrating his considerable skill at playing the saxophone. His eagerness for combat was such that having originally been posted to a bomber squadron, he had changed places with another pilot and, as a result, had gone to No. 80 instead.

For a man of Mason's fiery temperament, it must have been very frustrating that 80's Hurricane flight, of which he was a member, was held back to guard Alexandria and he was given no chance of engaging the enemy. He made up for lost time with 274. By the end of January 1941 he was the then highest-scoring British 'ace' in the Desert War, had been awarded a DFC and had been promoted to flying officer with an advance to flight lieutenant soon to follow. In March he led a flight of Hurricanes to reinforce 261 Squadron in Malta. Here on 13 April he boldly, if rashly, attacked four Messerschmitt Bf 109s and believed he shot one down; it is not recorded in German records but eye-witnesses reported that two aircraft had gone into the sea. The second was Mason's Hurricane that he was forced to 'ditch', having been attacked by the other 109s. He broke his nose in the process and was later evacuated to Egypt.

The other 261 pilots, who were now in desperate need of a rest, left Malta soon afterwards and re-formed in Iraq. In July Mason was promoted to lead them and in the following month, 261 took part in a joint British-Russian advance into Iran – or Persia for those like Churchill who preferred its older name – intended to secure a supply route to Britain's new ally. Typically, Mason was the only pilot to see combat when, on 26 August, he shot down an elderly Hawker Audax biplane.[1] In January 1942 he took command of 94 (Hurricane) Squadron but this shortly – and temporarily – converted to Kittyhawks with which neither Mason nor his men were familiar. On 15 February, he and three other pilots were killed in action.

Now a purely Gladiator squadron again, No. 80 saw much action first in the Western Desert and later, from November 1940 onwards, in Greece. It suffered inevitable losses and these included its Australian CO, Squadron Leader William Hickey, who was killed by Italian fighters while descending on his parachute. Flight Lieutenant Edward 'Tap' Jones, who had led 80's original Hurricane flight in Egypt, was promoted and succeeded him.

The squadron had far more victories than casualties, however, for even after the departure of those airmen who had formed the basis of 274, it still had many extremely capable pilots in its ranks. Flying Officer Richard Cullen, born in Australia but brought up in England, whose great size and strength had earned him the nickname of 'Ape', had been a skilful and daring racing motorcyclist before the war. As a pilot of 80 Squadron, he proved equally skilful and even more daring, so much so that his colleagues, all of whom liked him immensely, vainly implored him to be less reckless.

Pilot Officer William 'Cherry' Vale was very different in background and temperament. A slim, handsome Englishman who was the son of an officer in the Royal Marines, Vale had joined the Royal Air Force as an apprentice and qualified as a fitter before being taught to fly. As a sergeant pilot he flew Harts and Gladiators with 33 Squadron; then in July 1940 he was commissioned and posted to No. 80. In combat he was cool, poised and very competent, and in ability and number of victories alike, he was regarded as 80's finest pilot with only one exception: the brilliant and dynamic South African Flight Lieutenant 'Pat' Pattle, whose number of victories in Gladiators was the highest of any pilot in the war.

Neither Cullen nor Vale nor Pattle had experience of flying Hurricanes in combat, but in February 1941 they were given a rapid and unofficial conversion course on these. On receipt of six of the Hawker fighters, Squadron Leader Jones decided, as in North Africa, to form a separate Hurricane flight. The squadron was transferred to the aerodrome at Paramythia, situated in a mountain valley near the Albanian frontier, and here the Hurricanes were placed under Pattle's command with Cullen and Vale among his pilots.

In his biography, *Pattle: Supreme Fighter in the Air*, E.C.R. Baker gives an account, based on interviews with 80 Squadron's surviving pilots – Vale for one – of the reaction of the greatest Hurricane 'ace' to his new 'mount'. As an experienced combat pilot he was delighted by its speed, strength, fire-power and particularly its steadiness that made it such a marvellous gun platform. At the same time, it is a measure of his genuine joy of flying that he 'missed the quick loops and the tight turns of the Gladiator' and regretted that: 'The Hurricane could do everything that the Gladiator could do in the way of aerobatics, but it took a much bigger volume of sky in which to do it.'

In action, of course, there was no comparison between the types, as 80's Hurricane flight quickly demonstrated. On 20 February this flew its first combat sorties, escorting Blenheim bombers on a raid that hit supply dumps and an important road bridge. The Blenheims were attacked by Fiat G 50 monoplane fighters but Pattle pounced on the leading enemy aircraft and poured a vicious burst of fire into it, whereupon it 'exploded into flames'. This was the Hurricane's first victory in the Balkans and Pattle's men drove away the other Fiats and believed they shot down three more of these, much to the delight of watchers in the Blenheims.

The Greek army now advanced on the main Albanian harbour of Valona, the capture of which, it was hoped, would break Italian resistance. The Royal Air Force units in Greece provided full support and on 27 February 80's Hurricanes, together with Hurricanes of 33 Squadron, recently arrived in Greece, escorted Blenheims attacking Valona and its aerodrome. The formation was intercepted by Fiat CR 42s that damaged five of the bombers, one of which was 'written off'. The Hurricanes then counter-attacked. They suffered no losses and their pilots believed that seven CR 42s were shot down, all except one by members of No. 80, while two others were reported to have collided.

By contrast, the Italian official records indicate the loss of only two CR 42s. It may well be that the RAF made some duplicated claims but it is difficult to believe that they were mistaken to this extent, particularly as the crews of the Blenheims reported that 'the sky was full of crashing aircraft.' As was mentioned earlier, the RAF claims of Italian bombers are largely supported in enemy records but there are numerous instances of great disagreements in the case of Italian fighters, especially CR 42s. This may be because their losses were either ignored or reported through different channels, since it was intended to phase out the biplanes as soon as possible.

For that matter, it may be mentioned that the Fiat G 50 monoplanes, though superior to the CR 42s, were greatly inferior to the Hurricanes. On the outbreak of war, the Italians already had the Macchi MC 200 that was a much finer fighter than the G 50 and in June 1941 would receive the still better Macchi MC 202. They intended to replace their G 50s with these and the first MC 200s had, in fact, arrived in Albania by 7 March 1941. It is possible, therefore, that losses of G 50s are also not fully recorded.

These issues might be remembered as we turn to the controversial events of 28 February 1941. On that day, the full strength of 80 Squadron, both Hurricanes and Gladiators, together with the Gladiators of 112 Squadron, provided cover to the Greek army as it attempted to capture the important strategic town of Tepelenë. Almost continuous air battles raged across southern Albania, in the course of which the RAF pilots believed that they had destroyed twenty-seven Italian aircraft for the loss of a single Gladiator from 112, the pilot of which baled out unhurt.

In many accounts it is stated that there can be no doubt about the accuracy of the RAF's claims because the destruction of every Italian aircraft was witnessed and confirmed by the ground forces. It must be remembered, however, that these had more important matters to concern them than merely the exact number of aircraft to fall, and just as more than one pilot, in perfect good faith, might describe their destruction of the same enemy, so different army formations might confirm a 'kill' without realizing they were all referring to the same incident.

Nonetheless, the soldiers' reports do indicate that very considerable numbers of Italian machines fell and that alone casts considerable doubt on the official Italian figures. It may be accepted that the RAF pilots did somewhat overestimate the number of bombers they shot down, particularly since the records show several other bombers as damaged. It may, with more hesitation, be accepted that they considerably overestimated the number of Fiat G 50s brought down. It is impossible to accept the figures given for losses of Fiat CR 42s.

During the conflict, 'Pat' Pattle first shot down two Fiat BR 20 bombers in flames, but then had to return to Paramythia because oil from his victims had covered his windscreen, reducing visibility almost to zero. Taking off again in another Hurricane, he encountered and attacked three CR 42s, two of which were certainly destroyed since their pilots baled out and these are confirmed in Italian records. The third rolled onto its back and went down vertically with smoke pouring from it. Pattle followed it down until he was certain it was going to crash, but since he did not see it do so he claimed only a 'Probable' and we may be sceptical and accept that it pulled out of its dive and survived. It is surprising, though, that the official records do not report it as even damaged and frankly incredible that eleven other CR 42s claimed as destroyed were apparently untouched. It is suggested, therefore, that their loss was recorded elsewhere, rather than in the official records.

The early days of March saw 80's Hurricanes engaged in further aerial clashes. On the 3rd, 'Ape' Cullen, who had been credited with five victories on 28 February, assisted by Flying Officer Richard Acworth, temporarily transferred to No. 80 from 112, routed a formation of Cant Z 1007 bombers. On the 4th Pattle shot down three Fiat G 50s in flames. Sadly, though, also on the 4th, 80's Hurricane flight had its first fatal loss when Cullen failed to return from a sortie, having apparently been shot down by another G 50.

On 12 March the Squadron Diary recorded another 'sad day' but this time for a very different reason. 'Pat' Pattle left to take command of 33 Squadron, with which he would earn further fame and die in action. His value to No. 80 was well summarized in its diary: 'His great skill and determination as a pilot, combined with his sterling personal qualities had contributed in no small measure to the success of the squadron.'

By this time, 80 Squadron had retired to Eleusis from which some of its pilots were sent on to Egypt to collect more Hurricanes. By the end of the month, it was fully equipped with the Hawker fighters and handed over its remaining Gladiators to 112. It was just ready, though it did not know it, to meet the German invasion of Greece. This occurred on 6 April and that afternoon, 80 gained its first victory over the Luftwaffe when Flying Officer Dowding shot a reconnaissance Junkers Ju 88 into the sea. The squadron made several attacks on ground targets over the next week but did not have another clash with enemy aircraft until the 14th when three of its pilots engaged some Junkers Ju 87s bombing Allied troops, one of them being shot down by 'Cherry' Vale.

This was followed so far as 80 Squadron was concerned by six days of ferocious and almost continuous combat. It was not a good moment for a new recruit to arrive but on the evening of the 14th, a young man of Scandinavian descent landed at Eleusis with a brand-new replacement Hurricane. Pilot Officer Roald Dahl would later become a wing commander, an air attaché and security officer in Washington and, after the war, a famous author of children's books and scripts for television and films. At this moment, though, he was inexperienced, had had only seven hours' flying time on Hurricanes and was naturally anxious about what would happen next. According to Dahl in his book *Going Solo*, he was not reassured by an outburst from a Royal Air Force corporal who assured him that he had wasted his time in coming, that he would be shot down in flames or strafed on the ground by 109s and that his aircraft would not last a week.

Dahl published *Going Solo* more than forty years after the war's end and it seems that his memory must have tricked him. The massive Luftwaffe attacks on the RAF airfields did not begin until the following day and then on those in northern Greece, not on Eleusis, so this exchange must have taken place at a later date. It may also be exaggerated, for Dahl was not an easy man to get to know and he appears at this time to have been somewhat pessimistic. It is to his credit that this did not prevent him from carrying out his duties with skill and determination: he shot down a Junkers Ju 88 on his first operational sortie on 15 April and combined with AA gunners to destroy another on the 16th. It should be said, however, that his comments and descriptions are not echoed in any other accounts of the attitudes of either pilots or ground crews.

From 15 April to the 19th, 80's Hurricanes, despite very heavy adverse odds, inflicted considerable losses on German aircraft, particularly Junkers Ju 87s and Ju 88s. They were joined on the 17th by the Hurricanes of 33 and the two squadrons in effect combined their efforts; 80's Squadron Leader 'Tap' Jones acting as overall director of operations, and tactical command being exercised by 'Pat' Pattle who was, of course, well known to the airmen of both 80 and 33.

In *Going Solo*, Dahl has gloomy stories of his colleagues 'disappearing like flies' and of the only conversation in the mess being 'a few muttered remarks about the pilots who had not come back that day.' In reality, 80 Squadron had no more losses until the dreadful 20 April, already described, that saw the final great effort of the Hurricanes in Greece and the death of the heroic Pattle. Naturally 80 Squadron suffered as well: Pilot Officer Still was killed in the morning; Flight Lieutenant William Woods was killed in the afternoon; the Frenchman Flight Sergeant Wintersdorf baled out but was wounded in the leg; Flight Lieutenant Kettlewell baled out as well but injured his spine and spent several months in a plaster cast. There followed the destruction of most of the remaining Hurricanes on the ground on 23 April and the evacuation next morning of the last seven of them and the pilots of both 80 and 33 to Crete.

One of the airmen who flew out the Hurricanes was 'Cherry' Vale. He was now promoted to flying officer and it was he who recorded 80's first successes in Crete when he shot down a pair of Junkers Ju 88s on 29 April. He was also soon to be one of only two pilots from No. 80 still flying in the Hurricane Unit, Crete, because the rest of the squadron was transferred to Egypt and then to Palestine where it received fresh Hurricanes and Squadron Leader Jones reorganized and re-established it. Vale was certainly a worthy representative, for it is believed that he gained five more victories in Crete before being evacuated in a Sunderland flying-boat. The only other 80 Squadron pilot in Crete, Sergeant Maurice Bennett, left the island at the controls of its last serviceable Hurricane in the late afternoon of 19 May.

Vale and Bennett would enjoy only a short pause from combat before 80 Squadron was involved in a new campaign in a different theatre. On 1 April power in Iraq had been seized by Rashid Ali, a politician whose natural sympathy with Germany had been strengthened by generous donations. He had been defeated by the end of May but not before he had been assisted by Heinkel He 111s and Junkers Ju 88s that had reached Iraq by way of airfields in Vichy

French Syria. The British commanders were greatly concerned that Syrian airfields might be used by the Luftwaffe as bases from which to attack Egypt and their anxieties must have been increased when on 12 May the Vichy High Commissioner, General Dentz, formally gave notice that he would obey any orders to allow a German occupation of Syria.

On 8 June, therefore, British, Australian and Free French troops invaded Syria. It had been hoped that little or no resistance would be offered but it quickly became clear that the well-trained, well-equipped Vichy soldiers would not yield easily and they opposed with especial bitterness their fellow-Frenchmen whom they regarded as scoundrels and traitors.

Among the RAF squadrons supporting the advance was No. 80. Squadron Leader Jones had at first eight Hurricanes on strength, but on 9 June a flight of four more that Jones had sent to assist in the defence of Cyprus earlier in the month returned to him. One of 80's duties was to protect the 15th Cruiser Squadron that was guarding the soldiers' coastal flank and it was on 9 June that this task resulted in the squadron's most hectic day of aerial combat during the campaign. A raid on the cruisers by Vichy French bombers was driven off and two of the enemy aircraft destroyed but the Hurricanes were then attacked from above by Dewoitine D 520 fighters and two of them were shot down as well. Their pilots baled out but since neither was rescued, presumably they were drowned. Sergeant Bennett then collided head-on with a Dewoitine, both aircraft crashing. Bennett also baled out; he was rescued but was off the squadron strength for a time with severe burns.

These were the only losses suffered by 80 Squadron in combat, though on 12 June 'Cherry' Vale had a narrow escape when his aircraft suffered engine failure and he had to crash-land. Luckily the Hurricane's strength again proved immensely valuable: it was 'written off' but its pilot was unhurt. The squadron had other minor combats over the warships, but by far its most effective operations were directed against enemy aircraft on their own aerodromes, either escorting Blenheims or making strikes of its own. In one of these on 23 June it destroyed or damaged beyond repair at least nine Vichy French warplanes, as well as causing lesser damage to several others.

The attacks on their airfields, made of course by other squadrons in addition to No. 80, effectively crippled the Vichy French Air Force. Its remaining machines were withdrawn to Aleppo in the north of Syria and it seems that a raid on this – by 80 among other units – on 11 July was the last straw for General Dentz. That evening, he accepted the Allied terms and the formal armistice was signed three days later.

After that, 80 Squadron did have a quiet period during which it was engaged on protective patrols over Palestine. It also saw several changes of personnel: 'Cherry' Vale had already left on 5 July, taking up a series of administrative or instructional posts that ultimately led to his becoming a squadron leader; Roald Dahl was soon to be transferred to the United States; and the flight that had returned from Cyprus was sent back there and was incorporated into 213 Squadron. Finally, in September, 'Tap' Jones left the squadron, was promoted to wing commander and in due course became another of those former 80 Squadron pilots who reached very high rank; he would be Air Marshal Sir Edward Jones by the time of his retirement.

During this period also, 80 Squadron changed its duties. On 20 October its new CO, Squadron Leader Thomas Horgan, led his men back to Egypt and on 5 November they moved forward close behind the front line, ready to participate in Operation CRUSADER. For this, however, they would, according to the official Order of Battle of the Desert Air Force, be flying not just Hurricanes but 'Hurricanes (bombers)' or, as they were unofficially but universally known, 'Hurribombers'.

Hawkers had first experimented with fitting a pair of 250lb bombs, one under each wing, to a Hurricane I on 18 April 1941, and in the following month a similar installation was made on a Mark IIB. This would prove the ideal Hurribomber version and its first sorties – cross-Channel raids on targets in France – were flown on 30 October 1941 by 607 Squadron. As a Hurribomber, the IIB retained all its excellent handling characteristics and manoeuvrability and lost only 20 mph of its speed. It also frequently lost two of its twelve machine guns, one from each wing, in order to provide increased space for the bomb-racks and associated wiring, although some squadrons preferred to keep all the guns to provide better protection after dropping the bombs.

For 80 Squadron there was no choice to be made: it was still flying Hurricane Is. Nor was it equipped with 250lb weapons. Instead its aircraft carried eight 40lb bombs, four under each wing. These and even lighter 20lb bombs had been used by Hurricanes earlier, specifically by 126 and 249 Squadrons in Malta on strikes against targets in Sicily commencing on 20 September 1941. Despite these facts, 80's pilots were not pleased to be a Hurribomber unit. To a squadron that had, in the past, been noted for interceptor 'aces' of the calibre of Wykeham-Barnes, Lapsley, Pattle, Cullen and Vale, it seemed almost insulting to be classified as a 'bomber' unit.

In reality, 80 Squadron was about to embark on one of the most important and commendable periods in its career. If the Hurricane, as Air Marshal Sir Peter Wykeham acknowledges in his *Fighter Command*, had the honour of being 'the Royal Air Force's first true fighter-bomber', 80 Squadron had the honour of first using it in its most valuable fighter-bomber role. The more modern Hurribombers in Britain performed great service, attacking airfields, bridges, railway wagons, road transport, canal barges, merchant vessels and small warships such as minesweepers, but when on 20 November 1941, six Hurribombers from 80 Squadron attacked some of Rommel's motor vehicles, they made the first fighter-bomber strike in close support of Allied ground troops. It set a precedent that was to become of ever-greater importance for the remainder of the Second World War.

It was perhaps also the moment that marked an increasing divergence of the attitudes of German and Allied fighter pilots. In *Fighters Over the Desert*, Christopher Shores and Hans Ring state flatly that: 'Looking at the impressive personal scores of the top German pilots in the Desert, it is hard not to gain the impression that these men were sometimes conducting a private war of their own, divorced almost entirely from the actions of the main forces in the sands below.' Their contention is accepted, with admirable honesty, by the Luftwaffe's leading surviving desert 'ace', Werner Schroer, an oberleutnant (lieutenant: the equivalent of flying officer) at this time.

The fact was that the German airmen steadily succumbed to an 'ace' complex, regardless of other considerations. If, for instance, 109 pilots encountered escorted Allied bombers, they would eagerly attack the fighters, tied down as these were by their need to protect their charges, but they rarely tried to break through to the really important targets because, as Schroer frankly if cynically admits, 'they had tail gunners'.

Equally, the 109s rarely gave adequate cover to their own bombers, especially the vulnerable Stukas. This has been explained by the difference in speed but the 109s in the Battle of Britain had managed to provide reasonable protection and it is difficult to avoid the conclusion that the Luftwaffe 'aces' in the desert rather preferred to let Allied fighters engage German bombers so that they could then pounce on these afterwards with the advantage of height and a better chance of success.

Not only did the German fighters fail to protect their bombers but, as Schroer again admits, they 'shirked' coming down to low level themselves in order to strafe Allied troops. In consequence, British withdrawals were never seriously threatened by Axis air attacks that might well have turned them into routs.

By contrast, the Allied fighter pilots did protect their bombers, if sometimes at high cost. They did engage enemy bombers very capably, if sometimes at high cost. They did attack Axis ground forces, often, as Werner Schroer acknowledges, with 'devastating effect'. They never forgot that they and their own ground troops were fighting the same war.

Indeed, ever since the time of Operation CRUSADER, the whole Desert Air Force had been Eighth Army's partner in battle. Their partnership was broken only in July 1942, when General Auchinleck unwisely moved his headquarters away from that of the airmen – who did not approve of his action – to an area deep in the desert, dangerously far forward and with poor communications. Happily, under Auchinleck's successors, the partnership was renewed and strengthened until in January 1943, General Montgomery could declare from a captured Tripoli: 'I don't suppose that any army has ever been supported by such a magnificent air striking force. I have always maintained that the Eighth Army and the RAF in the

Western Desert together constitute one fighting machine, and therein lies our great strength.'

That partnership was first established by the Hurribombers of 80 Squadron. There had been army co-operation squadrons before but they did not carry bombs. There had been attacks on enemy land forces before but it was the conversion of a famous fighter unit so that it could make precision strikes on individual targets that first demonstrated the air force's total commitment to giving close support to the army. As a fighter-bomber squadron, moreover, 80 could also perform its usual interceptor duties. On 21 November 1941, the day after its original Hurribomber attack, it would be found escorting a raid by Blenheims and driving off enemy aircraft. Ironically, though, while the squadron had had no casualties from AA fire during its low-level strikes on the previous day, on the 21st Squadron Leader Horgan was hit by flak, crash-landed and was taken to hospital.

During 24, 25 and 26 November, the pilots of 80 Squadron were very much engaged in fighting the same war as the men of Eighth Army. Despite experiencing difficulty in telling friend from foe in the ever-changing complications of the land battle, they made frequent and effective attacks on Axis motor transport. They also struck at the Axis armour but although a direct hit from a 250lb bomb could destroy a tank, 80's 40lb weapons inflicted little damage. They did, however, cause some gruesome casualties among tank crews, who were decapitated when they opened their hatches to see what was happening or blown to pieces when caught by surprise outside their vehicles. On the 24th No. 80 also had a clash with Messerschmitt Bf 110s, destroying two of them but losing Flying Officer Tulloch.

On 27 November No. 80 welcomed a new CO and a very distinguished one at that. Squadron Leader (later Group Captain) Michael Stephens had first flown Hurricanes with 3 Squadron in the Battle of France. In this unit's final action in France, he had had 6in of one blade of his wooden propeller shot off but still managed to land safely. He was warned that if he tried to take off again, the vibration from the uneven propeller would shake his engine to pieces but, reluctant to see his Hurricane burned, he persuaded his ground crew to chop 6in off the other blade. He then somehow managed to get airborne and flew back to England where, in July, he became the first CO of the newly-formed 232 (Hurricane) Squadron.

In early 1941 Stephens became, in effect, a secret agent. The British had long been concerned that Turkey might be forced to join the Axis powers and fifteen Hurricane Is had been supplied to her immediately after the outbreak of war to help her resist if she was attacked. Stephens was now sent out to ensure that she would be ready to do so if necessary. He spent eight months in Turkey, during which he flew Turkish Hurricanes and on two occasions shot down Italian reconnaissance aircraft from Rhodes that had violated Turkey's airspace. Christopher Shores and Clive Williams in *Aces High* tell us that: 'He inspected the wreckage in each case, sending examples of ammunition etc. out in the diplomatic bag to the British authorities.' These victories were not included in his 'official' score but that is hardly surprising since Turkey was not at war with Italy and Stephens had flown not in uniform but in civilian clothes.

Stephens was an admirer of the Hurricane but not of its fighter-bomber version. He could, however, hardly complain of the actions of 80's Hurribombers during the sadly brief time that he commanded them. A particularly satisfying mission was flown by No. 80 on 8 December. While four of its Hurricanes, minus bombs, fought off Messerschmitt Bf 109s and Macchi MC 202s and believed they had inflicted losses on these, six Hurribombers struck at a German motorized convoy and left 'a trail of burning transports that stretched almost a mile along the main coast road.'

The next day, 80's Hurribombers again attacked Axis motor vehicles but were in turn engaged by enemy fighters. Stephens was wounded in both feet and his Hurricane set on fire but as he was about to bale out, his attacker overshot him. In spite of the intense heat, Stephens scrambled back into his seat, fired at his opponent and brought it down. He then took to his parachute, beating out his burning clothes during his descent. He was dangerously close to enemy lines but luckily was rescued by Polish troops who took him to Tobruk and confirmed his victory.[2]

Stephens had to enter a Tobruk hospital where he found himself in the same ward as his predecessor, Squadron Leader Horgan, and where he later learned that his 'great courage and devotion to duty' had been recognized by the award of a DSO. Unfortunately his injuries were such that he could not resume his command of 80 Squadron, which remained leaderless until January 1942 when it was taken over by Squadron Leader John Urwin-Mann who had formerly flown Hurricanes with 238 Squadron.

That did not prevent 80's pilots from continuing their Hurribomber attacks for the rest of the year, harrying Rommel's retreating troops. Flying at very low altitude, they were extremely vulnerable to flak or to prowling 109s and casualties mounted. On 9 December three more Hurricanes were lost; two of the pilots were killed but Flight Sergeant Rivalant, a Free Frenchman, baled out and made his way back some days later. On 12 December four Hurricanes were shot down and though all the pilots survived, they did so as prisoners of war. During the rest of the year four more Hurricanes were lost in combat, two pilots were killed and on 19 December there was a horrific accident when Warrant Officer Lamour crashed on take-off; the Hurricane's bombs exploded and he had to have both legs amputated.

By the time Urwin-Mann took charge, 80's pilots were badly in need of a rest. They retired to landing-grounds well to the east and, apart from driving away a raid on Tobruk on 16 January 1942, took no further part in the fighting until late March, thus missing Rommel's counter-offensive that drove the British back to Gazala. They now gave up their old Hurricane Is in favour of later versions but they also gave up their fighter-bomber activities. This was regrettable, for they had gained much experience in this role and their Hurricane IIs were well suited to it. As was mentioned earlier, the IIB was the ideal Hurribomber but the IIC could also carry two 250lb bombs. The weight of these, its four cannons and the effect of the tropical filter reduced the speed of a IIC in the desert to little more than 275 mph, but at least it had a formidable armament with which to defend itself.

It does seem that 80 Squadron was given little direction or sense of purpose at this time, probably because of frequent changes in its leadership. Both Horgan and Stephens, through no fault of their own, commanded the squadron only briefly. There was then a long delay before Urwin-Mann was appointed to take over from Stephens and he was transferred to a staff job in early April 1942. His successor, Squadron Leader Forsyth, was replaced by Squadron Leader Denison in June and he in turn was transferred in September.

Perhaps it was also for this reason that the squadron's duties varied considerably during this period. It strafed targets on the ground, flew tactical reconnaissance missions and attempted to engage high-flying Axis 'recce' aircraft by reducing the armament of some of its Hurricane IIBs to only four machine guns in order to save weight. Normally, though, it carried out interceptor patrols. On 19 March 1942 it clashed with Bf 109s in its first engagement for some time and in the course of this, one Hurricane was shot into the sea. Flight Sergeant Rivalant was again lucky: he baled out and was rescued a few hours later. In the same encounter, two other Hurricanes were badly damaged but both returned safely to base.

This ability of the Hurricane to endure battle-damage saved many of 80's pilots over the next two months. On 26 March, for instance, Flying Officer Frank Mason – 'Frank' was his real name – got back safely after his Hurricane had been damaged by both 109s and the Tobruk AA gunners. Yet during this time, 80 still lost six Hurricanes and all except one of their pilots in combat and three more with all their pilots in accidents. It did gain some successes but this was not an encouraging build-up to the Battle of Gazala.

For Eighth Army, the battle itself would be even less encouraging. Its course has already been described and it would result in the fall of Tobruk on 21 June. The Desert Air Force had nothing of which to be ashamed, however, and certainly delayed, if it could not prevent, Rommel's triumph by its attacks on Axis ground forces. One squadron that performed splendidly was No. 80 and mercifully, despite making a number of dangerous low-level strikes, it suffered less heavily than did many other units; six Hurricanes were lost but only two of their pilots died.

At the battle's end, 80 Squadron was briefly rested and when it re-entered the fighting, it had been much strengthened by Squadron Leader Wedgwood and fourteen other pilots of 92 Squadron. This was a deservedly famous Spitfire squadron but unfortunately it was still waiting to be provided with Spitfires,[3] so on 2 July it was decided that its men should fly with 80 Squadron in order to get experience of desert conditions. Until the first week in August, they would fight alongside 80's original airmen and their 'kills' would be counted as part of 80's score. By the time they left, 80 was officially credited with over 200 victories, though like all similar figures, this was undoubtedly an exaggerated one.

The enlarged squadron saw its first combat on 4 July, when it routed a large formation of Junkers Ju 87s. The determination with which the pilots engaged was exemplified by Flight Lieutenant John Sowrey who pressed home his attack to such close range that he collided with a Stuka and both it and Sowrey's Hurricane crashed. Sowrey baled out, was fired at while descending by parachute but survived and was able to reach Allied lines two days later. Pilot Officer Hill also baled out but he too returned safely.

As we saw earlier, by 4 July Eighth Army was attacking and during the rest of the month, General Auchinleck would make five major attempts to destroy or at least drive back Rommel's exhausted and vastly outnumbered soldiers. Unfortunately, the planning and execution of the attacks and the liaison between army and Air Force were all very poor and if describing 33's experiences was depressing, the same is equally true of those of No. 80. It did gain a few victories but by 5 August it had lost fourteen Hurricanes, while six more had crash-landed or been very badly damaged and seven pilots had been killed, with three others prisoners of war.

Eighth Army's fortunes began to change at the Battle of Alam Halfa, as did those of 80 Squadron, if not so decisively. The squadron got off to a bad start on 30 August when two of its aircraft collided, both pilots being killed, while Squadron Leader Denison had to crash-land when his Hurricane was damaged in combat, though he escaped unhurt. Thereafter, however, 80 did well, driving off several enemy raids. In the evening of 31 August, for instance, it encountered a formation of Junkers Ju 87s. In the gathering darkness, it was only able to damage a couple of these but it caused them all to flee, dropping their bombs everywhere except on their intended targets.

Complete recovery for Eighth Army came with Montgomery's

victory at the Battle of El Alamein. So indeed it did for No. 80. Now under the forceful direction of Squadron Leader Daniel Jack, it reverted to the duties it had performed in Operation CRUSADER, acting in close concert with the needs of Eighth Army, both protecting it from Luftwaffe raids and striking at Rommel's land forces. For the latter purpose its Hurricanes again became Hurribombers, but they were no longer equipped with the small 40lb bombs they had carried at the time of CRUSADER but with the much more effective 250lb ones.

On 3 November 80's value in the former role was especially emphasized when it dispersed another large Stuka formation, again causing the dive-bombers to jettison their weapons futilely and downing a number of them for the loss of one Hurricane that force-landed without injury to its pilot, Flight Lieutenant Russell Foskett. The following day, Eighth Army finally broke through the Axis defences and on the 5th, 80's Hurribombers hastened the enemy's retirement with their 250lb weapons, though they lost Pilot Officer Wilson who had to bale out and became a prisoner of war.

That was 80's last important contribution as a Hurricane squadron. At the end of November, it ceased to participate in the pursuit of the Axis army and settled down to protective patrols and the training of new pilots. As late as 3 March 1943 it repulsed a raid by Junkers Ju 88s on Tobruk, but such encounters were very rare and in the following month the squadron converted to Spitfires.

It was appropriate that 80's final really valuable appearance as a Hurricane squadron should have been on a fighter-bomber mission in close support of ground troops, for this type of work, first introduced by it on 20 November 1941, set an example for many a Hurricane squadron to follow. Nor was it an inspiration only for other Hurricane units, for in May 1942 No. 112, now a Kittyhawk squadron, also began operations over the desert in the fighter-bomber role and other Kittyhawk and Warhawk squadrons would do the same later.

It was also appropriate that the next Hurribomber squadron in North Africa after No. 80 was 274, since this, it will be remembered, had originally been formed from pilots and Hurricanes from No. 80. In June 1942 it began to operate as a fighter-bomber unit and as it was then flying Mark IICs, it could carry 250lb weapons. These it used to good effect in the Battles of Gazala, Alam Halfa and El Alamein, being joined at Alam Halfa by the Hurribomber IIBs of 7 Squadron South African Air Force and at El Alamein by the Hurribomber IIBs of the Greek 335 Squadron.

Elsewhere, two Hurribomber squadrons, 174 and 175, gave close support to the soldiers landing at Dieppe, flying so low that Flight Sergeant Brooks of 174 returned with the wireless aerial of a German tank wedged in his radiator. In Vichy French North Africa, the Hurribombers of 225 and 241 Squadrons saw similar action against Axis troops, including Rommel's men when they retired to Tunisia after the fall of Tripoli. The theatre where Hurribombers gained their greatest fame, however, was India/Burma.

Here, circumstances might have been designed to suit the Hurribombers. Any lack of speed was irrelevant, since by the time they were introduced, the Japanese Army Air Force in Burma was conspicuous by its absence and as Japan's fortunes in the Pacific continued to decline, no reinforcements could be sent out to it. On the other hand, the Hurricane's traditional strength, reliability and capacity to operate from practically any landing-ground, including rough strips hastily hacked out of the jungle, were of outstanding value.

Hurribombers began to appear on this front during the second half of 1943. Five Blenheim squadrons – 11, 34, 42, 60 and 113 – converted to them; they could carry the same bomb load as the Blenheim and were both faster and more manoeuvrable. Later, five fighter Hurricane squadrons – 30, 123, 134, 146 and 261 – also changed to flying fighter-bomber missions and the Hurribombers became the aircraft most loved by the Allied soldiers. Working in close accord with the needs of the army, they first played a decisive part in thwarting Japanese assaults during the twin battles of Kohima and Imphal and later made regular preliminary strikes of their own as essential preludes to Allied advances that eventually led to the re-conquest of Burma.

The pilots of 80's Hurribombers had certainly left quite a legacy.

Notes

1. To be strictly accurate, Mason's victim should be called a Hawker Nisr, this being the rather horrible name given to the Audax in the countries of the Middle East.

2. It is usually stated that Stephens shot down a Messerschmitt Bf 109 but none were lost during the day. It is, of course, possible that this was one more case where the enemy records are not complete. It has also been suggested, rather unkindly, that it was the Hurricane that the Poles had seen fall but in that case they would also have seen Stephens bale out and known it was not an enemy aircraft. Christopher Shores and Hans Ring in *Fighters Over the Desert* say that 'it would seem likely' it was a Macchi MC 202, similar in appearance and performance to the 109, and Stephens, on reflection, agreed with this suggestion.

3. The first Spitfires to reach the Mediterranean theatre had arrived – in Malta – on 7 March 1942. The first Spitfire squadron in North Africa, No. 145, did not get there until 30 April 1942 and did not become operational until 1 June.

Chapter 10

The Winged Tin-Openers
6 Squadron

The development of the Hurribomber provides an illustration of another of the Hurricane's qualities. It was extremely versatile and this, together with its great strength, allowed a number of effective adaptations. The Hurribomber was one. Another was the Hurricane 'Catafighter' or 'Hurricat' that was blasted by rockets down a 70ft-long steel ramp erected on merchantmen and naval auxiliaries to enable convoys to carry their own fighter protection. Still another was the Sea Hurricane that operated with great success from six fleet carriers and several smaller escort carriers.

Nor were bombs the only weapons that the Hurricane was converted to carry. Bombs could inflict considerable damage on larger targets such as airfields, bridges, railway engines, motor convoys, troop positions and naval and merchant vessels, but it required a direct hit to disable a tank and these, of course, were potent weapons on the battlefield. The Air Ministry therefore enquired whether Hawkers could adapt the Hurricane to mount anti-tank guns and on 18 September 1941, Z2326, the first Hurricane Mark IID, took to the air.

Like all the earlier Mark IIs, the IID was powered by a Merlin XX engine, but quite unlike them it was not an interceptor but a purely ground-attack aircraft. It retained only two 0.303in Browning machine guns and these normally fired tracer ammunition as an aid for sighting the IID's main armament. This was a pair of 40mm cannons, one under each wing, normally Vickers Type 'S' (for 'Simeon') and occasionally Rolls-Royce BF (belt feed), although the latter was not popular as it was less reliable and carried only twelve rounds per gun as against the fifteen per gun in the Vickers version. The IID's top speed was 304 mph but this declined to 288 mph when it was fitted with a tropical filter, as most of them were.

On the day following its first flight, Z2326 was delivered to the Aircraft and Armament Experimental Establishment (A&AEE) at Boscombe Down where its remarkable handling qualities were confirmed. Though the recoil when the guns were fired dramatically reduced the Hurricane's speed by some 40 mph and threw its nose down so that fresh aim had to be taken, it responded so quickly to the controls that the next salvo could be fired almost at once. Moreover, the guns were very accurate. The A&AEE pilots in attacks on a stationary tank scored twenty hits out of twenty-eight rounds and pilots who had gained experience on the type would later improve this percentage and make the Hurricane the most accurate anti-tank aircraft that the RAF had during the war. When it is added that the 40mm shells could penetrate the armour of any tank that the Germans possessed at the time of their introduction and were designed to break up into lethal fragments once they had penetrated, it can be seen just how deadly the RAF's 'secret weapon' could be.

It is also worth recalling that the 40mm was the second-largest calibre cannon to be carried on any RAF aircraft. Only the De Havilland Mosquito, one version of which had a 57mm cannon in the nose, exceeded the Hurricane and it had just one such gun while the Hurricane had two 40mms. More to the point, the Mosquito was a twin-engined machine. That a small single-engined aircraft could use its impressive cannons so effectively is a tribute to its steadiness and sheer rugged strength.

In the British Isles only a single squadron, No. 184, received IIDs and that not until December 1942. Most of them were sent abroad. At least sixty went to Russia and on the India/Burma front they equipped 5 and 20 Squadrons that recorded many successes against the light Japanese tanks. The first squadron to get IIDs, however, which it did in May 1942, was No. 6, then based at Shandur in Egypt. This squadron's badge was formally stated to be 'An eagle, wings elevated, preying upon a serpent.' It was a prophetic description of No. 6's work in the later campaigns of the Desert War, for in them it would attack and destroy another dangerous prey, the armoured vehicles of the German Afrika Korps.

During these campaigns, 6 Squadron would operate very closely with Eighth Army, and this also was appropriate. In the First World War, it had been an army co-operation squadron, mainly used for tactical reconnaissance and artillery-spotting; its motto translates as 'The Eyes of the Army'. When the war in the Western Desert began, it was still an army co-operation squadron, based in Palestine under Squadron Leader McKechnie and equipped with Westland Lysanders. Later, though, it moved to Egypt, then forward into Cyrenaica after the defeat of the Italians. Here, on 1 March 1941, one of its flights was re-equipped with Hurricanes, though it remained primarily a Lysander unit for several weeks and still had Lysanders on its strength as late as September.

Now commanded by Squadron Leader Rowland Weld, No. 6 was placed under direct military control and throughout its first month as a (partly) Hurricane squadron, it flew tactical reconnaissance missions for British armoured formations. These were normally routine and uneventful, though No. 6 did lose its first Hurricane on 17 March when Flying Officer Wilson was shot down by AA fire and became a prisoner of war. On 31 March, however, the situation altered abruptly when Rommel launched the first of his audacious offensives that by 3 April had driven back the British and Commonwealth forces in a chaotic retreat.

As the Allied soldiers withdrew, 6 Squadron found itself dangerously far forward and hastily retired. Some of its ground crews under Flight Lieutenant Sanders were unable to get clear and were taken prisoner. Despite its difficulties, the squadron continued to make its 'recce' flights and on both 3 and 7 April gave warning of enemy movements that would otherwise have cut off army units. On the 8th its Hurricanes, together with those of 73 Squadron, retired to airstrips within the fortified perimeter of Tobruk. Two days later, the port was completely isolated and its garrison was under siege.

While 73's Hurricanes battled against the enemy air forces, No. 6's pilots continued in their army co-operation role, keeping watch on the enemy ground forces and warning Tobruk's defenders of Axis moves such as a major but unsuccessful assault on 14 April. These lone tactical reconnaissance sorties were extremely perilous and their danger was increased on 19 April when Messerschmitt Bf 109s made their first appearance in the Desert War. That danger became horribly obvious to 6 Squadron on the 19th when their CO, Squadron Leader Weld, was shot down by 109s and killed.

Weld's men continued to carry out their difficult duties, even after 25 April when 73's exhausted survivors returned to Egypt. By then 6 Squadron had only five Hurricanes left and one of these was lost on 1 May. Flying Officer 'Pat' Pike was about to land after returning from a 'recce' flight when four 109s swooped down on him. His Hurricane's wheels had just touched the ground when a burst of machine-gun fire completely wrecked it and wounded its pilot. Members of his squadron rushed out to drag Pike clear in case the Hurricane caught fire. Mercifully it did not and Pike survived, though he had to be transferred to a hospital.

Over the next few days, 6's airfield was raided on several occasions with such determination and ferocity that even the Squadron Diary recorded that it seemed 'the German airmen had a personal grudge against us.' Clearly No. 6 could not remain in Tobruk without accepting total destruction, and on 8 May its four remaining Hurricanes were flown back to Egypt. Three days later, in a splendid gesture of defiance, Pilot Officer Griffiths, intercepted by three 109s, not only got away but is believed to have shot one of them down; its loss does not seem to have been noted in German records but it was seen to crash by army personnel. Unfortunately, this incident, on top of all the previous strain, may have had an adverse effect on Griffiths as on 21 May he crashed while landing and was killed.

By the end of May, 6 Squadron's strength had been increased to nine Hurricanes plus five Lysanders, although the latter were now rarely flown on operational missions. In early June it received reinforcements and throughout the month, now commanded by Squadron Leader Paul Legge, continued to fly its demanding and dangerous missions, losing six Hurricanes and three pilots including Flight Lieutenant McFall, one of its longest-serving members who had already earned a DFC and Bar for his exploits in both Lysanders and Hurricanes. He was shot down after a single-handed battle against three 109s but crash-landed in the desert and was able to scramble clear of his wrecked aircraft. Then, however, the Messerschmitts dived down and machine-gunned him. He was fatally wounded and died soon afterwards.

For the time being 6 Squadron could do no more and at the beginning of July it retired to Palestine where it replaced its Hurricanes with Gladiators. On 10 May 1942, however, it was moved to Shandur and began to re-equip with Hurricanes. It had originally been intended that it should receive Hurricane IICs but instead it was given six Hurricane IIDs, or 'tank-busters'.

This was the start of the most dramatic period in 6 Squadron's career. It would see 6's Hurricanes become the arch enemy of Rommel's armour and earn the nickname of 'The Winged Tin-Openers'. This in turn would give the squadron a new crest, unofficial but worn proudly not only on its Hurricanes but on the jet aircraft that it flew after the war, fighters and bombers alike, as a reminder of its greatest achievements.

They were also its most important achievements and it is a measure of their importance that 6's CO, Squadron Leader Roger Porteous, was raised to the rank of wing commander and his senior flight commander, Flight Lieutenant Allan Simpson, to that of squadron leader. These promotions may also have signalled an acceptance of the difficulty of their task. Porteous had gained all his previous experience on army co-operation squadrons and when he had taken over No. 6 in February 1942, he had believed it would be continuing in that role. His pilots were equally inexperienced in their new ground-attack duties and they now had to learn the capabilities and limitations of their Hurricane IIDs and the problems and dangers of the tactics that they would have to adopt. Moreover, they had at first few aircraft on which to learn and yet were ordered to be ready for action with the minimum of delay.

Fortunately, Porteous and his men proved as versatile as the Hurricanes they flew. It was obvious that attacks on tanks would require them to fly at a very low level – sometimes as little as 10ft off the ground and 40ft at the most – and to fire their 40mm cannons very accurately. The pilots originally used for target-practice a piece of canvas with the picture of a tank painted on it, secured between two lengths of railway track set up vertically in the desert sand. This provided useful preliminary information but was scarcely a realistic rehearsal and gave no information as to what damage any hits would cause or the best places in which to inflict them. Accordingly, 6 Squadron obtained first one old German tank and later several others and transferred its attention to these.

Thereafter, the skills of No. 6's pilots improved rapidly, though they may have been slightly discouraged by an early incident, amusingly described by Richard Townshend Bickers in *The Desert Air War 1939-1945*. A cat that was presumably a pet of one of the squadrons using the airfield at Shandur[1], wanting a cool and quiet place in which to shelter from the desert heat, had climbed into one of 6's target-tanks without, of course, having any way of knowing that this had been scheduled as an important item in a squadron exercise. The Hurricanes came in at low level and used their 40mm cannons with devastating effect. As the onlookers moved in to assess the damage, out jumped the cat, no doubt bewildered and shaken but quite unhurt.

If it took more than a few 40mm cannon shells to kill a cat, however, examination of their effect on tanks made it clear that for the more usual occupants of these the consequences of a hit would be horrendous. The pilots' trust in their Hurricanes and their own capabilities grew rapidly and by early June 1942, they were confident that any and all of them would have no difficulty in hitting Axis tanks or indeed any smaller but more vulnerable targets.

By this time, Porteous had eighteen Hurricane IIDs under his control and three liaison officers working with Eighth Army to advise on their use in ground-attack missions and to direct them on such missions. In every respect, 6 Squadron was ready for action and on 4 June it moved forward to Gambut airfield and later to a series of landing-grounds in its efforts to support Eighth Army. Disappointingly, its first sortie on 7 June proved abortive because the tanks on which it was directed were well dispersed and mingled with other vehicles and it was felt that they were most vulnerable when they were in the open and unsupported by other formations, especially mobile AA units. However, it was only a temporary setback. On 8 June the RAF's 'secret weapon' joined in the Battle of Gazala.

At this date, Rommel was directing his main efforts against the stubborn Free French defenders of Bir Hacheim and it was to assist them that 6 Squadron was sent into action. It flew sorties in both the morning and the afternoon against columns of Axis tanks and half-tracked troop-carriers and in the course of the day destroyed seven or eight of these. It did not escape unscathed, however, and in its second mission it was given a strong warning of the dangers presented by flak guns to aircraft flying as low as those of No. 6.

This mission was led by Allan Simpson, accompanied by Flying Officer Anthony Morrison-Bell and Pilot Officer Michael Besly. The column that they attacked was reported to be strongly protected by AA guns but in view of the pressure that was being put on Bir Hacheim, urgency was allowed to take precedence over prudence. It is therefore easy to imagine the concern in the squadron when none of its pilots had returned by the time they had been expected.

In fact, all three Hurricanes had been hit and it was only their sturdiness and reliability that kept losses within bounds. The Hurricane flown by Besly suffered only minor injury but he lost contact with his companions and had to land at Tobruk to refuel. Having done so, he flew back to base and reached it safely, if later than anticipated. Both the other Hurricanes were badly hit but both remained airborne long enough to get their pilots back behind Allied lines. 'Tony' Morrison-Bell was able to crash-land, was rescued by Allied armoured cars and returned to his squadron next day. Allan Simpson was hit on his approach to the target and wounded in the chest and arm. Though in considerable pain, he continued his attack and believed he had hit two tanks and a truck. He then turned back towards Gambut and was able to climb to 500ft where he baled out. Luckily he too was picked up by an Allied patrol that took him to hospital in Tobruk, and still more luckily he was quickly evacuated by air to Egypt and so did not become a prisoner when Tobruk fell.

To take Simpson's place as his second-in-command, Wing Commander Porteous asked for South African Squadron Leader

Donald Weston-Burt, an old friend and colleague from his army co-operation days, who had more recently become a flying instructor but was eager to be back on the front line. It turned out to be a brilliant choice, for Weston-Burt would prove an expert pilot and a fine leader but he did not reach 6 Squadron until 22 June and by that time much had happened.

Despite the efforts of 6 Squadron and indeed of the Desert Air Force as a whole to assist the defenders of Bir Hacheim, the fortress had to be abandoned on the night of 11/12 June, and its capture guaranteed the safety of Rommel's supply lines and restored his freedom of movement. He promptly struck northwards, taking the defences of the Gazala Line from the rear, and concluded his triumphant progress with the capture of Tobruk in the early hours of 21 June.

Throughout this period, 6 Squadron continued its assaults on Axis tanks and transport. One such attack on 15 June destroyed five tanks, five lorries and an anti-tank gun. Pilot Officer Lee's Hurricane was hit by flak and he had to crash-land but escaped unhurt. Flight Lieutenant Philip Hillier's aircraft gave a display of strength and reliability that was remarkable even for a Hurricane. Determined to make sure that his target was destroyed, Hillier pressed home his attack to such short range that, as he pulled away, his Hurricane struck the tank, knocking off the tailwheel and the bottom half of the rudder, in spite of which it remained airborne and returned safely to base. This aggressive determination was typical of 'Pip' Hillier, who would become an unofficial 'tank-buster ace' as the first pilot to destroy five of Rommel's precious panzers.

More anti-tank strikes were made on 16 June and on the 18th, despite the confusion caused by the Desert Air Force having to pull back hastily from its advanced landing-grounds, No. 6 attacked a column of tanks, half-tracks and lorries, destroyed eighteen vehicles of various kinds without loss, and compelled the enemy to retreat. During Eighth Army's withdrawal to El Alamein, the squadron continued to take its toll on the Axis armour. It was, of course, rarely possible for its successes to be confirmed on the ground and no doubt there were occasions when more than one pilot claimed to have destroyed the same tank or the damage inflicted was overestimated. Even so, it seems that by the end of June 6 Squadron had at the very least destroyed twenty-six tanks, thirty-one armoured troop-carriers and numerous other vehicles.

Losses like these were highly significant, for when Rommel reached the 'bottleneck' at El Alamein, he commanded only fifty-five German tanks – plus thirty Italian ones but these were useless in a tank-against-tank encounter – and it is not surprising that his advance ended abruptly. Moreover, throughout July his strength in tanks rarely exceeded fifty and sometimes fell to less than thirty. General Auchinleck, who had taken direct personal command of Eighth Army, had, by contrast, over 200 tanks by 10 July and almost 400 by the 20th. Unfortunately he handled them appallingly badly, persisted in dashing them against the Axis artillery, and on the 22nd and 23rd alone lost 118 of them as against a German loss of three. It was perhaps just as well that the Allies had such a superiority of numbers.

Nor could 6's 'tank-busters' do much to help balance the losses for, as indicated earlier, co-operation between the Eighth Army and the Desert Air Force was at a low level. Happily, if during July the squadron had scant success, it did at least have few casualties. Its IIDs had now been given additional protective armour – though this did reduce their speed – and although several were hit by AA fire, only one airman, Pilot Officer McKee, lost his life.

August was a quiet time but the first days of September saw 6 Squadron, now stationed at Amiriya, re-enter the fight at a crucial moment. Rommel had received large reinforcements, was once more on the offensive and believed that the coming Battle of Alam Halfa would result in 'the final destruction' of Eighth Army. Fortunately, Eighth Army's new leader, Lieutenant General Bernard Law Montgomery, had other ideas and his skilful defensive victory owed a good deal to his having sought a close relationship with the Desert Air Force. Its personnel responded by not just protecting their own troops but by making extremely effective strikes on those of the enemy. Naturally 6 Squadron played an important part, wrecking nine Axis tanks and suffering no losses, or at least none in combat.

Sadly, the squadron's satisfaction was marred on 6 September by a tragic incident well away from the battlefield. 'Pip' Hillier was then 6's most successful pilot with a score of at least nine tanks destroyed – some accounts, rather optimistically, credit him with even more – so he was the man chosen to demonstrate No. 6's technique to important army officers. It may be that he tried too hard to impress them. As in the case of 'Cobber' Kain, there are different versions of what happened. One is that he crashed into the old painted-canvas target and the rails supporting it tore off both his Hurricane's wings. It would seem unlikely, though, that this was still in use or that the onlookers would not have wanted the chance to examine the damage inflicted on a real tank.

Squadron Leader Weston-Burt, who was, of course, a member of No. 6 at the time, gives a less dramatic but almost certainly more accurate account in an article entitled 'Tank-Busters' in Chaz Bowyer's *Hurricane at War*. He confirms that the demonstration was made against a genuine tank and that 'Hillier banked away too steeply at the end of an attack, did a high-speed stall and was killed.'

In any case, Hillier's death was a great blow to his squadron. It was made worse by the loss of another leading pilot in a flying accident on the night of 2 October: Flight Lieutenant Julian Walford was killed while on a searchlight co-operation mission, having apparently been blinded by the lights.

During early October, No. 6 made the occasional sortie over enemy lines looking for trouble (and tanks), but its chief task was training the pilots of No. 7 Squadron South African Air Force to fly Hurricane IIDs. The South Africans had attacked Axis tanks with 'sticky bombs' during Alam Halfa but their gallant efforts had been costly and not very successful. They were eager to renew the fight with the far more deadly anti-tank 40mm cannons and by 20 October the second 'tank-buster' unit in the desert was fully operational. It was just in time to join No. 6 in the great Battle of El Alamein that would result in the enemy being driven out of Egypt, out of Libya and ultimately out of North Africa altogether.

At 2140 on 23 October 1942, a tremendous artillery barrage heralded Eighth Army's greatest effort. On the morning of the 24th 6 Squadron made its first appearance and, during the day, its pilots hit at least sixteen tanks or half-tracked troop-carriers and effectively put out of action 'Battlegroup Kiel', a German armoured formation using captured Allied tanks. Donald Weston-Burt personally hit three of the enemy's tanks and began what would be an impressive total of Axis vehicles destroyed, his best score in one day during the battle being six – two tanks and four lorries – on 3 November.

On 25 October the squadron hit eleven more tanks, but on this and the succeeding days it suffered heavy casualties. Alamein was a savage battle fought at close quarters and it was rare for the Hurricane IIDs to catch tanks in the open where they were separated from their mobile flak units and at their most vulnerable. The pilots adopted the device of flying past enemy columns and then turning back to attack from the rear in the hope of taking the Axis vehicles and particularly the Axis AA gunners by surprise. That this tactic did not always succeed is shown by the fact that in the battle and the immediate pursuit that followed it, 6 Squadron lost fourteen Hurricanes and seven pilots to ground fire.

In spite of these casualties, 6 Squadron remained in good spirits and was sustained by knowledge of the damage it was inflicting on the enemy. It is, as usual, impossible to be certain of exact figures but it appears that at the very least, No. 6 destroyed nearly forty tanks, several guns and not far short of 100 other vehicles of various kinds: troop-carriers, armoured cars, lorries and petrol vehicles. Weston-Burt even mentions a bus loaded with Italian soldiers that No. 6 wrecked on 3 November. The squadron also shot up ammunition and fuel dumps. No wonder its confidence was high and was increased as more was learned about the effects of its attacks.

On 4 November Montgomery's men broke through the last German defences. The Battle of El Alamein was won and prisoners started to pour in: 30,000 of them, of which 10,700 were Germans. They included panzer officers and crewmen and when these were interrogated by British Intelligence, several revealing facts came to light. It is normally stated that when attacked by the Hurricane IIDs, the tank crews would 'batten down and take their punishment' and some brave men would even fire back with their tanks' machine guns. That may indeed have been the case at first but once the lethal effect of the IID's cannons became known, it seems that different attitudes prevailed.

Thus Intelligence reports have prisoners admitting that the Hurricanes' strikes caused panic and confusion and even that the crews of some tanks abandoned them under attack and sought shelter elsewhere. These statements may have been exaggerated but that they were made at all shows the serious effects that the 'tank-busters' had had on the enemy's morale. Moreover, as former Axis bases were overrun by the Eighth Army, further information was received from captured documents and these were forwarded to No. 6 and incorporated into the Squadron Diary.

It must have been highly satisfying to 6's pilots to learn that they had caused such concern that reports on their activities and fragments of their cannon shells had been sent to both Rommel and Kesselring. The former appears to have taken no action – perhaps he felt that he had enough worries already – but Kesselring paid a special visit to inspect one of 6 Squadron's victims and must have been shaken to see that the tank's armour had been penetrated by every shell that had hit it. Nor could he do much to reassure the tank crews, apart from promising that they would be given stronger tanks in the future.

In fact, the panzers were now given a respite, for 6 Squadron was rested from its labours and in December was largely re-equipped with Hurricane IICs, with which it embarked on convoy protection patrols. Meanwhile, improvements were carried out on the IIDs and when they and some replacement machines were reissued to No. 6 in February 1943, they had still more protective armour and their engines had been re-rated so that, despite the additional weight, they could now show a 40 mph increase in speed at low level.

As well as having new aircraft, No. 6 had a new CO, Wing Commander Porteous having been posted to the Staff College, Palestine in January 1943. He would remain in the RAF after the war but a few years later, he was killed in a landing accident in a then-occupied Germany while flying a De Havilland Vampire. He was succeeded by his trusted second-in-command, Squadron Leader Weston-Burt, and on 22 February Weston-Burt took his men forward into Libya, ready to resume what he called 'our proper role of tank-buster'. The squadron's arrival was welcomed by a senior RAF officer who admired its earlier achievements and had every intention of using it as often as possible.

We left Harry Broadhurst as a group captain at the time of the

Dieppe raid in August 1942. In November he was an acting air commodore and joined the Desert Air Force as Senior Air Staff Officer to its leader Air Vice-Marshal Arthur Coningham. That officer was later sent to Algiers to become head of the North-West African Tactical Air Force, of which the Desert Air Force formed only one part, and Broadhurst, on 1 February 1943, succeeded him in his earlier command and at the age of 38 was promoted to acting air vice-marshal, the youngest in the Royal Air Force.

Broadhurst knew all about the Hurricane and especially appreciated its robust strength. He also greatly approved of the way Hurricane squadrons in general and 6's 'winged tin-openers' in particular had always been ready to operate at low level when engaging targets on the ground, whereas other squadrons of fighter-bombers and light bombers had tended to attack from a higher altitude, while other squadrons of fighters had been reluctant to come down and strafe. His beliefs were shortly to be confirmed by a brilliant achievement of 6 Squadron.

Having taken the whole of Libya, Eighth Army had reached the southern frontier of Tunisia, where it was confronted by a series of formidable natural and man-made obstacles. Any wide outflanking movement was blocked by a vast trackless salt marsh known as the Chott el Fedjadj and an almost equally impassable sea of sand called the Grand Erg. Eighth Army therefore had to advance along the Mediterranean coast and this led through two dangerous 'bottlenecks'. The more northerly of these – the 'Gabes Gap' between the marsh and the Mediterranean just north of the little town of Gabes – was heavily defended and only 15 miles wide. The one nearest to Eighth Army, between the sea and the Matmata Hills that ran parallel to it, was some 22 miles wide and guarded by the Mareth Line, a maze of mutually-supporting strongpoints and artillery posts protected by 100,000 anti-tank and 70,000 anti-personnel mines.

It was possible for troops to be moved west of the Matmata Hills through 'Wilder's Gap' – so-named after its discoverer, Lieutenant Nicholas Wilder of the Long Range Desert Group – but they would next have to move northward for some 150 miles through difficult, waterless country. They would then be blocked by the marshes and more hills called the Djebel Tebaga and the only way left for them to go would be eastward towards the coast. This would bypass the Mareth Line but would mean moving through the narrowest 'bottleneck' of them all, the Tebaga Gap – 'Plum Pass', as Eighth Army called it – just 4 miles wide, strongly defended and protected by guns, strongpoints, minefields and an anti-tank ditch.

Montgomery therefore decided that he would have to make a direct assault on the Mareth Line but that he would also send a force through Wilder's Gap to distract the defenders and perhaps divert part of their strength. To prepare the way, Wilder's Gap was secured by 'Force L', a group of French and colonial volunteers from French Equatorial Africa under General Philippe Leclerc. This then advanced along the west side of the Matmata Hills to a craggy massif called Ksar Rhilane. Here it was too far away to be assisted by the main body of Eighth Army and on 10 March its staff officers were horrified to hear that Leclerc had been attacked by a strong German unit that included tanks.

Mercifully, the Desert Air Force was able to assist and Broadhurst made sure that it did. A couple of Kittyhawk fighter-bomber squadrons were sent out but by far the most effective intervention was that of No. 6 Squadron's 'winged tin-openers'. As Squadron Leader Weston-Burt dived down to open No. 6's attack, a large shell hit his port wing with a tremendous bang. The Hurricane seemed to take no notice of this, however, so neither did the pilot and the thirteen IIDs that he commanded made repeated strikes on the enemy, being joined later by six more IIDs held in reserve under Flight Lieutenant Bluett.

Before 6's pilots had completed their attacks, the Germans were already starting to retreat. In all, the squadron hit six tanks, five half-tracks, thirteen armoured cars, ten lorries, a gun and a wireless van. The enemy recovered some of the disabled vehicles but, as Weston-Burt notes: 'A ground reconnaissance proved that our claims of almost complete destruction of the column were no exaggeration.' Not one Hurricane had been lost. On returning to base, the delighted Weston-Burt was strongly inclined to celebrate with a low victory roll but resisted the temptation, feeling that this would be too ostentatious. His restraint saved his life, for when his Hurricane was examined it was found that the shell that had struck his wing had punched a 9in hole through the main spar, which had a diameter of just 10in.

Air Vice-Marshal Broadhurst was equally delighted. Ever since he had taken over the Desert Air Force he had worked untiringly to improve its co-operation with Eighth Army. He had established excellent relationships with three of Montgomery's key officers: the Chief of Staff, Brigadier Francis 'Freddie' de Guingand; the Director of Operations, Lieutenant Colonel Charles Richardson; and Lieutenant Colonel Jock McNeill, directly responsible for army/Air Force liaison. Indeed, Broadhurst became almost an honorary member of Eighth Army and 6 Squadron's success at Ksar Rhilane encouraged him to get his pilots to participate to a still greater extent in the Battle of the Mareth Line.

The first move in this was made on the evening of 19 March when Montgomery's diversionary force passed through Wilder's Gap and headed northward for Ksar Rhilane. On the following day, the light bombers of the Desert Air Force delivered constant raids on the enemy defences; at 2230 Eighth Army's artillery began a heavy bombardment; and at 2345 the main direct assault on the Mareth Line was launched. The enemy offered stubborn resistance and on the 21st the Desert Air Force was called on to assist the ground troops. Once again, 6 Squadron was in action west of the Matmata Hills, dispersing a group of tanks threatening to check the progress of the diversionary force.

On 22 March German tanks made successful counter-attacks in the coastal area, and once more No. 6 was asked to intervene. Despite heavy AA fire and interceptions by Messerschmitt Bf 109s, the squadron made two separate strikes, destroying nine tanks and eleven other vehicles. It lost four Hurricanes but all the pilots survived, although Flying Officer Jones, another airman from the United States, was slightly wounded. Yet for all its efforts, the Germans continued to drive forward and by the early hours of the 23rd they had recovered virtually all the ground that Eighth Army had previously gained.

Montgomery, often blandly described as a cautious, unimaginative general, reacted with superb flexibility, switching the main weight of his armour to his subsidiary outflanking movement. It was in place by 26 March, ready to break through the Tebaga Gap; a manoeuvre known forever afterwards in Eighth Army as 'The Left Hook'. There remained, however, one major problem. It would simply not be possible to transfer the additional artillery needed for the breakthrough for several more days after the 26th.

To make good the deficit, de Guingand went to confer with Broadhurst. His proposals were startling, for not only did he want the Desert Air Force to provide the covering fire needed to 'keep enemy heads down' but Richardson and McNeill had urged him to request that its fighter-bombers and even its Spitfires, still pure interceptors, should go in and strafe at very low level where they would have the most disruptive effect. This was quite a favour to ask. Broadhurst had already considered the use of such tactics and had been greatly encouraged by No. 6's achievements at Ksar Rhilane, but the Tebaga Gap, both sides of which were covered with anti-aircraft guns, did not appear the best place at which to make the experiment. Moreover, Broadhurst's own superior, Air Marshal Sir Arthur Coningham (as he had become), was so concerned about the prospect that he sent a staff officer to warn Broadhurst that in the event of failure, his entire future career would be at risk.

Broadhurst, to his immense credit, took no notice. 'I will do it,' he promised de Guingand. 'You will have the whole boiling match – bombs and cannon. It will be a real low-flying blitz.' Army and Air Force staffs set to work at once to arrange the details of the assault, which included its direction by RAF officers sent to the front line in armoured cars, a technique later used most effectively in North-West Europe, Italy and Burma. To fulfil his aim, Broadhurst could call on six squadrons of light bombers, five of Spitfires and sixteen of fighter-bomber Kittyhawks or Warhawks. On 23 March he was also reinforced by the Hurribombers of 241 Squadron that had already made very low-level attacks on enemy transport on the northern Tunisian front and had knocked out a number of German tanks with its 250lb bombs. Most of all, he had his low-level specialists, the 'winged tin-openers'.

On the 23rd, fighter-bomber squadrons, including 241, attacked 'thin-skinned' Axis transports in the Tebaga area. Next day, No. 6 re-entered the fight, flying two main sorties and helping the fighter-bombers to inflict further losses. It again encountered heavy flak and Messerschmitt Bf 109s, having four Hurricanes shot down and a fifth damaged. Only one pilot, Sergeant Harris, was killed and the day provided another astonishing example of the Hurricane's strength. Warrant Officer Mercer was hit by AA fire in an attack on enemy tanks, his starboard wing was badly damaged and he crash-landed in open country at 200 mph. He walked away from the wreck unhurt.

The flak was even more ferocious on 25 March, and though No. 6 hit eleven more tanks, it lost no fewer than six Hurricanes. Once again, though, the Hurricanes' amazing toughness protected their important pilots; all were unhurt and returned safely later. On the following afternoon, the men of Eighth Army attacked the Tebaga Gap and, as Broadhurst had promised, the men of the Desert Air Force delivered a succession of assaults in support. In just two hours, they flew 412 sorties and though the doubters had predicted horrifying casualties, in reality only one Baltimore light bomber and thirteen single-engined aircraft were lost. These included two of No. 6's Hurricanes but both pilots were among the six who got back safely to their units.

Under cover of this barrage, Eighth Army burst through the Tebaga Gap, taking 2,500 prisoners, all Germans. By the evening of the 27th the troops that had been holding the Mareth Line were pouring back in a state of rout to avoid being cut off, while the triumphant airmen pounced on any concentrations of transport that could be found and 6 Squadron's pilots sought out tanks to raise the number of these they had destroyed in the battle to thirty-two.

Montgomery's pleasure was soon made clear. De Guingand would be promoted to major general, while Richardson, who as Director of Operations had played a major part in the rapid transfer of armour to Tebaga and the use of the Desert Air Force's 'flying artillery', would become a brigadier and receive a DSO. Montgomery was also quick to express gratitude to Broadhurst and admiration for the 'brilliant and brave work' of Broadhurst's pilots. Broadhurst's future had not been put in jeopardy. He would lead the Desert Air Force in Sicily and Italy before returning to Britain in early 1944 to command 83 Group in the 2nd Tactical Air Force, giving close support to the British Second Army in the North-West Europe campaigns. After the war, Air Chief Marshal Sir Harry Broadhurst would become Bomber Command's C-in-C in 1956 and Commander Allied Air Forces, Central Europe in 1959. His moral courage had deserved nothing less.

Broadhurst's 'spearhead', No. 6 Squadron, enjoyed a brief rest after the Mareth Line battle while it received replacement aircraft but it was back on the front line on 3 April, ready to assist Eighth Army to overcome its next obstacle, the Gabes Gap. This was taken after a short, savage battle on 6 April but No. 6's own experience was not a happy one, for it came under the usual very heavy flak and this shot down three Hurricanes. Yet again all the pilots survived but Flying Officer Ziliessen was captured by the enemy. Worse was to follow on 7 April when twelve of the squadron's Hurricanes were caught in a crossfire from two German formations. This time six of them were lost and three of their pilots died in action.

Fresh aircraft and new pilots reached No. 6 later in the month but its most splendid period had passed. During the campaign in Tunisia, the total number of tanks it destroyed was assessed at forty-six, not to mention a great many other vehicles and an occasional gun. In return, twenty-five Hurricanes had been shot down but twenty-one of their pilots had survived (one as a prisoner of war) and only four had lost their lives. In addition to its other virtues, the Hurricane IID had proved a staunch protector that could shield its airmen from all but the very worst of dangers.

On 5 May 1943 Donald Weston-Burt left No. 6 for a Kittyhawk wing. He tells us sardonically that it was felt he 'was staying alive too long and holding up promotion in the squadron', but it is clear that his superiors were not displeased with him for he was awarded a DSO for his 'leadership and determination' and also a Croix de Guerre recommended, no doubt with especial fervour, by General Philippe Leclerc. His senior flight commander, Flight Lieutenant Bluett, was also posted to a Kittyhawk squadron, No. 112, that he would later command, and 'Tony' Morrison-Bell who had flown with No. 6 at the time of its first 'tank-buster' missions back in June 1942 now became its new CO. He would lead it for a period of just over a year, by the end of which he was a wing commander.[2]

It must be admitted that only during the last two months of his leadership did Morrison-Bell's men see action, though their experiences in the preceding months were not without value. The squadron retired to the Middle East and here in July 1943 it began to be re-equipped with yet another new Hurricane adaptation. As the abilities of the Hurricane on ground-attack close-support duties became more and more appreciated, Hawkers, and later the Air Ministry, considered it would be beneficial to produce a version armed, like the IID, with only two 0.303in Browning machine guns but with a 'universal wing' on which could be mounted a whole variety of weapons or other external stores. The first prototype of this Hurricane IIE flew, without any additional armament, on 14 March 1943 and the second, with two 40mm cannons, nine days later.

The Hurricane IIE was very different from the earlier Mark IIs. Quite apart from the 'universal wing', it had 350lb of extra armour-plate, protecting the front fuselage and radiator, and the radiator had been deepened to improve performance. The additional armour and the variety of weapons carried naturally reduced the aircraft's speed, so to counteract this it was provided with a new Merlin 27 engine – or in the case of some later models, a Merlin 24 rated to give the same power – incorporating a redesigned oil system and driving a Rotol three-bladed, constant-speed propeller. These changes and particularly that of the engine prompted a different designation and the IIE accordingly entered squadron service as the Hurricane Mark IV.[3]

It was these Mark IVs that were received by 6 Squadron in July 1943 and it set to work learning how to manage them and which were the best weapons for them to use. The Mark IVs could carry two 250lb bombs, two 500lb bombs, two 40mm cannons, two Smoke Curtain Installations – these were used on several combined operations, particularly in Burma – and, best of all, rockets. A Hurricane IIA had first flown with six rockets, three under each wing, on 23 February 1942. This was, in fact, the first time rockets had been carried by any RAF aircraft and their number was soon increased to eight. They were crude but effective, consisting merely of an iron pipe approximately 3in in diameter, to the front of which was screwed the warhead, either a 25lb solid armour-piercing shot or a 60lb high-explosive shell, while on the back were bolted the tail-fins.

Compared with the anti-tank guns of the IIDs, the Mark IV's rockets were less accurate but far more destructive. The pilots of No. 6 came to prefer them to all other weapons and had the option of firing them in pairs, one from each side, or all at once in a single salvo. The effect of this can be judged from the fact that it was considered the equivalent of a full broadside from a light cruiser. The Mark IVs could also carry additional fuel tanks for long-range work and their steadiness and reliability enabled them to fly with an auxiliary tank under one wing and a bomb or an anti-tank gun or four rockets under the other. It was found, however, that it was difficult to aim a single 40mm cannon and firing it caused the Hurricane to lurch dangerously. By contrast, when the four rockets were fired, this had no effect on the aircraft. This, therefore, was the combination in fact used by No. 6 on most of its operations.

In February 1944 'Tony' Morrison-Bell, now a wing commander, took 6 Squadron to the airfield at Grottaglie in the 'heel' of Italy which, amazingly, was the first time that No. 6 had been based in Europe since 1919. It resumed active operations on 29 March when it attacked a German headquarters at Durazzo in Albania. From then until August 1944, it struck at targets on land and sea along both coasts of the Adriatic, moving on 4 July north-westward to Foggia, enabling it to cover the entire coastline of Yugoslavia.

During this period, 6's pilots hit radar stations, gun emplacements and even dockyard cranes, but their primary targets were enemy ships which they assaulted both by day and on moonlit nights when they would attack from the direction of the moon against vessels it had illuminated. As with all aerial operations, some exaggerated or duplicated claims were made but there can be no doubt that No. 6 destroyed or damaged over fifty vessels of various types including freighters, schooners, barges, ferries, landing-craft, dredgers and tugs. Its greatest success came on 6 July when four of its Hurricanes combined to sink a 5,000-ton merchantman named, with appropriate symbolism, the *Italia*.

Naturally, many of the vessels attacked and important targets like headquarters' buildings and radar stations were well protected by AA guns and 6 Squadron again suffered casualties, though these were reduced by the 'back-up' units of what was still called the Desert Air Force. As an example of this and perhaps a pleasant change from all the tales of death and destruction, we may turn to an episode that, at the risk of appearing facetious, might be entitled: 'The curious adventures of "Blondie" Walker.'

Flight Lieutenant Arnold Edgar Walker, to give him his correct name and rank, was a Yorkshireman who had previously flown Hurricanes with 94 Squadron and had then declined the chance of becoming an instructor, preferring to volunteer to join 6 Squadron instead. He quickly proved to be an expert at anti-shipping strikes and had already been awarded a Distinguished Flying Cross when, on 17 July, he was shot down by the vessel he was attacking and 'ditched' near the Yugoslav coast. Scrambling into his dinghy, he paddled away from the hostile shore under luckily inaccurate fire. Equally luckily, his misfortune had been reported and he was rescued by a Catalina flying-boat.

Undaunted by his experience, Walker resumed his anti-shipping forays but a fortnight later, he was again hit by AA fire, baled out and came down in the sea, fortunately close to an island. This proved to be unoccupied but a deserted cottage provided him with shelter and a supply of fresh water. He laid out seaweed on the beach to form the letters SOS and awaited results but four days passed before this was spotted, during which time he apparently lived on barley sugar and Horlicks tablets. He was then picked up by a Catalina that seemed familiar to him, as did he to its crew: 'Not you again!' exclaimed the airman who helped him on board. Walker was then sent back to Britain where he learned he had been awarded a Bar to his DFC.

Meanwhile, in June 1944 two important events had occurred. Rome was taken by the Allied armies and Marshal Tito, the leader of the Yugoslav guerillas who had been coming under heavy pressure from the Germans, was flown by Dakota to Italy where he appealed for close air support for his partisans. In response, a separate Balkan Air Force was formed to which 6 Squadron was transferred in August, as was another squadron of rocket-firing Hurricane IVs, No. 351, composed of Yugoslav personnel in September.

For the next few months, No. 6 rarely acted as a united squadron. Instead, detachments were stationed at a number of airfields in Italy and on Vis, an island in the Adriatic about halfway down the Yugoslavian coast that had originally been seized by the partisans and subsequently reinforced by the British. From their various bases, 6's pilots now flew their missions almost entirely on the eastern side of the Adriatic, striking at shipping, troop concentrations, roads and railways. By October 1944 these latter were important to the enemy mainly as escape routes, because in August and September the Russian armies had swallowed up Rumania and Bulgaria and made the Germans' position in Greece untenable, causing them to begin a slow, skilful withdrawal into Yugoslavia.

As the Germans moved out of Greece, British forces moved in and early in October 1944 half-a-dozen of 6's Hurricane IVs went to Araxos airfield, whence they harried the retreating enemy with bombs and rockets. The Germans continued their withdrawal through Yugoslavia, fighting off partisans and under constant threat from 6 Squadron which, among other raids in November, destroyed a railway bridge at Spuz that formed a vital link in the line of retreat from Albania.

The squadron also operated in close support of the partisans. On 1 December, for instance, three of its Hurricanes landed at Niksic airfield, north of Spuz and east of Vis, which had temporarily been captured by the Yugoslavs. On the 3rd they engaged a column of German tanks, destroying one and damaging two more. Next day, they were in action again, all scoring hits that wrecked another tank and two mobile guns. They then flew out again as German forces closed in on the airfield. Also during December, No. 6 attacked shipping, transport, troop concentrations and another German headquarters and its strikes continued without pause into the closing year of the war.

In February 1945 a few of 6's Hurricanes joined 351 Squadron at Prkos, an aerodrome in Yugoslavia further south than Niksic and close to the Albanian frontier but, unlike Niksic, permanently in Allied hands. On 9 April the rest of 6 Squadron moved there as well and, now reunited, resumed its assaults on the Germans in aid of the Yugoslavs' final advance. At the end of April, Tito's followers broke the last enemy resistance and, cutting off large numbers of Germans who had no choice but to surrender, they joined hands with the men of Eighth Army at Monfalcone, north-east of Trieste.

For the 'winged tin-openers', the end of their active service was near. The squadron destroyed its last tank and damaged another on 22 April and then flew its final mission on 1 May, just a week before the German surrender. It was a rather peculiar one, for the Hurricanes were ordered out against a troop convoy in the Gulf of Trieste but their pilots were advised that they might not have to attack this after all as Intelligence reports indicated that it was ready to surrender. This information proved correct and when 6 Squadron appeared, a total of twenty-five vessels, including sixteen troopships, hoisted white flags. It was a fitting symbolic capitulation to the aircraft that had been numerically the most important Allied fighter at the start of the Second World War and was still in action against its country's enemies when the war in Europe ended.

In May 1945 only two RAF Hurricane squadrons remained in the front line in Europe, 6 and 351, and the aircraft and personnel of the latter were transferred to the Yugoslav Air Force on 15 June. On the India/Burma front, eight Indian Air Force squadrons still retained Hurricanes and would do for some months to come but most of the RAF squadrons had converted or were converting to Thunderbolts, much to the distaste of almost all their pilots. Apart from 681, a photographic reconnaissance unit that had a variety of twin-engined aircraft to take its photos but used six Hurricane IICs to fly them from its bases to wherever they were needed, only five RAF squadrons still flew the Hawker fighters.

By the time the Japanese signed the formal document of surrender on board the American battleship *Missouri* in Tokyo Bay on 2 September 1945, there remained only 20 Squadron on ground-attack duties with its Hurricane Mark IIDs and IVs; 28 Squadron, a tactical reconnaissance unit that worked closely with No. 20, flying IICs; and the part-Hurricane 681. All of these had replaced their Hurricanes before the end of 1945, leaving only No. 6 with its Hurricane IVs.

In July 1945 it returned to Palestine, where for over a year it reverted to its old army co-operation role, carrying out internal security duties. In September 1946 it moved to Nicosia, Cyprus, where it was notified that it was to be re-equipped with Hawker Tempests. On 15 January 1947 it had received its full complement of Tempests and the last RAF Hurricanes retired from front-line squadron service. Just over nine years had passed since Hurricanes had first entered the RAF with 'Treble One'.

A great deal had happened in the interval between those two events and it is tempting to conclude with more tributes by its pilots to their 'faithful old "Hurrybus"', as 33's Squadron Leader Howell called it. That, though, would not really be appropriate. Sydney Camm had not designed his Hurricane to be a nice aeroplane to fly – though in fact it was – but to be a weapon that would protect its country and strike down its country's foes. That meant that he had, if unintentionally, designed it to fight the Second World War and it can only be assessed correctly by examining how well it performed that task.

For a judgement from a neutral source, let us turn to a man who never saw combat in a Hurricane but who flew it some 200 times, as indeed he flew the extraordinary number of 487 different types of aircraft altogether. In Brian Milton's *Hurricane: The Last Witnesses*, Captain Eric 'Winkle' Brown, the Fleet Air Arm's greatest test pilot, says of the Hurricane:

> This aircraft really was a stayer. It operated in virtually every field of operations. If you tally up at the end of the war, it actually destroyed more enemy aircraft than the Spitfire, throughout all the theatres of war. This is not just in the Battle of Britain, this was throughout the war.

Just how effective a weapon the Hurricane was is demonstrated by Francis K. Mason in *Hawker Aircraft since 1920*. He records that: 'In the entire war RAF and Fleet Air Arm Hurricane pilots destroyed 55 per cent of all enemy aircraft claimed by the fighter pilots of those services (compared with 33 per cent by those of Spitfires and 12 per cent by those of other fighters).' To this must be added the damage inflicted on the enemy by those Hurricanes that attacked land or seaborne targets, of which 6 Squadron was the most outstanding but far from the only example. Sydney Camm had created a war-winner and could therefore rest content.

Notes

1. The airmen had a surprisingly wide variety of pets, some of them most unusual. Richard Townshend Bickers records that the most extraordinary one was 'a Shetta spider, about four inches long.' This horror belonged to 73 Squadron which put it into fights with a growing number of scorpions, eventually as many as seven at a time, all of which the spider 'demolished'. 'Unfortunately,' we are told, 'somebody trod on it.' Whether this was deliberate or accidental is not revealed.

2. Since the next part of 6 Squadron's career is complicated enough in all conscience, it may be permissible to detail here the officers later appointed to command it: in May 1944, Squadron Leader Brown; in August 1944, Squadron Leader Langdon-Davies; in November 1944 and for the rest of the war, Squadron Leader Slade-Betts.

3. Not the Hurricane Mark III as one might have supposed. The Mark III was a Hurricane designed to receive the Merlin 28 engine then being produced in considerable numbers in the United States by the Packard Motor Corporation and used to power most of the Canadian-built aircraft. It was intended to introduce these Packard-Merlins into the production lines of British factories if the supplies of Rolls-Royce Merlins fell below the level required. Happily they never did, so no Hurricane IIIs were ever built.

Bibliography

Adams, Perry, *Hurricane Squadron: No. 87 Squadron at War 1939–1941* (Air Research Publications, 1988)

Allward, Maurice, *Hurricane Special* (Ian Allan, 1975)

Bader, Group Captain Sir Douglas, *Fight for the Sky: The Story of the Spitfire and Hurricane* (Sidgwick & Jackson, 1973)

Baker, E.C.R., *The Fighter Aces of the RAF* (Kimbers, 1962)

Baker, E.C.R., *Pattle: Supreme Fighter in the Air* (Kimbers, 1965)

Barker, Ralph, *The Hurricats* (Pelham Books, 1978)

Beamont, Wing Commander Roland, *Phoenix into Ashes* (Kimbers, 1968)

Beamont, Wing Commander Roland, *My Part of the Sky* (Patrick Stephens, 1989)

Beedle, James, *43 Squadron* (Beaumont Aviation Literature, 1966)

Bickers, Richard Townshend, *Ginger Lacey: Fighter Pilot* (Robert Hale, 1962)

Bickers, Richard Townshend, *The Desert Air War 1939-1945* (Leo Cooper, 1991)

Birtles, Patrick J., *Hurricane: The Illustrated History* (Patrick Stephens, 2001)

Bishop, Edward, *The Battle of Britain* (George Allen & Unwin, 1960)

Bishop, Edward, *Hurricane* (Airlife Publishing Limited, 1986)

Bolitho, Hector, *Combat Report* (Batsford, 1943)

Bowyer, Chaz, *Hurricane at War* (Ian Allan, 1974)

Bowyer, Chaz, *Fighter Pilots of the RAF 1939-1945* (Kimbers, 1984)

Chorlton, Martyn, *Hawker Hurricane Mk I-V* (Osprey, 2013)

Clark, Alan, *The Fall of Crete* (Anthony Blond Limited, 1962)

Collier, Basil, *The Battle of Britain* (Batsford, 1962)

Collier, Richard, *The Sands of Dunkirk* (Collins, 1961)

Dahl, Roald, *Going Solo* (Jonathan Cape, 1986)

Darlington, Roger, *Night Hawk* (Kimbers, 1985)

David, Group Captain Dennis, *Dennis 'Hurricane' David* (Grub Street, 2000)

Dibbs, John & Holmes, Tony, *Hurricane: A Fighter Legend* (Osprey, 1995)

Dick, Air Vice-Marshal Ron, *Hurricane: RAF Fighter* (Airlife Publishing Limited, 2000)

Forrester, Larry, *Fly for your Life* (Frederick Muller, 1956)

Fozard, Dr John W., *Sydney Camm and the Hurricane* (Airlife Publishing Limited, 1991)

Franks, Norman L.R., *The Greatest Air Battle: Dieppe 19th August 1942* (Kimbers, 1979)

Gleed, Wing Commander I., *Arise to Conquer* (Victor Gollanz, 1942)

Green, William, *Aircraft of the Battle of Britain* (Macdonald, 1969)

Halpenny, Bruce Barrymore, *Fight For The Sky: True Stories of Wartime Fighter Pilots* (Patrick Stephens, 1986)

Hiscock, Melvyn, *Hawker Hurricane Inside and Out* (Crowood Press, 2003)

Holmes, Tony, *Hurricane Aces 1939-40* (Osprey, 1998)

Howell, Edward, *Escape to Live* (Longmans, 1950)

Jackson, Robert, *Hawker Hurricane* (Blandford Press, 1987)

Jacobs, Peter, *Hawker Hurricane* (Crowood Press, 1998)

Kelly, Terence, *Hurricane and Spitfire Pilots at War* (Kimbers, 1986)

Lanchbery, Edward, *Against the Sun* (Cassell, 1955)

Lewis, Peter, *Squadron Histories RFC RNAS & RAF since 1912* (Putnam, 1959. New Edition, 1968)

MacDonald, Callum, *The Lost Battle: Crete 1941* (Macmillan, 1993)

Mackenzie, Wing Commander K.W., *Hurricane Combat* (Kimbers, 1987)

March, Peter R., *The Hurricane Story* (Sutton Publishing, 2007)

Mason, Francis K., *The Hawker Hurricane IIC* (Profile Publications Limited, 1965)

Mason, Francis K., *The Hawker Hurricane I* (Profile Publications Limited, 1966)

Mason, Francis K., *Battle Over Britain* (McWhirter Twins, 1969)

Mason, Francis K., *Hawker Hurricane Described* (Kookaburra
  Technical Publications, 1970)
Mason, Francis K., *The Hawker Hurricane* (MacDonald, 1962.
  Revised Edition, Acton Publications Limited, 1987)
Mason, Francis K., *Hawker Aircraft Since 1920* (Putnam, 1991)
Masters, David, *So Few* (Eyre & Spottiswoode, 1943)
McKinstry, Leo, *Hurricane: Victor of the Battle of Britain* (John
  Murray, 2010)
Middleton, Drew, *The Sky Suspended* (Secker & Warburg, 1960)
Milton, Brian, *Hurricane: The Last Witnesses* (Andre Deutsch,
  2010)
Moyes, Philip J.R., *Bomber Squadrons of the RAF and their Aircraft*
  (MacDonald, 1964)
Moyes, Philip J.R., *Hawker Hurricane I* (Vintage Aviation
  Publications, 1978)
Owen, Roderic, *The Desert Air Force* (Hutchinson, 1948)
Park, Edwards, *Fighters: The World's Great Aces and Their
  Aeroplanes* (Airlife Publishing Limited, 1991)
Pearson, Simon, *The Great Escaper* (Hodder & Stoughton, 2013)
Rawlings, John D.R., *Fighter Squadrons of the RAF and Their
  Aircraft* (Macdonald, 1969)
Richards, Denis & Saunders, Hilary St G., *Royal Air Force 1939–
  1945* (HMSO, Volume I: *The Fight at Odds*, 1953. Volume II: *The
  Fight Avails*, 1954. Volume III: *The Fight is Won*, 1954)
Richey, Wing Commander Paul, *Fighter Pilot* (Janes, 1980)
Robertson, Bruce & Scarborough, Gerald, *Hawker Hurricane*
  (Patrick Stephens, 1974)
Rys, Marek, *Hawker Hurricane* (Mushroom Model Publications,
  2006)
Saunders, Andy, *No. 43 'Fighting Cocks' Squadron* (Osprey, 2003)
Shacklady, Edward, *Hawker Hurricane* (Tempus Publishing
  Limited, 2000)
Shaw, Michael, *Twice Vertical* (MacDonald, 1971)
Shores, Christopher, *Hawker Hurricane Mk I/IV in Royal Air
  Force & Foreign Service* (Osprey, 1971)
Shores, Christopher, *Air Aces* (Bison Books, 1983)
Shores, Christopher, *Fledgling Eagles* (Grub Street, 1991)

Shores, Christopher, *Dust Clouds in the Middle East* (Grub Street, 1996)

Shores, Christopher, *Those Other Eagles* (Grub Street, 2004)

Shores, Christopher, *Air War for Burma* (Grub Street, 2005)

Shores, Christopher & Cull, Brian with Malizia, Nicola, *Malta: The Hurricane Years 1940-41* (Grub Street, 1987)

Shores, Christopher & Cull, Brian with Malizia, Nicola, *Air War for Yugoslavia, Greece and Crete 1940-41* (Grub Street, 1987)

Shores, Christopher & Cull, Brian with Malizia, Nicola, *Malta: The Spitfire Year, 1942* (Grub Street, 1991)

Shores, Christopher & Massimello, Giovanni, *A History of the Mediterranean Air War 1940-1945* (Grub Street, 2012. Volume I: *North Africa, June 1940-January 1942*. Volume II: *North African Desert, February 1942-March 1943*)

Shores, Christopher & Ring, Hans, *Fighters Over the Desert* (Neville Spearman, 1969)

Shores, Christopher, Ring, Hans & Hess, William N., *Fighters Over Tunisia* (Neville Spearman, 1975)

Shores, Christopher & Williams, Clive, *Aces High* (Grub Street, 1994). Supplemental Volume II by Shores, Christopher (Grub Street, 1999)

Sims, Charles, *The Royal Air Force: The First Fifty Years* (Adam & Charles Black, 1968)

Spencer, John Hall, *Battle for Crete* (Heinemann, 1962)

Stewart, Adrian, *Hurricane: The War Exploits of the Fighter Aircraft* (Kimbers, 1982)

Stewart, Adrian, *They Flew Hurricanes* (Pen & Sword, 2005)

Thomas, Andrew, *Hurricane Aces 1941-45* (Osprey, 2003)

Townsend, Group Captain Peter, *Duel of Eagles* (Weidenfeld & Nicolson, 1972)

Walters, Guy, *The Real Great Escape* (Bantam Press, 2013)

Wood, Derek & Dempster, Derek, *The Narrow Margin* (Hutchinson, 1961)

Wykeham, Air Marshal Sir Peter, *Fighter Command* (Putnam, 1960)

Index

Note: The ranks of the service personnel are those held at the time of the incident or incidents described.